"I was enthralled by this total‍ syn‍‍s that conceal the hidden truths that ou‍ ‍thoughtful exploration of the misuse of some‍ ‍ times is sobering and eye-opening. This‍ ‍ok that everybody needs to read to tru‍ w‍ nciples on which our country is foun‍ ii‍ future of the human species."

—Whitley Strieber, ‍ *nion* and *2012:* *Souls*

"…a book which every A‍ ‍uld read. It is a delic‍ some of the symbols, which enrich the‍ erica, stripped‍ ‍loying invention. It is a further delight tc‍ ‍poverished‍ eoning modern anti-American my‍ ‍ ‍informed way."

—David Ovason, auth‍ ‍ and ‍ *apital*

"Out of many symbols Dr. Hieronimus i‍ foun‍ one noble truth: America was created to enlighten the world. Here is her treasury of lost wisdom."

—William Henry, investigative mythologist, author of *A Nation Under God*

"*The United Symbolism of America* could not be more timely. It dispels several bizarre conspiracy theories regarding the symbolism reflected in the Great Seal, the Liberty Bell, the Statue of Liberty, and other American icons, revealing the profound wisdom involved in their creation. This book transcends party politics and religious sects; it contains a patriotic message for all people who would defend liberty and uphold freedom."

—Stanley Krippner, PhD, professor of psychology,
Saybrook Graduate School and Research Center; coauthor of
Haunted by Combat: Understanding PTSD in War Veterans

"Is our Statue of Liberty actually a monument to the Egyptian goddess, Isis? Does the arcane symbolism of our dollar bill hide a satanic conspiracy or archetypes for freedom? Is our Constitution really indebted to the Iroquois Indians for its existence? I found Dr. Hieronimus's answers to these and many other provocative questions as shocking as they are insightful and uplifting."

—Frank Joseph, editor-in-chief of *Ancient American* Magazine and author of *Discovering the Mysteries of Ancient America*

"I am a devoted follower of Dr. Bob Hieronimus. His book, *The United Symbolism of America,* is a 'must-read'! I have seen these diversified symbols all of my life, and wondered about their meaning, but never took the time to study their background. Reflecting an enormous dedication to the 'cause,' this is a valuable, informative book with touches of humor. It grabs your attention and holds it through to the final page!"

—Bill Mack, "The Satellite Cowboy," Grammy award–winning songwriter, and XM Satellite Radio Host

Praise for *Founding Fathers, Secret Societies*

"A vision that can unite, guide, and inspire us is increasingly possible when we know more of the rich history that helped launch our nation. Too much of this history has been unknown; too many facts have been hard to come by. It is a special delight to learn more of our history with Robert Hieronimus who is so careful to not exaggerate sources or certainty."

—David A. Burnet, Grand Councilor Emeritus and former Treasurer of the English Grand Lodge, Rosicrucian Order, AMORC

"*Founding Fathers* is a breath of fresh air.... [Hieronimus] corrects errors and offers superb summaries of available evidence."

—*Living Tradition*

"...makes an intriguing case that combines a number of historical threads to provide a new interpretation of the United States founding. Most importantly, Robert Hieronimus starts at the beginning, with our truly American founding, notably with the Great Law of the Haudenosaunee (Iroquois) Confederacy. This work should put to rest any remaining notions that the founding was a result of spontaneous intellectual combustion in a Philadelphia meeting room."

—Bruce E. Johansen, author of
Forgotten Founders: How the Iroquois Helped Shape Democracy

THE UNITED SYMBOLISM OF AMERICA

The United Symbolism of America

Deciphering Hidden Meanings in America's Most Familiar Art, Architecture, and Logos

Robert Hieronimus, PhD
with Laura Cortner

New Page Books
A Division of The Career Press, Inc.
Franklin Lakes, NJ

THE UNITED SYMBOLISM OF AMERICA
EDITED BY JODI BRANDON
TYPESET BY MICHAEL FITZGIBBON
Cover design by Howard Grossman/12e Design
Printed in the U.S.A. by Book-mart Press

To order this title, please call toll-free 1 800 CAREER-1 (NJ and Canada: 201-848-0310) to order using VISA or MasterCard, or for further information on books from Career Press.

The Career Press, Inc., 3 Tice Road, PO Box 687,
Franklin Lakes, NJ 07417
www.careerpress.com
www.newpagebooks.com

Library of Congress Cataloging-in-Publication Data
Hieronimus, Robert.
    The united symbolism of America : deciphering hidden meanings in America's most familiar art, architecture, and logos / by Robert Hieronimus ; with Laura Cortner.
    p. cm.
    Includes bibliographical references and index.
    ISBN 978-1-60163-001-8
    1. Emblems, National—United States. 2. Signs and symbols—United States. I. Cortner, Laura. II. Title.

JC346.H54 2008
929.9--dc22

2007048060

To my wife and partner, Zohara Meyerhoff Hieronimus. Prophetesses are rarely honored in their homeland, but this one will always be honored in mine. A flower of the universe in the garden of my heart.

ACKNOWLEDGMENTS

Having been a student of the ageless wisdom teachings and perennial philosophy for about 40 years, I have learned that there is always a lot more to learn. What little I have glimpsed, however, gives me hope to continue this work. Many souls have helped and encouraged me through the years. Starting with those no longer in their physical bodies, I need to thank the philosopher Lord Bertrand Russell, author Henry Miller, and Beethoven for his 9th Symphony, for feeding me when I was desperate and hungry. Former secretary general of the United Nations U Thant for introducing me to my spiritual teacher, U Maung Maung Ji, a Buddhist scholar, statesman, diplomat, and disciple of Master Koot Hoomi. Also my beloved best friend, coworker, author, and researcher, Christopher Bird; my patron and friend Mari H. Milholland; and my "uncle" Thomas Galen Hieronymus for gracious and continual encouragement. And finally to my late mother-in-law, Lyn P. Meyerhoff, who made it possible for me to share what I knew about the Great Seal with former Egyptian President Anwar El-Sadat. All of these helpers taught me why I needed to transform from just a visual artist to one using words as well as images and symbols in order to express this vision.

With the humblest of gratitude I acknowledge the Queen of my heart, Zohara Meyerhoff Hieronimus, whose extraordinary courage, brilliant leadership, generosity, and love of all living things is an inspiration to all. Connected by our goals for planetary regeneration, she has time and again pulled me up from despair and pushed me back to building the roads.

Endless thanks to my collaborator on this book, Laura Cortner, who is also the executive producer for our media production company, Hieronimus & Co. Laura added original research and spent hundreds of hours reworking these chapters for more fluidity and touches of humor. All the conclusions are mine, but she helped me reach them in much more clever ways than I would have if writing alone. Thanks also to her sister, Jennifer Cortner, whose photos, experience, and advice were freely shared. Thanks to Meghan Bowen and Alden Brigham for their help at Hieronimus & Co., and particularly to Meg for her help with the illustrations and some research. I'd also like to thank my friends who have kept me on my feet through their various professions and support, including Dr. Peter Hinderberger, Dr. George Yu, photographer Stuart Zolotorow, Linda and Robert Gassaway, Margie Herskovitz, and Paul and Bernadette Trattner. Guiding my research and studies have always been my alma mater, the Saybrook Graduate School, and my doctoral committee doctors Stanley Krippner and Willis Harman. Special thanks to David Ovason for his continuing friendship, research, and advice. And though I met all of them only briefly, I give special acknowledgments to broadcasters Bill and Cindy Mack and to Willie Nelson for their support of the American farmer, especially through the promotion of biodiesel fuel; and also to Nobel laureate and Oscar winner Al Gore, who really did win the presidency in 2000, for shifting the mindset in this country toward action to forestall global warming.

Much love to my family for their patience with me, especially my children, Anna, Maré, and Plato. Also to Vicki, Dolly, and Barbara, and the entire extended families of the Meyerhoffs, Rubensteins, Hendlers, Minkins, Katzes, Pearlstones, Cutlers, and Pancoes. A special thanks to Walter and Beth Pancoe for resurrecting and reproducing my "American Beauty" painting series.

And finally, thank you to our New Page Books editors, Jodi Brandon, Kirsten Dalley, Kristen Parkes, and Michael Pye, director of product development, who originally suggested this topic.

May the rebirth of our nation and our planet be one of enlightenment for all.

CONTENTS

CHAPTER 1

INTRODUCTION TO SYMBOL STUDY: WHY LACKING A COHERENT SYMBOL SYSTEM IS BAD FOR YOUR HEALTH

The problem with writing about symbols is that it is done with words. Words, language, and even letters are attached to trillions of different thoughts and associations in our brains, and each of us has a slightly different understanding of reality based on our own unique perceptions. Images, on the other hand, speak directly to our subconscious minds, allowing information to be conveyed without the baggage of words and interpretations. This applies especially to images that can be identified as archetypal, or those that convey fundamental truths about our physical and non-physical realities at a glance. Certain symbols are even theorized to have been "hard-wired" into our very being by our Creator. In that case, the symbols used by the first-known artists of the world, the pre-historic cave painters, would transmit the same messages they did 35,000 years ago.

When it comes to reading symbols, the first thing that must be considered is that *every symbol has more than one layer of interpretation.* Some schools say there are seven levels of interpretation to everything (divine, spiritual, intuitive, mental, astral, etheric, physical), whereas others hold to a three-level approach. G.A. Gaskell in *The Dictionary of Scriptures and Myths* outlines the "Five Planes in the World Systems" showing a remarkable five-pronged similarity to mythological interpretation around the world, for example:

△ **China**: (Heaven) Water/Fire/Metal/Wood/Earth

△ **Egypt**: (Ra) Osiris/Isis/Thoth/Set/Nephthys

△ **Greece**: (Zeus) Apollo/Hera/Hermes/Hades/Hestia

△ **Christian**: (Father God) Son of God/Holy Ghost/Mental Faculties/
Lower Emotions/Sensations

Oftentimes symbols are defined and understood differently by different strata of society. In ancient Egypt, for example, the sun to the common man would have symbolized God. To the nobles of the land, the sun symbolized a channel though which God manifested. But to the priests and those in the inner temples, the sun stood for the star Sirius, which they may have viewed as the origin of the lifestreams on Earth. What is certain is that they used its annual rising at dawn just before sunrise as the beginning of the sacred year and the commencement of the Nile's inundation.[1] In the Hebrew tradition there are four ways of studying the holy writings of Torah: *Peshat,* the literal translation, is the external form of Torah; *Remez* or allusion is the internal form; *Derush* or the homiletical meaning is how it is used in teaching; and *Sod* for the Kabbalah and Gematria, the most internal and mystical of the studies of Torah.[2] In Freemasonry the first or Apprentice degree teaches the physical or material interpretation of the symbols of the craft. In the second degree of Fellowcraft, the same symbols are given psychic interpretations, and in the third degree of Master Masonry they are given the spiritual level of meaning.

J.E. Cirlot in *A Dictionary of Symbols* demonstrates that the many levels in which a symbol can be appreciated do not negate one another. People who cling to just one interpretation often fall into this trap. Consider, for example, the many ways in which a sacred structure can be enjoyed: One could marvel at its beauty or its architectural construction, or consider its geographical and historical implications. Neither of these would be invalidated when one notices how a certain arch falls directly under a rose window, symbolically representing the soul. This realization would rather enrich the significance of the structure by "identifying it with an inner form."[3]

The Deliberate Selection of American Symbols

The young men and women of America who determined some truths to be self-evident a couple hundred years ago were deliberate in their selection of symbols to illustrate their cause. These were days of low literacy rates, and the great majority of people were attuned to learning through symbols with highly illustrated morality guides known as "emblem books." (See the illustration in Chapter 6.) The planners of the revolution tried to be careful in their

Humanistic psychologists agree that, without meaningful symbols, a society will be unstable and anxious—as symbols supply both the psychological and organizational foundations of social life. Our Founding Fathers intuitively knew this and adopted images from classical mythology to illustrate their cause. This is the reverse of the Libertas Americana medal, designed and ordered by Benjamin Franklin to commemorate the successful conclusion of the war and sent to many leaders in Europe. Executed by the great French medalist Augustin Dupré in 1782, it shows the infant Hercules strangling two serpents representing the British armies at Saratoga and Yorktown. To the left is Minerva, whose shield is decorated with the lilies of France, ready to strike the British lion to protect the young America. Courtesy of the American Numismatic Society.

selection of symbols for the new country, but at the same time, they had extremely pressing physical concerns in the years leading up to and through the actual war. Many of the symbols we will discuss in this book took several years of modifications by many people before they were approved or became well-known. The first "Stars and Stripes" flag had many unknown contributors, whereas the U.S. Great Seal had many well-documented contributors. The Liberty Bell, on the other hand, was designed purely for utilitarian purposes, only to later take on symbolic and mythological meanings. Most of our symbols did not come with any interpretive text, and the legendary myths of their meanings and origins (which we all "know so well") have been added later.

Note: for consistency and brevity, in this book we will refer to the government created by the white men in the 1770s as a "new" country, but we must also acknowledge that the word *new* is, of course, inaccurate. For hundreds or thousands of years before colonization by the Europeans, native tribal peoples lived on this continent. It was "their country" long before the European Colonists claimed it. Also, we must acknowledge that by "freedom" of the individual, our founders were defining freedoms only for white male property owners. The total population of the Colonies in 1776 is estimated at 2.5 million, and more than one-fifth (500,000) were held in slavery. Thanks to America's ability to evolve, we have slowly learned to extend the concepts of freedom, liberty, and enlightenment also to women and people of all color and means.

Those responsible for creating our pseudo-history of American symbols come from at least two schools: enthusiastic patriots with a flair for a colorful story, and symbol readers like myself. Most speculative interpretations of American symbols are rejected by mainstream academics due to the lack of documentary evidence indicating the intentions of the designers. However, this lack does not invalidate our search for archetypal resonance patterns to explain why these particular symbols have become icons. Many of the American symbols discussed in this book were either designed or popularized long after the Revolutionary War ended, though all of them have antecedents that predate colonization. I find it significant that at the end of the Civil War, as if the country needed psychic healing, several of our American symbols and myths came into existence or experienced a rebirth. The decades surrounding the 100th anniversary of the Declaration of Independence saw the first appearance of the Betsy Ross legend, the Liberty Bell gaining a national reputation, the birth of the Statue of Liberty, and the completion of the Washington Monument.

The biggest influence on the designs that were intentionally created for this country was the classical education of the designers. The United States of America was born during the Age of Enlightenment, and indeed our revolution is often cited as one of the best by-products of these new ideas of freedom and knowledge spreading all over Europe. The architects of our government were excited by the democratic and educational ideals of ancient Greece and Rome, and they boldly took the next step beyond what was only being theorized upon in Europe: They put the experiment into action. Our Founding Fathers declared they would live and operate under self-rule, and dreamed of recreating earlier democratic societies where men had lived in general peace and self-governance without the fear of religious and intellectual intolerance. They determined that their new country would carry this torch of freedom forward. As a natural course the symbols they chose, and the art and architecture they left behind, were styled mainly after ancient Greece and Rome. Symbols of enlightenment from other cultures were also used, but most often it's the Greco-Roman influence that we see in early American art, architecture, and symbolism. The largest example of this neoclassical trend in design is our capital, Washington, D.C. (See Chapter 7.)

One of the mottoes our founders chose for the U.S. Great Seal declared a new order for the ages. (See Chapter 2.) As far as they were concerned, they were witnessing the beginning of the end of oppression, the end of the church-state alliance and government-promoted religion, and the beginning of rule by the people. The religious right who currently sit in power have tried to rewrite this essential element of our history. They claim that their authority for legislating morality according to their own narrowly defined ideas is derived from our Founding Fathers and the so-called "Christian nation" they founded. Though the majority of them were Christians, to be sure, what the Founding Fathers deliberately did *not* create was a Christian nation. They created a land of *religious tolerance,* so that *all* faiths could worship as they choose without persecution from the state. Christianity was not being promoted. Religious tolerance and liberty were being promoted. These are also Christian ideals, of course, as in the story of the Good Samaritan, but our Founding Fathers were declaring the American way was to be respectful of those who worship differently.

The same concept of tolerance should be applied to the interpretation of any symbol anywhere. The first rule of symbolism is that there is more than one layer of interpretation. Don't accept my conclusions or anyone else's without question. Acceptance can lead to non-thinking, crystallization, and bondage. Opposition, on the other hand, can lead to thinking, questioning, and involvement. I'm hoping that a deeper and more timeless appreciation of American symbols can be gained when we account for the classical inspirations of the designers together with a humanistic archetypal interpretation.

My Approach With This Book

I will be reexamining and shedding fresh light on images that have become commonplace and dear in an attempt to show why each of them resonates so resoundingly with our collective psyche. Because we would be remiss to offer you just one interpretation of any symbol, for most of them, we will provide at least three different layers of perception. Where possible, we will provide a brief sketch of the historically documentable information pertaining to its origins. My own interpretations will usually be based on a humanistic psychological perspective. We will attempt to look behind each symbol or design for the archetypal connection, and how each relates to the American experience. And finally, where relevant, we will also examine the fundamentalist-conspiratorialist interpretation, a concept I will explain in more detail later.

My perspective is based on many decades of studying symbols. I have studied symbols psychologically, mythologically, numerologically, religiously—and all kinds of symbols interest me. Some of the best information comes from esoteric sources, which are not generally acknowledged by modern educators. It is possible, however, that these same sources were available to some of the founders of this nation, many of whom were demonstrably familiar with the esoteric tradition. Throughout this book I include examinations that might be classified as divination arts, such as numerology and astrology. In the past few decades, the trend has been to discount these types of systems that are not based on empirical evidence. This is an old paradigm way of thinking, and I believe, as the new paradigm emerges, we will once again recognize the value of these divinatory arts, which have been used and improved upon for millennia. Having made almost a lifetime of study of some of them I will often include at least a cursory glance at how our familiar American symbols can be seen in a new light by taking them into account.

For example, numerology has been practiced by many ancient wise men, including Pythagoras in sixth century BCE Greece. Philosophers of the time believed that numbers were the fundamental language of the universe, and everything was vibration. Geometry was the ultimate truth. Everything was related on a numerical basis. There developed several different schools of thought for how to achieve the numerical value of a thing. The process of numerology we will follow in this book is adding together the digits in the number until you can consider it as a single digit. To demonstrate: $1776 = 1 + 7 + 7 + 6 = 21 = 2 + 1 = 3$. We would then suggest that the number three has been associated with the theme of the trinity and the triangle, and go from there.

Most other authors on America's symbolism use the interests shown by some of the Founding Fathers in esoteric subjects and spirituality to conclude they were either: A.) Initiates in the ancient wisdom teachings (conclusions of Hall, Case, and Heline, for example); or B.) Satan-driven Illuminati Masons intent on world domination (conclusions of Icke, Marrs, and Epperson, for example). Because I try to use primary sources, I have found that the historically documentable evidence often calls into question the conclusions of both groups. My interpretations of these symbols will usually conflict with the conclusions of Group B, whom I've decided to call the fundamentalist-conspiratorialists.

The Fundamentalist-Conspiratorialists

In my doctoral thesis and 2006 publication, *Founding Fathers, Secret Societies: Freemasons, Illuminati, Rosicrucians and the Decoding of the Great Seal,* I demonstrated how the evidence does not support a Freemasonic influence on the design of the United States Great Seal. As I browsed the Web in preparation for this new book, however, I was amazed to realize that, almost without exception, most other people posting interpretations about our Great Seal *all make this fatal error in assumption.* And it is an error, there is no question about it. It is factually incorrect. *There is NO direct connection between the Freemasons and the creation of the Great Seal.* There is a *relationship* between the Freemasons and the Great Seal, and an indirect connection in that regard, as we will discuss in Chapter 2, but it is entirely untrue to say, "Freemasons designed our Great Seal," or "There is a Freemasonic message or intent behind the Great Seal."

The irrational fear that a vocal group of people has of the secretive Freemasons infects everything they say about the Seal. This means that everything they say about the Seal is based on a false assumption. We will find this situation repeats itself frequently as we look at the astoundingly negative interpretations that have been proposed for some of our beloved American symbols. For the most part the fundamentalist-conspiratorialist assumptions are based on jumps in conclusion resulting in faulty interpretations that apply to only one level of the symbol.

What is a fundamentalist-conspiratorialist? It is a loose term I invented for this book to describe the sub-group of the religious right that believes everything that does not fit their strict definition of "Christian" is *a priori* therefore "of Satan." Anything that is non-Christian in their definition is not only to be feared and avoided, but also removed or destroyed, sometimes violently. This would include any cultures that existed before the time of Christ, and all the art, philosophy, and science that they advanced. There have been numerous violent upheavals during the past 2,000 years as Christians tried to exterminate various non-Christians (for example, the pagan massacres in Greece and Rome throughout the first millennium, the Crusades, and the Inquisition). Other non-religious conspiracy promoters see a conspiracy of evil intentions all around us, organized by an ultimate tempter and the powerful ruling elite. They simply enjoy searching for clues that a mysterious "them" is responsible for all that is wrong with the world. It is this mindset today that is attacking our beloved American symbols.

Nova Constellatio Copper 1785. One example of the many uses of the single eye as a motif in early American art.

The symbols most often lied about by the fundamentalist-conspiratorialists are the reverse of the Great Seal and Washington, D.C. I say "lie" because the great weakness of these writers is a deliberate clouding of documented history. They selectively filter information to support their perspective, because they believe they already have the truth. They are merely searching for examples to make a showy case for others. Fundamentalist-conspiratorialists fear our American symbols because they are under the assumption that *the leaders of the American Revolution were motivated by evil intentions.* I know this will sound anathema to the rational and educated majority of our readers, but it's an important point to make and refute, because this is the key difference between my interpretations and the majority of all other symbolic interpretations out there today. One of the purposes of this book is to put the brakes on some of the negative shifts happening in America's appreciation of her own symbols.

Each successive Republican administration that has assumed power in the past 25 years has grown increasingly closer to the fundamentalist-conspiratorialist school of thought, and, as a result, this small but vocal group has grown even more powerful and widely quoted. The average American may not know why, but *they think they know* there is something spooky about the Great Seal, probably because they've caught a whiff of the well-spread rumors on TV documentaries and the Web that are inspired by the fundamentalist-conspiratorialists. It's almost as if a conspiracy campaign has been launched to defame these uplifting and empowering symbols. Some Americans are now afraid of anything that is even remotely "symbolic." No matter what it is, if it appears ancient or mythological, it has been accused of being motivated by Satan and thus worthy of being purged. I have been absolutely astounded at the evil intentions and negative interpretations being attributed to the Statue of Liberty, the eagle, the Washington Monument, and even the Liberty Bell, which you will read about in each of their respective chapters.

There are an estimated 20–80 million Fundamentalist Evangelicals in America today[4] who are being exposed to these claims. There is no way of knowing how many fundamentalist-conspiratorialists are out there, and the numbers of fundamentalist Christians is presented merely as a reference point. For the record, I would like to emphasize that I am not critical of Christ's teachings, just of the lies that are presented in His name. I believe the Master Jesus Christ was the ultimate expression of compassion, unconditional love, and being our brother's keeper. I agree with Thomas Jefferson who said in an 1813 letter to John Adams that the words of Jesus are as easily distinguishable from those of his evangelists "as diamonds in a dung hill." Christ is a new dimension of love. I believe it is important to present the historical and contextual origins of America's symbols as a balance to the lies currently being circulated about them.

Creating a sense of fear about our Founding Fathers, or about the Freemasons, or about any of our American symbols *is a waste of time.* Those who are really in control behind the scenes are probably pleased to see this misrepresentation continue as a diversionary tactic. These connect-the-dots conspiracy theories that rely on a hyper-analysis of our national symbols using the entire world as a reference point divert people's attention from our real duty of keeping a close eye on the current administration and preventing them from abusing their positions of power. The George W. Bush administration was elected in large measure thanks to the support from the fundamentalist evangelical voting block. Now we have an administration that is driven by war profiteering interests and is ignoring the world scientific consensus regarding needs for environmental safeguards threatening even the short-term future for our children. Instead of standing up to vote them out, many of our fundamentalist-conspiratorialist friends concentrated on this behemoth of a conspiracy theory.

An Irrational Fear of the Freemasons

The fear about our symbols basically boils down to an irrational fear of secret societies and, in particular, the Freemasons. Keep in mind that most of the criticism of Freemasonry is based on insinuation and jumps to conclusion, as only a minute handful of its critics through the centuries have joined a lodge or done any true primary research into what Freemasons do and teach in their ceremonies. In 1971 I decided to do just that, and, as an active Co-Mason for several years, I can attest to the sincerity of this group. The Freemasons are what they say they are: a community service organization founded on principles of brother hood and altruism and tolerance. Personally, I was drawn more to the Co-Masonry branch of the order, which allows for female membership, believing as I do that equal rights for both sexes, particularly in the search for truth and the performance of rituals, provides balance in all things.

It is the Freemasons' insistence on secrecy and their penchant for elaborate and unusual play-acting rituals that trigger such suspicion and fear in the ill informed. For hundreds of years Freemasons have been accused of being anti-Christian. For the most part this is because one of the main tenets of Freemasonry is the practice of *religious tolerance,* and they have adopted the use of universal terms and rituals to express their concept of the Creator. This practice makes all members from all faiths welcome and comfortable in dedicating themselves to their common bond of serving their fellow man and community. Fundamentalist-conspiratorialists say these altruistic statements and philanthropic activities are merely a "front" calculated to conceal from us their true intentions that include world domination, mind control of the masses, and the eradication of Christianity. They believe that, around the time of the American Revolution, the Freemasons were infiltrated by the infamous Bavarian secret society called the Illuminati, and that since then the Masons have served as the cover organization for men of power to control the rest of humanity. I am not about to deny the existence of covert groups of powerful men who meet for shadowy purposes of mind control of the masses. Unfortunately, I believe that really does happen. However, I am wholeheartedly of the belief that this is not being done through the auspices of the modern Freemasons.

Nor can I believe that the Founding Fathers in question—Benjamin Franklin and Thomas Jefferson are prime examples—who did not worship in the fundamental Christian fashions, had anything *but* religious freedom and tolerance for all in their plans for this country. Of course, none of our founders was perfect. Jefferson owned slaves and Franklin was a philanderer, but I think their biographers and the general consensus agree that overall they served to the best of their abilities to create a nation where *freedom* was the overarching theme.

At the same time, we should also acknowledge that not all Freemasons are perfect either. In any large group of people through several hundreds of years, odds are a few will not live up to the expectations of society. But most of the outrageous and scandalous crimes you will hear attributed to "Freemasons" are outright hoaxes, as we discuss further in Chapter 8. Weighed against the enormous good the Freemasons do and have always done in contributing services and funds to the community and charities, the few members who have done bad deeds should not be indicative overall of this organization of do-gooders.

What Is a Symbol?

Writers in the humanistic tradition, such as Rollo May, June Singer, Joseph Campbell, and Carl Jung, define myths, symbols, and archetypes as a significant force in the psyche of humanity. Symbols may also be sources of historical or factual knowledge of the objective world, but many of them are far more than that. Symbolism is "the art of thinking in images," according to Hindu philosopher Ananda K. Koomaraswamy.[5] J.E. Cirlot says this art is now lost to civilized man, "notably in the last three hundred years.... [T]his loss—as anthropology and psychoanalysis have shown—is limited to consciousness and not to the 'unconscious,' which, to compensate, is perhaps now overloaded with symbolic material."[6]

The *affect-image* is a term applied by John W. Perry to a living mythological symbol, and his description accurately addresses the physical power of a symbol:

It is an image that hits one where it counts. It is not addressed first to the brain, to be there interpreted and appreciated. On the contrary, if that is where it has to be read, the symbol is already dead. An "affect image" talks directly to the feeling system and immediately elicits a response. When the vital symbols of any given social group evoke in all of its members responses of this kind, a sort of magical accord unites them as one spiritual organism.[7]

Edward Edinger described symbols as carriers of "psychic energy" and spontaneous products of the archetypal psyche, which cannot be discovered or manufactured. He goes on to observe that without the symbolic life the ego is alienated from its suprapersonal source and falls victim to a kind of cosmic anxiety. The ultimate goal of Jungian psychotherapy is to make the symbolic process conscious.

June Singer cites the ability of the symbol to facilitate wholeness through its power to attract and lead the individual on the way to becoming what he or she is capable of becoming: "That goal is wholeness, which is integration of the parts of his personality into a functioning totality. Here conscious and unconscious are united around the symbols of the self."[8]

Rollo May regarded the original root meaning of the word *symbol,* deriving from "drawing together,"[9] as an echo of the process of integration and wholeness. The individuation process facilitates a homogeneous being, leads us to the missing part of the whole person, and heals our split and alienation from life.

Carl Jung was convinced that symbols are formed out of the unconscious by way of revelation, intuition, or dreams. Jung further stated that slowly evolving symbol formations are responsible for the development of cultural ideas and behavior. He believed that symbols are the formative agents of communities and supply both the psychological and the organizational foundations of social life.

Joseph Campbell said that the most important effect of a living mythological symbol is an energy-releasing and directing image, which awakens and gives guidance to humanity and is conducive to participation in the life and purpose of a functioning social group.

All these modern philosophers and psychologists agree that the symbol plays a central role in the integration of the personality. When a symbol system is missing, society grows increasingly estranged. Without meaningful symbols, a society will be unstable and anxious, as symbols are the very formative agents of communities, supplying both the psychological and organizational foundations of social life. As Paul Tillich put it:

> Symbols cannot be produced intentionally.... They grow out of the individual or collective unconscious and cannot function without being accepted by the unconscious dimension of our being. Only the symbol can convey our ultimate concerns, unlike signs, which do not participate in the reality of that to which they point. Symbols cannot be replaced.[10]

The Meaning of Mythology

For the most part, the contemporary world identifies the word *myth* with fictional, made-up stories for fireside entertainment. The humanistic tradition, on the other hand, sees myths as a significant force in the human psyche. From the anthropological, intellectual, or sociological view, the content of a myth is of minimum value, as the historic facts and timetables within the myth are often paradoxical and contradictory. Many believe, as Carl Jung did, that myths require a psychological interpretation. As products of the unconscious archetype and therefore symbolic, myths could be interpreted no other way. The universal similarity of mythological motifs has been well documented by Campbell, Kerényi, Neuman, Singer, and others. Deities and heroes in the myths are actually productions and projections of the psyche. Joseph Campbell said in *The Hero with a Thousand Faces* that mythology was simply psychology misread as biography, history, or cosmology:

> Mythology has been interpreted by the modern intellect as a primitive, fumbling effort to explain the world of nature (Frazer); as a production of poetical fantasy from prehistoric times, misunderstood by succeeding ages (Muller); as a repository of allegorical instruction to shape the individual to his group (Durkheim); as a group dream, symptomatic of archetypal urges within the depths of the human psyche (Jung); as the traditional vehicle of man's profoundest metaphysical insights (Koomaraswamy); and as God's Revelation to His children (the church). Mythology is all of these. The various judgments are determined by the viewpoints of the judges. For when scrutinized in terms not of what it is, but how it functions, of how it has served mankind in the past, of how it may serve today, mythology shows itself to be as amenable

as life itself to the obsessions and requirements of the individual, the race, the age.[11]

Myths describe the psychological development of humanity and provide a method by which people can stabilize and grow in an unfavorable environment. The historian of myth Karl Kerényi said that the basic property of mythology is a return to origins and primordiality, and its paramount theme is foundation.

Paralleling the development of science has been the disintegration of our mythological systems, and this has contributed to the alienation and fragmentation experienced in our contemporary period. The distant historical past provides little of the technological comforts by which the contemporary person has made himself the center of the universe. Campbell points out that man today finds the past unworthy of imitation and ritual meaningless:

> ...[I]t may well be that the very high incidence of neuroticism among ourselves follows from the decline among us of such effective spiritual aid [as mythology]. We remain fixated to the unexorcised images of our infancy, and hence disinclined to the necessary passages of our adulthood. In the United States there is even a pathos of inverted emphasis: the goal is not to grow old, but to remain young; not to mature away from mother, but to cleave to her.[12]

A living mythological symbol awakens and gives guidance to the energies of human life in order to become conscious of the unconscious. Through individuation (to use Jung's term) one can establish one's own foundation and center. We must learn to turn inward to acquire meaning, purpose, and destiny, in order to overcome our anxieties, fears, and suffering, and discover our reason for being.

It's All in the Archetype

As stated earlier, symbols may be derivatives of archetypes, an idea popularized by Carl Jung in recent decades, although he acknowledged it was not a modern expression. In use before the time of St. Augustine, the archetype is reminiscent of Plato's "Ideal," a primordial image reposited in a supracelestial place as an eternal, transcendent form. According to Wallace Clift, archetypes are potentialities, whereas symbols are actualizations conditioned by individual and social situations.[13] Tillich notes that symbols are the infinitely variable expressions of the underlying static archetypes. Jung and Neumann say symbols and mythological motifs are derivative of the archetypes of the collective unconscious.

My favorite example of an archetype as it relates to the founding of this nation is the persistent story of the unknown man or "professor" who anonymously aided the revolution. Appearing and disappearing at key moments of decision, always rallying and leading the new republic on, this mysterious man fits the archetype of the magician or wise old man. Most of these stories did not appear until the late 1800s, but they still demonstrate Americans' collective desire to believe that we are being led by Divine Providence. There are several uncorroborated accounts of the mysterious professor influencing the design of the American flag, the signing of the Declaration of Independence, and the design of the Great Seal.[14] Theodore Heline wrote of an "influential person" called "the Professor" who was apparently known to both Franklin and Washington and "who submitted to the Cambridge Committee a design for a flag with the notion that if it were accepted, little or no alteration would be necessary when the colonies would secure their independence." Another mysterious man reportedly rallied the Continental Convention at a low point of indecision, by closing his "appeal for decisive action with the ringing words: 'God has given America to be free.'"[15] A third mysterious visitor is said to have granted George Washington a vision for the future of our country. Even though none of these accounts can be factually substantiated, all of them can be considered expressions of the magician archetype, and thus explored in a useful manner. Functioning as an archetype, the unknown man or stranger could be a centering device, restoring meaning and purpose to life, a role formerly filled by ancient myths.

Examining the notable elements within the story told about the Great Seal and the mysterious man, we can see expressions of the "magician archetype" as defined by Jung. The setting is a dark night in a garden where Thomas Jefferson has walked to clear his head. A black-cloaked stranger appears who is fully aware of the committee inside struggling to devise an American seal. He hands Jefferson a design for the seal that the committee immediately recognizes as perfect, and then he vanishes forever before they can thank him. According to Carl Jung, the magician archetype does not express human or personal qualities, but is instead a mythological figure possessing unknown or inhuman characteristics.[16] The stranger in this account was entirely cloaked, making him, in effect, an invisible source possessing unknown or inhuman characteristics. He both enters and exits mysteriously without identifying himself or discussing the design of the seal. As we'll see in the next chapter, the Great Seal *was not* designed by the committee on which Thomas Jefferson sat, so this story cannot possibly be true on a factual basis. The various authors repeating it have inadvertently created a mythology, perhaps inspired by an archetype. Though irrational in nature, the centering capacity of these types of stories continues to be sought by some.

Approaching the word *archetype* etymologically, we learn that "arch" signifies beginning, origin, cause, primal source, or a "dominant." "Type" means a blow, as in the striking or the imprinting on a coin. It also means form, image, order, prototype, model, or primordial form. Putting them together we have a primal dominant order or prototype. Compared by Jung to the axial system of a crystal that preforms the structure of the crystal (although it has no material existence of its own), archetypes mediate the primal chaos in the first stratum of the psyche in which the psyche and the natural world are fused together in an undifferentiated mass. They are vehicles through which order is transmitted from the collective unconscious into the personal unconscious. The archetype acts as an ordering principle or constellating hub around which experiences reappear again and again. Providing us a means to perceive and experience correlations between larger patterns of the universe and the destiny of the individual, archetypes tend to manifest through the "synchronistic" process.

Jung lists the principle archetypes affecting human thought and behavior as: the self, the persona (the role-playing personality), the shadow (the unconscious), the anima (feminine characteristics), the animus (masculine characteristics), the wise old man or magician (spirit who provides guidance in a meaningful direction), the earth mother (who brings forth all life from herself), and the child (the young undeveloped aspect of the personality). The self is the central archetype, the archetype of wholeness, or, as Ira Progoff regards it, the self is the archetype of archetypes.

Intentionally or not, the founders of the United States of America chose national symbols that depict the individuation process using archetypal images. This demonstrates a basic human need to identify with the archetypal process of regeneration, rebirth, self-realization, and synthesis. The need to become whole was just as great to archaic society (note the transformation of Osiris) as it is to contemporary humanity. Wholeness occurs through the union of opposites—basically a creative process—and symbols facilitate this union. The reverse of the Great Seal is an excellent contemporary expression of an ancient archetypal process that resolves human fragmentation. In desperate need of uniting their countrymen and of overcoming the fragmented state of the American colonies, the Founding Fathers agreed upon symbols that expressed both their predicament and its resolution.

Self-Actualization Is the New Order of the Ages

Many believe that the world today is on the verge of an evolutionary change in consciousness. America was designed to lead the way into this enlightened state by creating a situation of self-governance that engendered freedom of speech, freedom of religion, and the room these freedoms guaranteed for reflection and spiritual growth. In order to claim our destiny, we must demand a new type of leadership able to reflect this change. It is possible that this shift in consciousness is something for which our Founding Fathers were hoping and planning as they selected these symbols and designs to identify us.

As psychology returns to its primary business of an examination of consciousness, and as the Eastern methods of problem-solving mix with the Western traditions, more people are learning to turn within. Becoming quiet to listen to the "still, small voice" of God within, becoming conscious of the unconscious, these activities result in individuation and allow us to manifest our potential. This process is sometimes called self-actualization or self-realization. Self-actualization means experiencing life fully, vividly, selflessly, with full concentration, and with total absorption without immature self-consciousness. It is an ongoing process, often involving struggle and pain, and is experienced by everyone to some degree.

There are many parallels between our contemporary age and the revolution for American independence. In describing this new era of the currently shifting paradigm, June Singer could almost be describing the goals of the Founding Fathers to set forth a new nation of liberty and justice for all:

> The new era we are entering will require a shift from the exclusively personal viewpoint to one that includes the transpersonal, a shift from an egocentric position toward a universal orientation. The new consciousness is founded in a deeply felt awareness that our being in and of the universe means that the universe is in and of ourselves.[17]

Although many point to modern technological values as responsible for the loss and destruction of the symbolic and mythological systems of humanity, others see the old paradigm as a necessary stepping stone on our way to becoming what we are meant to become. A worshiping of objects definitely leads to a loss of humanism and the view of the individual as an object. If it's true what Campbell and others conclude, "that we are at this moment participating in one of the very greatest leaps of the human spirit to a knowledge not only of outside nature but also of our own deep inward mystery, that has ever been taken, or that ever will or ever can be taken,"[18] then I believe that a new appreciation for American symbols can help us take this step. I also believe our Founding Fathers knew that, at least on some level.

Has America Lost Its Way?

The news media report daily on the belief around the world that the United States of America is an imperialist nation. "Making the world safe for democracy" in one person's description is seen as "forcing capitalism by gunpoint" in another's. I am greatly disturbed at the American people's gradual acquiescence to the corporation to whom we have granted more rights than any individual ever had. Because the corporations mostly control the media, they have been able to bend our minds to their will, until most of us believe that the economy and consumerism are more important to this country than individual freedoms. When we ask too many questions, we are told to "shut up and sit down."[19] In our current political climate patriotism is proved by wrapping oneself in the flag, and torture has been condoned by our highest elected leaders. Questioning authority can label you a terrorist and get you thrown in jail for years without a trial. Most Americans are enslaved to a Madison Avenue chimera called the American dream. We worship at the bank and take on several jobs, struggling with debt and the illnesses that result from this intense concentration on material gain. Our goals are renewed nightly through the hypnotic appeal of television. This is nothing new, of course. What has changed is that, in the past, those enslaved were still comfortable enough to believe it was all worthwhile.

I paint cars because they become moving billboards for the ageless wisdom teachings. Working in this medium, it is best to teach through symbols, because most people only view the car fleetingly as it rolls by and therefore only their subconscious is able to grasp the message. Symbols speak directly to our subconscious minds, and I find it the most gratifying medium for most of my artwork. This is the Biodiesel Founding Fathers Artcar, completed in 2006. Photo by Stuart Zolotorow.

When we allowed the presidential election to be stolen in 2000 (and probably again in 2004)[20] we invited in a new monarchy. This new brand of fundamentalist patriotism, with its restrictions on our personal liberties in the guise of protecting us, is something our Founding Fathers would have certainly rebelled against. Remember Ben Franklin's popular slogan: "They who would give up an essential liberty for temporary security, deserve neither liberty or security." Most disturbing to me is that our new monarchy has co-opted our beloved symbols of freedom and independence, turning many in this country and around the world against these powerful icons by unfairly associating them with this current administration.

As we shift from an old paradigm to a new, our inherited social systems are being questioned while we gradually synthesize the humanistic tradition with contemporary scientific technology. In the new paradigm, our technological prowess will no longer menace our very future on this planet. Only recently has humanity sought the development of technical power over the internal growth of moral integrity, resulting in this imbalance. The new paradigm allows for more so-called feminine and nurturing characteristics to enter the mainstream consciousness. Doors of opportunity for women are opening as never before, and new emphasis is being placed on values of cooperation over competition, for the team approach to problem-solving, and to using our intuition.

Technology has led to a loss of humanism (Singer), a worshiping of objects (Fromm), viewing the individual as an object (Progoff), and an estrangement of people from their true nature (Tillich), but the main reason we feel so disoriented and pointless is because we have lost the glue that holds together nations, societies, and civilizations: We have lost our appreciation for our collective symbols and myths. The most famous American symbols could reestablish a symbolic and mythological system for our nation as a whole, which could then awaken and give guidance to the energies of human life. The symbol contains both conscious and unconscious elements and relates to the entire psychic system; it can therefore be assimilated by consciousness with relative quickness. As June Singer pointed out, "Today we are beginning to understand that how we live and what we do may have a profound effect upon forces that we formerly thought of as inexorable. We are not only the products of creation; we are also the co-creators."[21]

A Reason for Hope: The Cultural Creatives

Despite the destruction and dismay caused by the old paradigm, and despite the current political climate of domination, there are still reasons to feel optimistic, if for nothing else, for change. Seed changes can happen rather quickly, as seen by mid-term elections. Thanks to Al Gore, we now have a most promising change in mindset regarding how we as a nation abuse the environment. *Finally,* there is a growing state-by-state active determination for change, overruling the "stay the course" policies of the W. Bush administration that is firmly entrenched in the old paradigm in terms of environmental sustainability. That alone is reason for hope.

If we embrace a collective mythological and symbolic system, and appreciate our symbols on their deeper and more profound levels, they can actually stimulate higher consciousness. People will come together and ethical leaders will be elected who will serve to embellish the common good. And most importantly, as we face this coming century that promises great climate changes globally, America can continue to be a leader in the West, the lifted torch of hope and refuge, the promised land for right stewardship, a helpful neighbor. In this new paradigm, American symbolism will suddenly make a lot more sense. The motto on the Great Seal, *Novus Ordo Seclorum* (literally translated: the New Order of the Ages), indicates the American experience was consciously identified by our founders to be a momentous step in the evolution of the human species. The American revolutionary period was also a theoretical paradigm shift in the fields of politics, government, and economics, and our contemporary transitional interval mirrors that shift.

There is a new sub-culture of people evolving in America, dubbed the "Cultural Creatives" by psychologists Sherry Ruth Anderson and Paul Ray. After a 13-year statistical study, Anderson and Ray identified a growing shift in values that crosses all ethnic, economic, political, and spiritual boundaries. These people identify themselves as part of what we have been calling the new paradigm: They are more compassionate, creative, spiritual, and ecologically aware. But the stunning revelation in Ray and Anderson's work is the sheer size of the group. More than 50 million Americans, or one in four of all adults, fall into the category of "Cultural Creatives," according to this study. "These 50 million people are trying to create a new American culture," says Ray, "and to a large extent, they are succeeding.... As they come to appreciate their numbers, there's no telling what kind of impact they will have."[22] Ray and Anderson estimate the group to be growing at a rate of 1–2 percent a year, and cultural analysts and marketers are already predicting shifts in behaviors in response.

If you are one of these 50 million, then you should be able to relax and enjoy this book. It will hopefully instill a new sense of pride in being American and a resolve to use your political will to do something about correcting the course we are on. If you are uncomfortable with the idea of changing paradigms, and with symbols having more than one level of meaning, then I hope this book is able to expand your awareness. New levels of interpretation about the symbols of the American experiment can be beneficial to all Earth people.

CHAPTER 2

THE EYE, THE TRIANGLE, AND WHOSE EYE IS IT, ANYWAY?

As long as man has been drawing on caves, he's been representing the human form, and eyes are some of the oldest symbols known to man. Acknowledging their power, we call them "windows to our souls." They are considered sacred and supreme all over the world. In learning how to deal with other humans we learn that often the eyes will reveal the truth, even when the mouth is speaking falsely. When two symbolic eyes are together, it obviously conveys meanings associated with vision, seeing, and this powerful physical sense. But what does one single eye mean?

The Master Jesus spoke of it, saying, "If therefore thine eye be single, thy whole body shall be full of light" (Matthew 6:22, King James Version). This scripture is teaching us to shift the focus from the personal, physical self (two eyes) to that of spiritual attainment (single eye). In the Eastern traditions, the single eye has been identified with the third eye, or spiritual eye, seeing within or, in other words, with clairvoyance. The single eye is related to the inner light, intuitive power, and illumination. Hindus and Buddhists often depict the third eye with a dot or an eye symbol painted in the center of the forehead. The legend of the Cyclops is theorized by the Theosophists to be based on memory of a time when there was a race of beings that had a powerful third or psychic eye. They believe that the pineal gland is what remains of this third eye or psychic center. Jung compares the eye to the mandala, the structure of which symbolizes the center of order in the unconscious.

The Eye = God

In Christianity, as in many other religions, the single eye is used to represent the all-seeing, all-powerful God. Several times in the Bible, God is referred to as a single, all-seeing eye, as in, for example, Psalm 33:18 and throughout Ezekiel. It was a popular symbol in the Renaissance and during the 1700s. The Revolutionary generation was familiar with it and associated it with God. It has since waned in popularity, as have many of the symbols and neo-classical artistic choices of our Founding Fathers, and, as a result, their meanings have become obscure. The more mysterious, the more open they are to misrepresentation. It is crucial to remember that these symbols were not at all mysterious to our forefathers who chose them to represent America. They were chosen partly *because of their popularity* and their immediate understanding by people of all classes in America, as well as the people they were trying to impress in Europe. A single eye, especially when it had a radiant light or *glory* surrounding it, meant instantly to the Founding Fathers: "God." Enclosing the eye in a triangle reinforced the Trinitarian concept of the Christian religion. The single eye and eyes in triangles are depicted in many Christian churches, but the single eye was a popular symbol in pre-Christian religions as well, which is apparently the main reason the fundamentalist-conspiratorialists fear this symbol today. The stylized eye, or *Udjat,* is one of the best recognized of Egyptian symbols and is known as the Eye of Ra or the Eye of Horus. Both Ra and Horus were gods of the sun or sky, and thus the single eye became also a symbol for the sun.

The Egyptian *Udjat,* the right eye of Ra, also identified with Horus. Egypt is one of many cultures that depicted their idea of God as a single eye. Illustration from Petrie, *Amulets.*

The new Congress approved the radiant eye in a triangle for the Great Seal of our nation because there was a consensus belief among them that God had played an active role in the founding of this new country, and they wanted to honor that in the design of their seal. Today, there is a contemporary conspiracy theory, spreading quickly, thanks to the Internet, based entirely on misinformation surrounding this seal. It goes like this: There is a mysterious group of "Them," often called the Illuminati, but known by many names, controlling the world behind the scenes. They like to sprinkle eyes and triangles and pentagrams all over the place in logos and public designs as clues to their existence. This theory can be toppled quite literally, by kicking out just one leg: the connection between the reverse of the Great Seal and the Freemasons or the Illuminati. It is not there, and it was never intended to be there. The only connection between the Freemasons and the reverse of the Great Seal is the 1935 dollar bill, which we will get into a little later in this chapter.

I find it painful to realize that tens of millions of Americans now believe that the reverse of the Great Seal is Satanic or somehow otherwise menacing. I offer the following historical and symbolic interpretation to prove otherwise: that it is a noble symbol worthy of our reverence and respect. Yes,

The reverse of the Great Seal is a noble symbol worthy of our reverence and respect. The eye shows the favor of Providence (God), and the pyramid shows the strength and duration of America. Department of State pamphlet 8868, July 1976.

there is a relationship between it and symbols used in Egypt and Babylon and other ancient civilizations. Yes, the Freemasons use these types of symbols, too, borrowing as they do from the same ancient civilizations. No, this is not proof of a Satanic connection. The eye on the reverse of the Great Seal is just the opposite, in fact. It stands for God.

The Triangle = The Trinity

The triangle represents the number three and thus a trinity, where two opposites combine to create a third. Many religions possess trinities or triads—for example, the Father, Son, and Holy Spirit in Christianity. In esoteric Judaism there are Kether, Chokmah, and Binah. Ancient Egypt venerated Osiris, Isis, and Horus, and the Hindus venerate Brahma, Vishnu, and Shiva. There may be a deep-seated tendency to organize temporal or developmental events into three-fold patterns. Freud saw psychological development in three states: oral, anal, and genital. Hegel understood the historical process from the threefold cyclic pattern of thesis, antithesis, and synthesis. Other common triune expressions in nature include solids, liquids, and gases; animal, vegetable, mineral; and space, time, and measure. Joseph Campbell's monomythic process, which is similar to Jung's individuation process, is also threefold: separation, initiation, and return. Buckminster Fuller considered the tetrahedron, a three-dimensional triangle, to be the building block of the universe. The triangle is often used to symbolize the pyramid, which in turn is an archetypal symbol for the mountain, or the breast, or the mother. In the case of the reverse of the Great Seal, the triangle was placed around the eye most likely as a means of connecting it more strongly to the Christian tradition. By placing the eye in the triangle, the symbol for the Trinity, most people of that time would have immediately identified it as a Christian symbol for God. Though the vast majority of Americans were Christians themselves, it was paramount among the founders' intentions to protect freedom of religion, and thus they regularly used terms such as *Divine Providence,* a term that Protestants, Catholics, Deists, and Jews alike could relate to.

A single eye with a radiant light surrounding it meant "God" to the Founding Fathers. Enclosing the eye in a triangle reinforced the Trinitarian concept of the Christian religion, and is a common symbol in churches such as this one in the Aachen Cathedral in Aachen (western Germany).

The Pyramid = Strength, Duration, and Possibly Initiation

The pyramid has sprouted a whole school of theory as to its inclusion on an American seal because of its obvious connections to Egypt. Unbeknownst to most contemporary Americans, the symbol of the pyramid was already popular in Revolutionary art before its use on the Seal. Early American designers used the pyramid symbol to indicate endurance and unity.

Academic historians will consider as verifiable fact only the words of Secretary of Congress Charles Thomson and artist William Barton regarding the interpretations of what they included in the final design of the Great Seal (which we cover in more detail in Chapter 6). Thomson and Barton gave us just this one sentence for why they chose the pyramid for the Seal: "The pyramid signifies Strength and Duration." That's it. The founders chose the pyramid because they wanted to associate these two qualities with the new United States. As I demonstrated in *Founding Fathers, Secret Societies,* however, the pyramid on the Great Seal of the United States is not just any pyramid. It was probably modeled after the Great Pyramid of Giza, a sketch of which was available to the founders in a book that was in the Library Company of Philadelphia. *Pyramidographia,* published by John Greaves in 1646, contains illustrations that compare favorably to the William Barton/Charles Thomson 1782 pyramid of the Great Seal, especially in that they are both missing the capstone at the top.

Part of the reason the Founding Fathers were interested in ancient Egypt was their appreciation for a civilization that could last so long and build monuments that were geometrically significant. So far today, archeologists and historians cannot agree on the original purpose for the pyramids, nor how they were constructed. But we have been able to prove that there was an advanced geometry that went into their design and construction, incorporating measurements of pi, the golden section or phi, and measurements for the center of the galaxy.

Geologist Robert Schoch, following the leads of Schwaller de Lubicz and John Anthony West, is one of a handful of brave academics going public with their conviction that a culture more ancient than pre-dynastic Egypt developed the Sphinx and the pyramids. Schoch's addition to the puzzle is his geological interpretations of the water marks on the Sphinx proving it was once underwater— a *really* long time ago for the Sahara desert. Their calculations take advanced civilization further back than we can comprehend. "Giza isn't the birth of something new," says Schoch, but rather, "it is the full flower of something old."[1] Though there is no documentation indicating that any of our founders were aware of this, tradition has long held that the Great Pyramid of Giza was used as an initiation chamber where aspirants would enter a sort of isolation chamber to go on a vision quest and determine their life purpose.

The Pyramid and the Eye Were Everywhere

Possibly more important than the 18th-century interest in Egypt was the heavy influence of the neoclassical school of art. Symbols used by the ancient Greeks and Romans appeared all over early American symbolism, not just in the

Great Seal. As we discuss in Chapter 4, from the time of the Revolution until at least the War of 1812, personified depictions of "America" were always portrayed in the vicinity of some other object of classical antiquity. Symbols including pyramids, obelisks, temples, and altars were meant to link the grand American experiment of republicanism with these earlier successful attempts. For example, in an 1807 engraving entitled *The Goddess of Liberty with the Portrait of Jefferson,* the goddess is holding a portrait of Jefferson while gazing respectfully at a portrait of George Washington *on a pyramid* in front of her. In an 1815 print entitled *Peace of Ghent and Triumph of America,* the Goddess America is riding *toward an obelisk* inscribed with the names of American military heroes. An 1808 publication entitled *America* depicted the Goddess Columbia *next to a pyramid* with portraits of Washington, Franklin, and Hancock. We also recently located another piece of Colonial currency showing the pyramid: a 1776 Colonial bill for $8 that features the truncated 13-step pyramid with the Latin motto *Majora Minoribus Consonant.* Translated loosely, this means: "The greater are in harmony with the lesser," referring to the strength in the union of the Colonies.

A 1776 Colonial bill for eight dollars featuring the truncated 13-step pyramid demonstrates that this symbol meant the strength of the union to the Colonists.

Similar to the pyramid, the single eye was also in frequent use in early American art and symbolism before it was chosen for the Great Seal. The 40-dollar bill of 1778 designed by Francis Hopkinson featured the single eye with rays of light coming from it, over a circle of eight-pointed stars and an altar. It was Francis Hopkinson's 50-dollar bill of the same year that included the image of an unfinished pyramid, which most likely served as the inspiration for the final design of the reverse of the Great Seal. Mr. Hopkinson's appreciation for these two symbols—even though when he worked on the Great Seal committee he did not suggest either one of them for the Seal—calls for a further examination of this intriguing fellow later in this chapter. The *Nova Constellatio* coin of 1783 showed a single eye surrounded by a circle of 13 six-pointed stars. As we'll see in Chapter 3, the same words—*New Constellation*—were used to describe the star spangled blue canton on the new flag adopted in 1777. As with the first flag, the stars in earlier renditions of this coin are three intersecting tapered lines, rather than two interlocking triangles. The *Immunis Columbia* coin of 1787 originally had the Eye of Providence on the obverse before it was changed to the Goddess Columbia.

The single eye was a well-established artistic convention for the Revolutionary generation seen on Colonial money. This 1778 40-dollar bill shows the single eye with rays of light coming from it, over a circle of eight-pointed stars and an altar.

The point here is that neither the pyramid nor the eye were exclusive to the design of the Great Seal, though in none of these earlier uses were the two symbols used together. The combination of the radiant eye inside a triangle acting as a capstone to finish an incomplete pyramid is *a uniquely American symbol*. When Charles Thomson put them together to form the reverse of our Great Seal, individually they were commonplace devices, and because of that, the seal would not have appeared strange at all to that generation. As the decades passed, however, and the neoclassical style of art was replaced by more Victorian sensibilities, Americans lost their ability to interpret many of our early symbols as meaningful. The concepts of liberty and republicanism gradually became more commonplace and taken for granted, and the more dramatic artistic interpretations of these hard-won ideals faded from popularity. When they are resurrected today they sometimes appear strange and mysterious to our modern eyes, and into that mystery step the fundamentalist-conspiratorialists making up answers to satisfy the curious.

Today's Seal Is Not Yesterday's Seal

As is the case with much of what the founders did, the Great Seal was somewhat cobbled together from ideas and suggestions by people during the course of many years. For example, the radiant eye in the triangle had actually been suggested for the front of the Great Seal six years before the pyramid was suggested for the back. When the pyramid was first placed on the reverse, the eye above it was not encased in a triangle. The first artistic rendering of the reverse, which historians believe was done under William Barton's supervision, did not give the impression that the eye was the missing capstone for the pyramid as it appears today. They still looked like two distinct symbols rather than two pieces of the same puzzle. The eye was described as being connected *to the motto above it* to stand for the concept of God. The pyramid was connected to the date *and the motto below it,* or the hoped-for longevity of the new republican undertaking they had launched in 1776.

Many of the details to which clue-finders point when examining the Great Seal, including any measurements of its angles, were added in later renditions, and were not intended by the founders. My purpose with this book is mainly to examine the original intentions for these symbols as proposed by our Founding Fathers. Fundamentalist-conspiratorialists delight in pointing out Freemasonic correspondences found in "clues" on the dollar bill, but these details are meaningless in telling us anything about the Founding Fathers, whose original designs and descriptions called for no such details. There is no reason to believe that the Founding Fathers were thinking about geometry when they chose the Great Seal. They were interested in *the idea* of a pyramid and what the image conveyed. *And it did not mean "Freemason" to the people of this generation.*

The Birth of the Reverse of the Great Seal

This is the main subject of my earlier book, *Founding Fathers, Secret Societies,* and I urge the reader to check that publication for more details on the origins and interpretations of the Great Seal. The best official source of information on the Great Seal is *The Eagle and the Shield* by Richard Patterson and Richardson Dougall, published by the State Department in 1976 and released in 1978. John MacArthur's terrific Website, *GreatSeal.com,* is an organized and encapsulated history of the Great Seal, factually based on *The Eagle and the Shield,* and it is highly recommended.

The radiant eye in the triangle (though not with a pyramid) was included in the design for the Great Seal from the very beginning. The first committee was called immediately after the Declaration of Independence was signed in 1776. Though their suggestions were rejected by Congress, four elements from the first committee's designs did survive through to the final design. All four were suggested by the artistic and heraldic consultant on the job, Pierre Eugène du Simitière, whose sketch called for the motto *E Pluribus Unum,* a shield, a radiant eye in a triangle, and the date "MDCCLXXVI."[2]

In *The Eagle and the Shield,* Patterson and Dougall demonstrate how the radiant eye was used as a symbol for an "omniscient ubiquitous Deity" in the medallic art of the Renaissance and was a "well established artistic convention" of the time.[3] All three artists on the three Seal committees (du Simitière, Hopkinson, and Barton) were familiar with heraldic and ornamental devices, and used the single eye to imply that God, or Providence, was watching over this new nation. This is the *only* official interpretation of the eye, from the Remarks by Secretary of Congress Charles Thomson: "The eye over it & the Motto [*Annuit Coeptis*] allude to the many signal interpositions of providence in favor of the American cause."[4]

Annuit Coeptis = God Favors Our Enterprise

William Barton's original motto suggestion instead of his eye was *Deo Favente.* Latin teacher Charles Thomson changed it to *Annuit Coeptis,* which means basically the same thing. Seal historians have traced it back to Virgil's *Aeneid* book 9, line 625, and *Georgics* book 1, line 40. In both cases, the phrase was *Annue Coeptis,* which was translated as an appeal to the Roman god Jupiter to *favor these undertakings* or enterprise. David Ovason has made a convincing case that Thomson changed the conjugation to the third person, so it would read *Annuit* (or "[He] favors") instead of *Annue* (for "[please] favor") in part so that the phrase would have 13 letters. It does seem as though they were trying to reflect 13 as many as 13 times in the Great Seal for the ostensible reason of celebrating the 13 united colonies or states. As we discuss in Chapter 5, it is probable that some of the Founding Fathers were familiar with the ancient symbolic associations of the number 13 with themes of renewal. It's likely they called such attention to the number not only for the 13 states, but also to link America to the theme of rebirth. They saw our new nation as being born anew out from the shackles of Britain's tyranny. *Annuit Coeptis* does NOT translate to "announcing the birth of," as you will see in many fundamentalist-conspiratorialist writings mistranslating this symbol. Thomson specifically states that the radiant eye of Providence works together with this motto, *Annuit Coeptis*. There can be no doubt that the intention of this device is to symbolize the eye of God looking favorably over the new American experiment.

Novus Ordo Seclorum = The New American Era

The other half of the motto refers to those undertakings our founders believed God was looking upon so favorably. They called it the *Novus Ordo Seclorum,* which translates as the "New Order of the Ages." In his official Remarks, Thomson indicated that this motto works together with the date underneath the pyramid, 1776: "The date underneath is that of the Declaration of Independence, and the words under it signify the beginning of the new American era, which commences from that date."[5] *Seclorum* is a poetic form of *Seculorum* or *Saeculorum* meaning "of the ages," or "generations," or "centuries." Again, the peculiar spelling may have been chosen for numerological purposes, as Ovason surmises. He shows that a combination of the 17 letters in *Novus Ordo Seclorum* with the nine digits in the Roman numeral used to depict 1776 (MDCCLXXVI) produces a total of 26 (or twice 13), and Ovason uses these as the final two to achieve 13 thirteens in the Seal.[6]

Seclorum does NOT translate to "secular," as many fundamentalist-conspiratorialists would have you believe. Using their version of specious Latin translations, fundamentalist-conspiratorialists will tell you that *Annuit Coeptis* and *Novus Ordo Seclorum* translate to "announcing the undertaking (or birth) of a New Secular (or World) Order." They want you to be afraid that the Founding Fathers were infiltrated by Satan-worshipping Illuminati who now control this country through the Freemasons. For proof they say all you need to do is notice how many people and organizations use symbols similar to the reverse of the Great Seal with eyes or triangles in their logos. This argument, of course, fails to recognize that these symbols are universal and have always been used by all kinds of people. Until the last few decades when this anti-American-symbol conspiracy took hold, these symbols have been interpreted on the surface to mean pretty much the same thing by all the different groups who used them: the eye is God, the rays are illumination or enlightenment from the Divine, the triangle is the Trinity, the pyramid is ancient strength.

A Brief Symbolic Interpretation of the Reverse of the Great Seal

In my previous books and my 1981 doctoral dissertation, I spent hundreds of pages offering deeper, archetypal interpretations of these symbols and combinations of symbols. So as not to overly repeat myself here, I'll provide just a brief summary. When we apply the humanistic psychological and archetypal under-standings to the different elements in the reverse of the Great Seal, we see a union of opposites that creates a new whole. The radiant eye represents spirit, and the pyramid (an archetypal mountain) represents matter. Put the two to-gether and you have the cosmic soul or spirit coming down into the body to create the enlightened human. It is my belief that this overly simplified state-ment sums up the spiritual vision of our Founding Fathers for this nation: create a land of liberty and freedom for the individual so that both the republic and the individual can evolve to their next logical step in evolution. That step is Self Awareness.

Were the Freemasons or Illuminati Involved With the Great Seal?

The simple answer is no. More to the point: Of the 14 men assigned to the various committees between 1776 and 1782, Benjamin Franklin is the only con-firmed Freemason among them. Franklin was a member of the first committee on the Great Seal, but, instead of looking to Masonic symbolism, Franklin suggested themes from the Old Testament of the Bible. The scene he wanted to see im-pressed on official documents being authenticated with America's seal was de-scribed as Moses next to the pillar of fire, indicating Divine Providence, as the Red Sea swells over Pharaoh's army. I love the motto he chose so much I painted it down one side of my car: "Rebellion to Tyrants is Obedience to God."

His fellow committee member, Thomas Jefferson, who also loved that motto, is sometimes listed as a Freemason. There is no evidence that "the Father of American Cryptography" ever joined any secret society, though he did come in contact with them and was certainly a secretive individual. His opinions on the Bavarian Illuminati have been preserved in his collected writings and are par-tially reprinted in the section titled "Thomas Jefferson and the Illuminati."

Jefferson's vision of America's official seal suggested the pillar of fire leading the Israelites out of the wilderness, also from the Old Testament. He is also the one who first suggested a two-sided seal, and on his reverse he wanted to see the Anglo-Saxon heroes Hengist and Horsa.

Their third committee member was the upright John Adams, who was so straight-laced that he is usually spared when the other Founding Fathers are accused of pagan idolatry or Satanism. Adams, too, however, was influenced by the current themes of the time in poetry, art, and literature, as well as in the rhetoric that was spawning the revolution for independence. This is evident in his choice for the U.S. Great Seal: a scene from classical Greek mythology called the Judgment of Hercules where the young hero must choose between the path of sloth or the path of virtue. Adams was not being original here, as Hercules, like the pyramid and obelisk mentioned earlier, was routinely depicted as the allegorical young nation "America." Artists wanted to associate our new country with Hercules's qualities of strength and divine guidance.

None of these three suggestions were used, obviously, though as we noted, their artistic consultant, Pierre Eugène du Simitière, did make a number of suggestions that stuck. Swiss-born du Simitière was well known for his collection of "Americana," including paintings, coins, newspapers, handbills, a special collection of books of American history, flora, and fauna. He went into debt purchasing items for his collection, and died in poverty in 1784. His collection was the basis for the first American Museum of Natural History, which he opened in 1782.

The second committee in 1780 consisted of founders not nearly as famous as the first committee: James Lovell, John Morin Scott, and William Churchill Houston. But again, the only significant contributions came from the artistic consultant they called in for help on the job, Francis Hopkinson. The suggestions Hopkinson made that stuck were the olive branch, and—straight from his 1777 flag—red and white stripes with a blue background for the shield, and a radiant constellation of 13 stars. The same thing happened with the third committee in 1782, which consisted of Arthur Middleton, John Rutledge, Elias Boudinot, and Arthur Lee. Again, the artistic consultant, William Barton, had the only lasting effect, with Barton's suggestions including the unfinished pyramid and an eagle (though just a tiny one on the shield). This committee's renderings were taken over by the Secretary of Congress Charles Thomson who we've written about extensively in

Chapter 6. Thomson deserves the credit for both rearranging and reinventing the final designs for both sides based on ideas of his own. Thomson's and Barton's sketches and descriptions made up the final accepted design on June 20, 1782.

Were the Artists Freemasons?

Only one of the men on any of the committees was a verified Freemason: Ben Franklin. One other is often mis-identified as a Mason: Thomas Jefferson. And a third, and perhaps the most significant, considering he made lasting suggestions, is also rumored to have been a Freemason: Francis Hopkinson. As with with Jefferson, no record of initiation has turned up to verify Hopkinson was a Freemason, but unlike Jefferson there is circumstantial evidence for Hopkinson. The fires of war destroy many records, and we can assume that there were probably more Freemasons among the Founding Fathers than can be certified by the surviving papers. When no records exist, historians will look for other indicators, such as attendance at lodge meetings or events, or close relations who have documented lodge initiation records, or certain characteristics in their lives and activities. In the case of Francis Hopkinson, his father, Thomas Hopkinson, was not only a Freemason, but also the Grand Master of the Grand Lodge of Pennsylvania in 1736.[7]

We will get to know Francis Hopkinson better in Chapter 3, but in brief, of the signers of the Declaration of Independence, Francis Hopkinson was the only one who was a professional artist. His work graced several pieces of Colonial money and other official seals and ornaments, and can still be seen in the Seal of the Treasury Department, which appears on the front side of the current dollar bill. He was better known among his contemporaries as a composer of popular songs, poetry, satire, and propaganda, including a very funny piece about the deliberation over the 1787 Constitutional Convention called "The New Roof." Some historians give even more credit to this piece than to *The Federalist Papers* for helping convince voters in several states to ratify the Constitution for the new national government.

It is assumed by the official Seal historians Patterson and Dougall, that Hopkinson's design for a $50 dollar bill in 1778, featuring an unfinished, 13-tier pyramid, was the inspiration for William Barton's pyramid design that remained on the reverse of the final Great Seal in 1782. Barton even assigned the same motto, "Perennis," as seen on Hopkinson's bill, and the drawings are nearly identical. Barton would certainly have seen the Hopkinson $50 bill when he wrote an essay on the nature and use of paper credit. *If* Hopkinson was a Freemason, it could be argued that his pyramid was in turn influenced by the use of the pyramid as a symbol in *some* Masonic regalia, where it represents the great builders of the past. But we must remember that the pyramid on Hopkinson's money was used as propaganda, advocating the union of the 13 states through the symbolism of the tiers of the pyramid, and that the pyramid was used elsewhere in Colonial and Revolutionary art as a popular reminder of endurance.

William Barton was the artistic consultant for the third committee who also worked with Charles Thomson to create the final accepted designs in 1782. Just 27 years old when asked to help on the Great Seal, he had already attained a reputation as an artist and a scholar. A student of heraldry, he had written another essay on the proper use of coats of arms in the United States, and he later wrote the first biography of America's famous astronomer, David Rittenhouse, who happened to be his uncle. He attempted to establish the American Heraldic Institution and was a member and counselor of the American Philosophical Society. Barton was *not* a Freemason, though he is sometimes confused with a Rhode Islander of the same name who *was* a Mason.

The radiant eye with the triangle around it was suggested first by Pierre Eugène du Simitière, whom we previously discussed. There is no indication that he was a Freemason.

This brings us finally to Charles Thomson, the originator of the symbol combination featuring an unfinished pyramid topped by a radiant eye in a triangle. That's right: American Charles Thomson originated this symbol combination, not the Freemasons, not the Illuminati, not the Egyptians or the Babylonians. Before it was done by Charles Thomson, no other group had ever combined these symbols together in just such a way. We will return to Charles Thomson in Chapter 6, but suffice it to say there is no indication that Thomson was a Freemason. He was friendly with the earliest group of Rosicrucians in America at the Wissahickon and Ephrata communities outside of Philadelphia, but there is no verification that he was a member. Rosicrucians also used the single eye in their symbolism, and sometimes also the pyramid, but never the two together.

The Dollar Bill

The only verifiable Freemasons who appear in the history of the Great Seal are the ones who decided to put it on the dollar bill in 1935. This is not a conspiracy and is all part of the official history of the dollar bill. Here's how it happened.

After all the careful deliberations over the designs, the Continental Congress of 1782 decided they really only needed to cast a die for the front side of the seal, and the design for the reverse was put away in a drawer. Two-sided national seals were sometimes created to impress hanging pendant seals, but by the end of the 18th century these were already fading from popular use. A die has never been cut for the reverse side of the U.S. Great Seal, and official public documents have always been authenticated by the front side only. As the decades passed, popular taste fell away from the idealistic visionary art styles used proudly by the Revolutionary generation, and the reverse of the seal was virtually forgotten. One group of patriotic Americans, however (the Freemasons), still enjoyed these romantic types of images, having adopted many of the same symbols as the founding Americans had. It's not surprising then, 153 years later, that it was two Freemasons who resurrected the design for the reverse. In 1935 they recognized the value of its symbolism as intended by our Founding Fathers, because privately they had continued to use similar symbolism all along.

These weren't just any two Masons, of course, but the President of the United States, Franklin Delano Roosevelt, and his secretary of agriculture, who later became his vice president, Henry A. Wallace. Wallace had just read the 1909 publication by government official and historian Galliard Hunt, *The History of the Seal of the United States,* where he learned of the little-known reverse side. Wallace took the design to Roosevelt, proposing they mint a coin showing the two sides of the Great Seal on either side. Roosevelt was equally impressed with the image, and liked Wallace's idea so much that he decided to put the two sides on the new one-dollar bill instead. They enjoyed how the words in the motto *Novus Ordo Seclorum* could be compared to Roosevelt's program of the "New Deal."

Two other important Freemasons were involved with the design of the new dollar bill: Henry Morganthau, secretary of the treasury, and Edward M. Weeks, the chief designer of the bill. A much more thorough study of the life and inspirations of

Edward Weeks is called for in order to do justice to an analysis of his beautiful dollar bill. For now we will refer to the brief biographical study done by author Ken McGrath in his *Secret Geometry of the Dollar.* According to McGrath, Weeks was also a Sunday school teacher and vestryman at his Episcopalian church, a Republican, and a member of his local chess club. In his 1952 book, *Letters Analyzed and Spaced,* Weeks displayed a mind of exacting care and accuracy, and McGrath proposes that he included geometric proportions in his design for the dollar bill that would allow a student of geometry to endlessly enjoy puzzling them out and reading meanings into the numbers. Even those without an appreciation for the meaning of symbols or training in geometry are able to sense the symbolic weight in this design. Mason and surveyor McGrath used geometry, the golden ratio, letter/number logarithmic codes, and some of the number theories of 19th- and early-20th-century pyramidologists to show a striking geometric intricacy on the back of the bill, but unlike the fundamentalist-conspiratorialists who have examined the bill almost as intensely, McGrath sees only positive codes and messages embedded therein.

Esoteric writers have linked the reemergence of the reverse of the Great Seal in 1935 to the great social changes that have occurred in this country since the mid-1930s. Women's rights, the civil rights movement, and a developing concept of environmental stewardship have all taken enormous strides forward in the last few generations. It has been my argument all along that the reverse of the Great Seal represents the collective feminine consciousness of our country, its more intuitive side, more compassionate and nurturing qualities, whereas the obverse of the Seal represents our masculine natures of bold courage, justice, and martial energies. The two sides of the seal illustrate our internal and our external personalities. Virtually unknown until 1935, the reverse of the Great Seal suddenly leapt into prominence by its inclusion on a vehicle that passes through countless hands every day. It is my belief that its qualities slowly began to assimilate themselves into our national psyche assisting these paradigm shifts. What might we expect to happen if the American government were to officially cut the die for the reverse of the Seal and use it as the Founding Fathers intended on official documents? Because of the law of similars and the theory of synchronicity, I believe we would see a corresponding balance assert itself in our national policies demonstrating an increased sensitivity to feminine values, more cooperation and less competition, more intuition and less dogmatic control.

The Owl on the Dollar and the
Bohemian Grove

When the reverse of the Great Seal became erroneously linked to the Freemasons, it began to develop a pseudo-history that has twisted all its positive interpretations around to suit the anti-Masons' agenda. Because of its placement on the dollar bill, every element of this intricately beautiful design has been scoured. Every millimeter of the eagle side of the Great Seal, every letter and every angle has been interpreted as "proof" that an ultimate secret society is in control of everything and everyone. They discovered you can draw a hexagram over the reverse of the Great Seal on the dollar bill, and the letters at five of the points would spell out "Mason." (They also spell out "No Sam" or "So Man" or "O Mans.") A great fuss is made over a tiny corner of the webbing in the background of the design of the bill and how various junctures resemble spiders or owls. These symbols are then given their most nefarious meanings as if there is only one level of interpretation possible. See the illustration where the webbing hits the top left of the border around the numeral 1 in the top right corner on the front of the dollar bill and perhaps you will also see the "owl" or "spider." It is unlikely that this "owl" is anything other than a trick of the eyes at a point where the spirograph pattern of the background webbing joins together. But if Weeks had intended this pattern to be an owl, it's much more likely that he would have seen it as a symbol of wisdom, which is the most commonly accepted interpretation of an owl. Fundamentalist-conspiratorialists, however, have constructed a complicated scheme based on this tiny mark on the dollar bill. By digging deeply, they found some symbolic meanings of the owl that match their preconceived evil interpretations. The one they like best links this tiny "owl" on the dollar to the mascot of the Bohemian Grove, a summer camp in California for the elite and powerful. According to eyewitness accounts by journalists who have infiltrated the Bohemian Grove retreats,[8] the activities during the two-week camp are nothing more than an attempt to bond the attendees in a spirit of exclusive togetherness. Their opening ceremonies are rather bizarre, however, apparently cobbled together from many different traditions. It began back in 1872 as a "spoof of ceremonies"[9] to encourage participants to put aside their thoughts and concerns about business. As infiltrator Philip Weiss concluded, "Bohemian Club literature boasts that the Cremation of Care ceremony derives from Druid rites, medieval Christian liturgy, the Book of Common Prayer, Shakespearean drama and nineteenth-century American lodge rites."[10] Participants are meant to feel even more elitist and separate from the general public, who are kept guessing that the members are up to something more powerful than they really are. I think they like it that way. Weiss reports that the rest of the time at camp is spent relaxing and acting extremely silly while drinking enormous amounts of alcohol and telling endless pee-pee jokes. The majority of the famous powerful people attending these secret retreats probably have no interest in the archetypal or ancient symbolic meanings of any of these rituals or symbols. Although its critics continue to protest outside the Bohemian Grove for their policy of excluding women and allegedly making important behind-the-scenes deals between global powerbrokers, it seems their mysterious rituals have no more occult significance than the high school plays so much of the rest of their activities resemble. Conspiracy theorists have picked up on the sophomoric rituals of this summer camp for grown men, and used their pastiche of ritualism to fabricate a new symbolic meaning for the owl. Thanks to the fundamentalist-conspiratorialists, you can now find plenty of Websites that will tell you the owl is an evil symbol for human sacrifice, an interpretation based entirely on the made-up rituals of the Bohemian Grove.

Conspiracy theorists have found what they believe to be an owl in the filigree background design of the one dollar bill. Some interpret this as "proof" that this country is controlled by the secret society known as the Bohemian Grove who also use the owl symbol.

The Illuminati

Throughout history we have used "light" to describe the "a-ha!" state of having a good idea and the "enlightened" state of an individual in communion with the Supreme Being. We depict saints and holy people with light radiating around them in halos. Ecstatic union with God causes one to be "illumined." The first baptized Christians were called "Illuminati" as were higher initiates in the Rosicrucian Order and other mystery schools of the East. The name "Alumbrados" was used by a Christian mystery sect in 15th- and 16th-century Spain, where they were some of the earliest victims of the Inquisition. To be illuminated means to be full of light, the symbol for knowledge, or the Christ Consciousness, if you prefer, a way out of the darkness of confusion. Illuminati originally described those who were "awakened" or "enlightened" or "illuminated," referring to the light of knowledge received from an exalted or higher source. Ironically, the meaning of this word has been turned on its head in contemporary understanding, thanks to the fundamentalist-conspiratorialists co-opting this term to describe their fabricated construct of an evil "them" bent on world domination.

In the same sweep that has condemned the reverse of the Great Seal for completely erroneous reasons, the label "Illuminati" has been so perverted that the average citizen today who has even heard the word before assumes it is linked to an evil cult. Instead of holy people being illuminated by the light of cosmic consciousness, the light has been redefined in these conspiracy theories to symbolize the secret knowledge of the cabal itself. "Illumined ones" are supposedly those "in the know" or members of the mysterious "them." According to this theory, any symbols associated with light—torches, radiant eyes, or suns, for example—are interpreted as a clue that the dreaded Illuminati are in the vicinity. Fundamentalist-conspiratorialists go to great lengths to identify various leaders in politics and industry as Illuminati by scrutinizing their clothing, jewelry, and photo ops for items or gestures that could be called symbols of light.

Anyone promoting union, brotherhood, peace, or particularly socialistic ideas such as public education or universal healthcare, is especially suspicious, because these goals are interpreted as stepping-stones to a global dictatorship. Photos of eye logos, eagle lapel pins, and pentagrams on coffee cups are used to "prove" that the politician or corporation in question is a member of the cabal, and has a secret agenda to overthrow all world religions and establish a one world government. These "illumined ones" allegedly enjoy toying with the rest of us by identifying themselves to each other through popular culture and mass media using symbols. Sound familiar? That's because one reason this conspiracy theory is so popular today is that it was the subject of Dan Brown's prequel to *The DaVinci Code,* called *Angels and Demons,* which became a coattails best-seller. The Illuminati are also the bad guys in the *Lara Croft: Tomb Raider* film and in countless comic books, video games, and other fictional entertainment.

The first fundamentalist-conspiratorialist in print that we could find misidentifying the reverse of the Great Seal as an insignia of the Illuminati was William Guy Carr in his *Pawns in the Game,* first published in 1955. Carr capitalized on the anti-Communism scare of his time by updating the anti-Semitic conspiracy theories of Nesta Webster and the proven hoax, *The Protocols of Zion.* We are currently looking into the possibility that Carr appropriated these connections between the Great Seal and the Illuminati from an earlier source, possibly from an anti-Roosevelt backlash generated by the 1935 dollar bill design, in an attempt to tie his reforms to a Jewish-inspired Illuminati conspiracy.

The design of the dollar bill almost became a campaign issue in 1936 when Wallace was linked to Nicholas Roerich, a controversial Russian mystic and artist, though Wallace had already fallen out with Roerich by then. Their full relationship was not revealed in the press until 1948, when Wallace ran for president on the Progressive ticket, and the story was dredged up and publicized for the first time. His political enemies used his unconventional religious interests to their advantage, and Wallace was said to have believed the reverse of the Great Seal had "kabbalistic" significance. It may have been this 1948 media coverage that started the fundamentalist-conspiratorialists thinking there was a connection between the reverse of the Great Seal and a secret society.

Identifying the Illuminati with the Great Seal, or anything remotely resembling it showing a pyramid or an eye, is a complete fabrication. Unfortunately this erronious link has effectively filtered into the consciousness of our nation to the point that today, though they may not know quite why, many people think the reverse of the Great Seal is a little bit spooky. Much of this is thanks to works of fiction such as the popular role-playing game developed by Steve Jackson in the 1980s, and a series of novels by tricksters Robert Anton Wilson and Robert Shea in the 1970s, both elaborately detailed tongue-in-cheek satire.[11] There is no documentation linking the eye in the triangle with the Bavarian Illuminati, and the best the conspiratorialists can do is claim that documents proving the Bavarian Illuminati used this symbol were formerly on display at the British Museum until they mysteriously disappeared.[12]

Traditional historians consider the official "Illuminati" (or the Perfectibilis) to have been formed in Bavaria in 1776 by Adam Weishaupt, a former professor of canon law. This group was dissolved less than 12 years later, and anything claimed about them after that is pure speculation. Many conspiratorialists believe the historical group went underground when officially banned, and that it continues to function in secret today. The Bavarian Illuminati was a secret society similar in many ways to the Freemasons, but with more radical and somewhat anarchic ideas. Many of their goals centered on throwing off the oppressive monarchy and church rule, which were particularly strict in Bavaria, but were also stifling the growing interest in intellectual and religious freedoms across Europe. Weishaupt became a Mason in 1777 and recruited from their lodges men who were attracted to his utopian goals of a secret network of influential people designed to reform the world. Internal fighting by rabble-rousing members is generally credited for their collapse, though the Bavarian government officially disbanded them in 1784. Weishaupt lived in exile for many years after the dissolution, writing apologetic histories of his failed order. Many wonder about the disproportionately large impact such a short-lived organization had on history and conclude their work must have continued in secret.

There is circumstantial evidence linking the influence of certain ex-members of the Illuminati to the bloody French Revolution,[13] even though the club was officially defunct before 1789. When the violence of the Reign of Terror died down and the survivors started looking around for someone to blame, secret societies in general were cast in a cloud of suspicion. After surviving years of horrific violence, many French people were attracted to the old order. People who encouraged free thought and universality were suspected as *agent provocateurs,* and it became popular to claim secret plots provoked the revolts, rather than the mean truth that their poor people were revolting against deplorable living conditions. These ideas were largely a result of two scurrilous books published in 1797–98. Jesuit priest Abbé Augustin Barruel and Scottish natural philosopher John Robison wrote convincing and somewhat lurid tracts detailing their convictions that secret societies, in particular the Illuminati and the Freemasons, were intent on destroying the Christian religion and taking over the world. These authors were afraid that the ideas of the Enlightenment regarding political rights for the individual were leading to a breakdown in society.

None of the American Founding Fathers can be identified by any evidence as having been a member of the Illuminati, though "Illuminati" became a smear word thrown around during the rancorous political divisiveness of the late 1790s and early 1800s, and Jefferson, in particular, was labeled as such by his political enemies. When questioned about whether or not Illuminism had spread to Masonry in America, George Washington answered that he "did not believe that the lodges of Freemasons in this country had as societies, endeavored to propagate the diabolical tenet of the former [Illuminati] or pernicious principles of the latter [Jacobinism]."[14] He condemned the Illuminati and the Jacobins as "self-created societies," which dealt them a blow that led to their disappearance in America.

Thomas Jefferson and the Illuminati

With Jefferson's quirky lifestyle and rather independent approach to religious services,[15] it was tempting to lump him together with the group currently under attack for their very liberal beliefs. Jefferson answered his critics in a letter to Bishop James Madison in January of 1800 where his astute mind made a clear distinction between the emotional opinions of Barruel and the philosophies of Weishaupt:

> I have lately…got sight of a single volume…of the Abbé Barruel's *Antisocial Conspiracy,* which gives me the first idea I have ever had of what is meant by the Illuminatism against which "Illuminate Morse," as he is now called, and his ecclesiastical and monarchical associates have been making such a hue and cry. Barruel's own parts of the book are perfectly the ravings of a Bedlamite. But he quotes largely from Wishaupt [*sic*] whom he considers the founder of what he calls the order…. Wishaupt seems to be an enthusiastic philanthropist. He is among those…who believe in the infinite perfectibility of man. He thinks he may in time be rendered so perfect that he will be able to govern himself in every circumstance, so as to injure none, to do all the good he can, to leave government no occasion to exercise their powers over him, and, of course, to render political government useless…. [T]his is what Robison, Barruel, and Morse have called a conspiracy against all government.[16]

Jefferson felt affinity for Weishaupt's goals of spreading information and morality, indicating that, if Weishaupt had been an American, he would not have had to resort to the formation of a secret society in which to perpetuate these aims. Rather it was the "tyrannical" rule of "despots and priests" that necessitated the spread of perfection and enlightenment under the cloak of secrecy. He continued in the same letter:

> The means [Weishaupt] proposes to effect this improvement of human nature are 'to enlighten men, to correct their morals and inspire them with benevolence.' As Wishaupt lived under the tyranny of a despot and priests, he knew that caution was necessary even in spreading information, and the principles of pure morality…. [I]f Wishaupt had written here, where no secrecy is necessary in our endeavors to render men wise and virtuous, he would not have thought of any secret machinery for that purpose.[17]

Charles Heckethorn, author of *The Secret Societies of All Ages and Countries,* and other traditional historians follow Jefferson on this conclusion, stating that the Illuminati "was instituted for the purpose of lessening the evils resulting from the want of information from tyranny, political and ecclesiastical."[18] Although these may have been the laudable goals of Weishaupt, the goals of the nefarious fictional groups called "the Illuminati" that followed, as depicted in the writings of conspiratorialists and satirists, were more about establishing a tyranny *by controlling information.* What has lived on into the 21st century is the belief that a secret society of anti-government, anti-religion power brokers are working behind the scenes to control world events to their own benefit. The *Illuminati* has become a catch-all label for those controlling this alleged conspiracy.

The Great Seal, the Illuminati, and the Freemasons

Freemasons did not officially use the all-seeing eye as one of their symbols until several decades *after* the approval of the U.S. Great Seal.[19] Likewise the pyramid. It's more a case of the Great Seal influencing the Masons to adopt these symbols than the Masons influencing the symbols used in the Great Seal. Masons do not usually depict their all-seeing eye encased in a triangle, but rather floating alone among clouds, just as a lot of Christians do. Masons have long admired pyramids as incredible *structures built by ancient stone masons,* but they did not become popular on regalia until after the adoption of the Great Seal. Masonic symbolism and popular American symbolism run parallel sometimes, choosing as they did from the same pool, but the pyramid-with-the-eye-in-the-triangle-above-it is not a Masonic symbol. It was not an Illuminati symbol. It was not an Egyptian, Phoenician, Babylonian, or any other kind of symbol. It was designed by an American, and a non-Mason, Charles Thomson. The reverse of the Great Seal is an American symbol.

Fundamentalist-conspiratorialists see a similarity between the U.S. Great Seal and contemporary corporate logos as "proof" of an Illuminati or Freemasonic world domination conspiracy. The popularity of eyes in corporate logos is probably due more to the logo designers wanting you to think about vision and far-sightedness than they do about the all-seeing eye of God (or Satan, for that matter). I'm convinced that the popularity of circles and triangles in corporate logos is because these are basic shapes that resemble so many things in our world, including the letters in our alphabet that are very often incorporated as part of a company's graphic designs.

This may seem obvious to you now, but if you ever come across a documentary or a Website demonstrating how similar are the symbols used by secret societies and corporate logos, it can tend to suck you in. When in doubt, always look for the sources behind the claim. The fundamentalist-conspiratorialists who attack the reverse of the Great Seal and call it a template for the Illuminati to reveal themselves through corporate logos usually rely heavily on the writings of Nesta H. Webster, William Guy Carr, Texe Marrs, and David Icke, all of whom in turn list *The Protocols of the Elders of Zion* as one of their own main sources. The Protocols is a proven anti-Semitic hoax that was first published in the early 1900s in Russia, probably by the Russian secret police in an attempt to justify their violence against the Jews.[20] It is considered by many to be the first book outlining the modern conspiracy theory that implies a secret group is manipulating global events by controlling banking, the media, and politics. In this early version, instead of the Illuminati pulling the strings, it is the Jews who are cast as the evil bad guys.

Despite being thoroughly debunked as a hoax by several independent investigations, *The Protocols of the Elders of Zion* continues to make an impact today, especially in anti-Semitic audiences. Icke, Carr, and others interchange the word *Illuminati* for the word *Jew* in their interpretation of "Them." Many of today's fundamentalist-conspiracy writers have retained this anti-Semitic streak. They seem more interested in mongering a fear about a persecuted minority than they are in fact-checking. Webster and Carr perpetuated the erroneous conclusions of Barruel and Robison that the Illuminati were directly responsible for the French Revolution and almost all other uprisings since then. When reference sources are cited at all on current Websites and books connecting the Freemasons to the Illuminati and revolutions, these writings are usually the original sources. Though the nature of symbolic interpretations is that several differing layers can all be correct at the same time, any correlations must first pass the test of historical accuracy.

The Skull and Bones, the CFR, the TLC, and the Other Modern "Thems"

There is no question that groups of rich and powerful people gather on a regular basis to plot out the course of the immediate future of the world. Many of my esteemed colleagues have written books about this shadowy conspiracy that has probably run parallel with official history all along. There are many, many critics of this kind of behind-the-scenes power brokering who are at the opposite end of the spectrum of what we would call fundamentalist-conspiratorialists. Libertarians and liberal intelligentsia, and other opponents of the neo-conservative religious right can (unlike the critics of the fabricated construct called "the Illuminati") actually name the names of the power brokers doing the manipulating. The missions of the Council on Foreign Relations (CFR), the Trilateral Commission (TLC), the Bohemian Grove, the Bilderberger Group, the Brookings Institution, and the Skull and Bones are to control what we see in the mass media, and even trigger certain events to persuade passage of certain policies they support. They have members in high positions of power and authority in the fields of politics, entertainment, media, and business. This is all true, and many people more qualified than I am have tracked and documented the revolving doors between the power elite, politics, and the media.

It is an established fact that our own government has dabbled, and probably still is dabbling, in mind control as revealed in their own archives and in congressional hearings in the 1970s. The CIA was forced to admit they had administered LSD and other psychoactive drugs to unwitting participants, as well as experimenting with sensory deprivation and conditioning in attempts to control behaviors.[21] Nick Begich is among many who have done an admirable job of documenting the latest in advances in technology designed to assist the government in this goal.

Groups of powerful people have always met in secret with the goal of controlling the masses, but, fortunately, I believe human beings are far too unpredictable and resilient for great success in this venture on a wide scale. Advertisers will keep trying, however, and there is no question that they are choosing symbols they hope will control human behavior (that is, purchase their product, vote for their candidate). But as stated repeatedly, their penchant for choosing eyes, circles, and triangles can be explained by the strength of these symbols to "strike a chord" based on their archetypal foundations, not based on their questionable link to Satanism. If you are worried about having your mind controlled by any of the "thems" out there, the best thing you can do is turn off your television set. Mind control works best on brains that are in a non-participatory state of semi-hypnosis that develops from regular TV viewing.

The problem arises when fundamentalist-conspiratorialists debase whole ethnic groups, religions, or social clubs by identifying them as minions of these corporate CEOs and bankers motivated by personal greed and power. This whole speculation that somehow the Freemasons are involved in a global conspiracy based on clues left by our Founding Fathers is offensive, but I do understand how the Masons make a perfect scapegoat. Freemasons love their secrecy clauses and oaths. They enjoy play-acting and dress-up rituals that are so old-fashioned they lead to all kinds of speculation by outsiders. They strive for the perfectibility of man through service to the community of mankind. Yes, they had a lot to do with the founding of this nation. That is because Freemasons tend to be very civically active people, and naturally would be the ones founding the post offices and fire departments, arranging for the street lights, and laying the foundations of community buildings—after volunteering to fight on the front lines to establish the liberty and freedom to do so. Unlike the goals of many in the elitist organizations listed previously, which are devoted to achieving more power, the goals of the Freemasons are all about service.

It is my contention that if you substitute the name "Skull and Bones" wherever you see the word *Freemasonry* as the inheritor of the nebulous "Illuminati," you would be much closer to the truth. Researcher Antony C. Sutton was one of the first to connect the Yale University secret society to the Bavarian Illuminati, noting that the year the latter disbanded coincided with the dating system used by the Skull and Bones regarding their own origins. If there is any truth to the idea that radical members of the Bavarian Illuminati went underground after 1784 to continue with a goal of secretly controlling world events, then their descendents would likely be attracted to the Skull and Bones. Author Alexandra Robbins says Skull and Bones is the only society at Yale University that exists exclusively for its own good: "No community service, no donations to anybody.... It is the only society that has this very specific agenda, which is to get members into positions of power, and to have those members hire other Bonesmen to positions of prominence and prestige."[22] Skull and Bones are particularly prevalent in our media, and some of the most popular news outlets—*Time* and *Newsweek,* for example—have Skull and Bones at their foundings.[23]

Ostensibly founded in the 1830s, the most infamous fraternity at Yale University has nothing to do with the founding of our nation. Three members of this powerful club have become president of the United States, however, including both presidents George W. Bush and George H.W. Bush, and William H. Taft, whose father was one of the original founders of the society. The Bush family dynasty in Skull and Bones (W's grandfather, Prescott Bush, was also a member) is only one of many prominent and recognizable power-family names on the register of the society, including also Bundy, Buckley, Harriman, Rockefeller, Taft, and Whitney. The 2004 presidential election was unique in that both candidates, John Kerry and George W. Bush, were Bonesmen.

According to the legends, the Order of Skull and Bones started with Yale student William H. Russell. After returning home from studying abroad in Germany in the early 1830s, Russell found that Phi Beta Kappa, the national honor society, had been stripped of its secrecy in an anti-society fervor. He was so incensed that he installed Skull and Bones at Yale University as the American chapter of a German secret society he had encountered while abroad. They allegedly called their organization the Brotherhood of Death or, more informally, the Order of Skull and Bones, and are said to have plotted an underground conspiracy to dominate the world. Though there is ample reason to fear a group whose sole mission is to get members into positions of power in order to aid other members, fundamentalist-conspiratorialists tend to miss the mark when they focus on their symbolism or the meanings of their rituals. I've heard one fundamentalist-conspiratorialist critic describe one ritual where participants drink wine out of a skull, nodding his head and saying, "and we all know what *that* means." We do?

To many of us today the skull symbol with crossed bones beneath it means "danger" of poison or death. The skull and crossbones on a black flag means a pirate ship, which most of us probably assume is because the pirates would often kill people, so it was an allusion to death, as well. Or was it? Author Steven Sora says the insignia had a deeper meaning to the original Knights Templar who sailed under this flag. To them it symbolized resurrection. The skull and crossbones is also seen on Washington's Masonic apron, preserved in the collections of the Grand Lodge of Pennsylvania. Once again we have the Freemasons appreciating a very old symbol for reasons very different from the modern spin. A skull is an obvious symbol for death, yes, but death is not necessarily a symbol for something negative. Death can also be symbolic for a big change, as in transcending the physical world and reuniting with the Creator.

I have no idea what is the intention behind the selection of this symbol by the Skull and Bones fraternity. Unlike the Freemasons, there are no great exposés of their literature, nor can just anyone join who wants to. Although I was initiated into Co-Masonry in 1971, I will never be able to experience the Skull and Bones firsthand, and thus I can only speculate on what they are up to. To do this, I look at their behaviors and activities in the community rather than getting hung up on their symbolism and one particular meaning that could be attributed to it. Without a historical record to study, no one on the outside can be sure what these symbols meant to their founders or current members. We can only look at the reports of the few investigators who follow the people identified as members. The activities of their currently most famous member, George W. Bush, speaks volumes about their goals, in my opinion.

Fear of the Symbols Instead of What's Really Behind Them

Mythology, ritual, and symbolism are important to the psychological health of the human being, as has been amply demonstrated by humanistic psychologists Joseph Campbell, Rollo May, Carl Jung, and many others described in Chapter 1. That human beings tend to want to join together into groups of like-minded people to perform ceremonies that tie them to the past, can be explained as a method of giving meaning to their lives. Unfortunately, some groups are formed to satisfy greed at the expense of others, and it's possible that some of these may be misusing the eye or the triangle or the circle in their symbolism. Connections may appear to exist between power groups of today and ancient societies through the use of such symbolism, but it is most unlikely that the known leaders of these groups are consciously practicing black magic of any sort. Most of our political leaders and entertainment figures who are identified as members of the groups such as the TLC, the CFR, and so on, do not believe in the power of symbols or ceremonial rituals. Anything that resembles these kinds of activities is probably being done for the shared bonding experience and to give themselves an air of mystery. Occult trappings of modern groups are meant to distract you or to make them seem more powerful than they really are.

It is unfair and unnecessary to drag the honorable Great Seal of the United States into this debate. Attaching it to a group that doesn't even exist has smeared its reputation, and now it is beginning to stand for some of the worst things about this nation. More and more often we see it in political cartoons and editorials to exhibit the proclivities of the W. Bush administration to spy on its own people. The Great Seal was chosen as a symbol for early Americans to emulate, and to remind us that we are not complete as humans or as a nation without God or the conscious soul. It was not designed as a clue that any one particular group was secretly in charge. Secret and non-secret societies for centuries have honored the individual symbols that make up the reverse of the Great Seal for the same reasons Americans today should still honor them. It reminds us that illumination from the Creator source gives knowledge of the purpose of the soul or nation, which, when achieved, creates a balanced whole individual, or unified nation.

The Eye and the Triangle in Corporate Logos

The fundamentalist-conspiratorialists are very busy compiling lists of all the companies that use symbols of eyes, triangles, pyramids, torches, pentagrams, and other ancient symbols they have decided to interpret one way only. They declare with an exclamation point that everyone using such logos is in league with Satan! The eye and the triangle are the symbols most often cited on these lists, possibly because the eye, the circle, and the triangle have been represented in corporate America for as long as there has been advertising, giving them far more ammunition to use for examples. The fundamentalist-conspiratorialists say the hundreds of companies and groups who use the eye or the triangle in their logos proves the "Illuminati" are all around us. These theories prey on the socio-logical aversion we all have of being lied to and laughed at. Because most of us do not have the classical education that our Founding Fathers had, it is easy for many to be swayed by the ominous-sounding interpretations of the radiant eye, the triangle, and the pyramid. Add the spin that the "Illuminati" are deliberately flaunting these symbols in plain sight to make fun of the rest of us, and our emotions take hold with a "Wow! These symbols really ARE all around us. I must have been blind before, but now I see!" Allow me to repeat: These symbols are all around us because the eye, the circle, and the triangle are fundamental building blocks of the universe, not because a Satan-worshipping cabal is controlling everything and laughing in your face.

According to conspiracy theorists like Alex Jones, the corporations using these types of logos are doing so deliberately to align themselves with symbols they know to be Satanic and that they believe will bring them power. The unconscious public is theoretically being conditioned to dark magic through repeated association with these "Satanic" symbols on everyday products and services. Although there is truth in the concept of mind control through media and advertising, and even in the concept of sending secret messages within headlines, the idea that these symbols were chosen by corporate graphic designers to condition us for the coming Antichrist is about as far-fetched as the concept of our Founding Fathers being Satanists. And don't forget the first rule of interpreting symbols: You must allow for many levels.

Here are some examples of how widespread are the circle, the eye, and the triangle in advertising logos: The Pinkerton National Detective Agency, known today as Pinkerton Consulting and Investigations, still uses a modified version of the single eye they devised for their logo back in the 1800s to illustrate their motto: "We never sleep." The Alliance of Guardian Angels uses a radiant eye in the triangle with wings in their motif on their T-shirts as part of their uniforms. Columbia Records has a logo they call the "walking eye," which looks like a record album with two little stick legs on the bottom. The logo of the National Film Board of Canada resembles a person with arms joined overhead, creating the image of an eye. The FEMA logo until 2003 (when it adopted the Homeland Security Logo) was very similar to the eagle side of the Great Seal, except over the eagle's head was a circle with a triangle inside it, a symbol recognized by the rules of International Humanitarian Law for civil defense.

The triangle is an equally popular choice for logos, in large part because it is often used to stand for the letter "A" in a company name. We find this pattern in the logos for Adidas, the German sportswear manufacturer; Avery/Dennison, the label makers; and Adobe Systems, makers of Acrobat reader and Photoshop, which also uses the eye in their software logo. The triangular Greek letter Delta, a symbol for change, is also the reason behind a number of corporations choosing the triangle as their symbol, most obviously with Delta Airlines and Delta Faucet manufacturers. Others use the triangle as a symbol for a mountain, as in Marlboro cigarettes and the Paramount Motion Picture Company. Columbia Pictures Industries deserves a special prize for incorporating several of our favorite symbols (and those most feared by the fundamentalist-conspiratorialists) in one logo. We have the goddess Columbia, who is holding a torch, while standing on a pyramid pedestal. Oh, my!

Because of their dominance at the top of these lists, we will focus on three logos: CBS-TV, AOL, and DARPA. When presented with the official company line about the origins of these logos, the fundamentalist-conspiratorialists will probably dismiss them as mere cover stories devised by the Satanic elitists in control of these corporations. It is this same selective disregard for the historical record that lies behind their mistaken claim that the Illuminati identifies itself with the eye in the pyramid. "Close enough" is "close enough" for the fundamentalist-conspiratorialists. Even if the official explanations of the corporations proved conclusively that their logos were not intended to be symbols for the Illuminati, I'm afraid many would still insist otherwise.

CBS—Eye on the World

The eye used in a logo, such as this one from CBS-TV, is often interpreted by conspiracy theorists to link the company to the "all-seeing Illuminati." ® and © 2007 CBS Broadcasting Inc. All Rights Reserved. Used by permission.

Whereas the logos for most other companies have changed significantly throughout the years, the "eye" logo for CBS Television has remained virtually unchanged for more than half a century. The official time line and interpretation of their logo is told in some detail at *CBS.com,* where we learn that a promotional designer at the Columbia Broadcasting System named William Golden devised the eye logo for CBS in 1951. Golden remembered driving through the country in Pennsylvania and drawing inspiration from the folk symbols painted on Shaker barns to ward off evil spirits. He was struck with an idea for a new logo for CBS that was a stylized eye similar to these Pennsylvania Dutch symbols, to show that CBS had its eye on the world. The first versions of the logo even had the eye in motion with the pupil opening and closing as a camera shutter lens.[24] In looking for connections to prove their theory that eye logos are meant to be Satanic, fundamentalist-conspiratorialists could choose from any program CBS has run since the 1920s to demonstrate evil intent. Because they are a communications company, it's easy to whip up paranoia about the possibilities implied by the logo of the CBS eye: It could be spying on us, filtering our knowledge, and controlling our behavior. Or it could simply be keeping an eye on the world for news.

AOL—America Online

 Despite their seeming similarity, the AOL logo was not designed with the intention of resembling the Great Seal. The universal appeal of these geometric shapes, and their resemblance to the letters "A" and "O," explain their popularity in corporate logos. AOL and the AOL triangle logo are registered trademarks of AOL, LLC. All Rights Reserved. © 2007 AOL LLC. Used with permission.

The original logo for America Online (AOL) resembled the reverse of the Great Seal, making them another prime target for the fundamentalist-conspiratorialists. If you do a Google image search for "AOL logo" on the first page of hits you'll find at least one site that claims the "all-seeing eye of the Illuminati appears in the AOL logo." Unlike CBS, however, when the people at America Online first designed their logo, they were still very much a fledgling company, and no one bothered to keep a record of how the logo originated. The original triangle with a swirl inside of it was devised in 1988 when Quantum Computer Services changed their name to America Online. This was back when they were still mainly providing limited BBS services and game downloads. As Elizabeth Ellers, senior vice president of brand development and consumer research, told us, "Things were changing rapidly, and in those days we didn't spend a lot of time worrying about history. We were moving ahead at full speed."[25] Along with Ellers, I interviewed Danielle Marcey, director of brand development, and they gave us the history of their logo and how it has changed.

According to company legend, the concept for the original logo was scrawled on a napkin during a meeting in a restaurant. In 2004, when AOL decided to upgrade their logo, they spent a lot of time trying to find out more details about the original concept, but to no avail. Marcey related how they couldn't even locate the name of the design firm that was hired to finalize the napkin design into what became the famous logo. All they had to rely on was anecdotal company stories that recalled that the triangle symbolized the A in "America" and the swirl inside it symbolized the O in "Online." This was long before the company became known as AOL. The swirl of the "O" also symbolized the movement associated with connection to the Internet. As Ellers described it, "swirls were very big in the 80s."[26]

Through the years, as the company exploded in popularity, they made it a policy to follow customer feedback very closely. When they decided to update their logo to reflect their new direction, they consulted numerous focus groups that told them to keep the triangle, as it projected a sense of stability, but the swirl had lost its appeal. Consumers today relate the swirl more to a hurricane or another danger symbol. It projected a sense of unease, which is why in the updated AOL logo, designed by Desgrippes Gobe in New York, the swirl or the "O" has been filled in to become an unbroken circle. They also turned the triangle on its side to show that the company was moving in a forward direction.

Notice we are calling the symbol a *triangle,* because that is what it is, and that is what consumers perceived. It is not a *pyramid,* as the fundamentalist-conspiratorialists have claimed. Despite their resemblance, a pyramid and a triangle are not the same thing. But fundamentalist-conspiratorialists look at symbols on only one level, and when they see something that looks *like* a pyramid with an eye in it, they don't need to do any further research. It looks like it, so it must be related.

It was encouraging to me that these rumors had not reached the officials I spoke to at AOL. "It just throws me for a loop," said Marcey. "Some of these questions are just so funny."[27] Ellers went on to explain that no one in the company, as far as she knew, had ever noticed the similarity of their logo to the reverse of the Great Seal, much less heard that because of it, their company was being linked to a global, elitist conspiracy of Satan-worshippers. Ellers and Marcey were surprised these accusations had not surfaced in their many focus groups employed to gage the public's interpretation of their logo. "Everyone called it a triangle," said Marcey, "never a pyramid." And for the record: "I think it is fair to say we deny being part of any conspiracy."[28]

It's a Waste of Time

It is most unfortunate that fundamentalist-conspiratorialists are wasting their energy by examining corporate logos to make invalid associations with these symbols. They are right to keep a strict eye on the large corporations that control our communication and access to knowledge, as I believe strict attention to protecting our liberties is entirely warranted in maintaining them. I am also a vocal critic of the ever-shrinking base of ownership in the media since Ronald Reagan's deregulation measures. But to waste time making up stories about the AOL logo resembling the reverse of the Great Seal to prove that they are led by some imagined version of the Illuminati is pointless and results in other enormous leaps in conclusion. Accusations that result from such hysteria are easily debunked by good investigative reporters, who, after doing so, will be less inclined to investigate truly valid claims of media monopoly or threats to our privacy.

May I take this opportunity to remind you that the fundamentalists made a big impact in the elections of George W. Bush who professes to be an evangelical Christian? Some of the fundamentalist-conspiratorialists have since turned on him, and now accuse him of being the devil,[29] but they sure were singing his praises back then, identifying with his speeches as they would with an evangelical preacher prophesying the end of the world rapture. The kinds of people who fixate on one singular interpretation for a symbol are also the kinds of people who want to escalate the war in the Middle East because they interpret the outcome will fulfill biblical prophesy for the second coming.

America was founded as a country where freedom of religion was to be sacrosanct. People who follow fundamentalist-conspiratorialist teachings have every right to believe and worship as they choose. When they start inaccurately attacking American symbols, however, something I've made a lifetime of appreciating, I am going to stand up and defend them by exposing the inaccuracies in these claims. What bothers me the most is how this mindset—not this religious denomination—has invaded the policies of our country. In the international theater we are driven by fear in the wars in Iraq and Afghanistan. In the domestic theater, fear is mongered to bully us into policy changes that suppress more of our civil liberties than has been done in all our 230-plus years. Worse still is President Bush's miserable shirking of responsibility to reduce our effects on climate change in the face of international scientific pressure. By subjecting us to an endless campaign of fear and deceit, the Bush administration has instead busied itself convincing Americans to give up our rights, as well as our responsibilities to leave a sustainable planet for our children. To illustrate this point, see the examination of the DARPA logo for how a bad interpretation of the reverse of the Great Seal can backfire.

DARPA

The immediate reaction of many when they saw this logo designed for the Big Brother–sounding Defense Department organization called the Total Information Awareness Program, was, "Are they joking?" The logo was discontinued soon after its unveiling in 2003.

DARPA is the Defense Advanced Research Project Agency, a research and development team for the Department of Defense. Their official history on their Website says they were created in 1958 in reaction to the "surprise" launch of the Soviet's *Sputnik,* a surprise that was blamed on a lapse in intelligence-gathering capabilities.[30] Their stated mission is to develop the latest technology for use by the military, and that means a lot of spying to find out what the enemies have and know. With the new directives from the Patriot Act, when it was decided that everyone could be a potential enemy, information-gathering gained much more support. To handle the extra work, DARPA formed a new sub-agency called the Information Awareness Office (IAO), which funded the Total Information Awareness (TIA) Program. The TIA later changed its name to the *Terrorism* Information Awareness Program because so many people were comparing them to the Orwellian newspeak version of Big Brother. For good spies, they sure missed a beat when they decided on a logo using the reverse of the Great Seal in such a provocative manner that it seemed they were just asking for trouble. It didn't help that their mission statement fit the description of all that's bad about the alleged Illuminati.

The IAO was charged with improving intelligence-gathering on American citizens with everything from facial recognition software, to laser machines that pierce your clothes to show clear images of your body. They proposed a closed-loop information system to link all our daily computerized activities, allowing them to spy on everyone instead of just suspicious characters. The danger of this approach is that those in power can then decide who is suspicious according to changing criteria.

The description of their mission was enough to ruffle feathers in Congress, and the program was soon de-funded. Most of us only learned of it in hindsight, as if watching a bad movie, learning they had tapped convicted Iran-Contra felon John Poindexter to head this new agency. Then we see the logo they used for the Information Awareness Office, and it seems designed deliberately to invite criticism from conspiracy theorists. I have a hard time assuming they did not know how controversial that logo would be. But that would mean they adopted a cartoon-ish logo, knowing it would be interpreted as part of this "Illuminati conspiracy." Why? Warped sense of humor? Wanting some paranoid people to think they were more powerful than they really were?

    Their logo consisted of the eye in the triangle over the unfinished pyramid, directly off the U.S. Great Seal. (See the illustration.) These two symbols were placed behind the Earth, with the rays from the eye enveloping it. Their motto was Latin for "Knowledge Is Power." From the opinion commentaries of the time, it seems that when most people saw this symbol, their reaction was: "Are they joking?" Not many did see it while it was current, however. The public reaction against the logo and the whole concept of a Total Information Awareness Program was vehement and swift. The agency was immediately attacked by the American Civil Liberties Union and half of Congress for overstepping the civil rights to privacy held dear in our constitutional bloodstream. Congress defunded the whole outfit in 2003 and Poindexter was dismissed, but, in typical fashion, conspiratorialists say their research projects live on under other umbrella organizations. One is rumored to be called the "MATRIX," for Multistate Antiterrorism Information Exchange. If that's true, then the man behind the curtain apparently does have a sense of humor.

    Before it was de-funded, the IAO actually posted this explanation about their controversial logo and why it had been removed:

> DARPA offices have traditionally designed and adopted logos. However, because the IAO logo has become a lightning rod and is needlessly diverting time and attention from the critical tasks of executing that office's mission effectively and openly, we have decided to discontinue the use of the original logo.
>
> For the record, the IAO logo was designed to convey the mission of that office; i.e., to imagine, develop, apply, integrate, demonstrate,

and transition information technologies, components, and prototype, closed-loop information systems that will counter asymmet-
ric threats by achieving total information awareness useful for
preemption, national security warning, and national security decision making. On an elemental level, the logo is the representation
of the office acronym (IAO) the eye above the pyramid represents "I," the pyramid represents "A," and the globe represents
"O." In the detail, the eye scans the globe for evidence of terrorist
planning and is focused on the part of the world that was the source
of the attacks on the World Trade Center and the Pentagon.
"Scientia est potentia" means "Knowledge is power." With the
enabling technologies being developed by the office, the United
States will be empowered to implement operational systems to
thwart terrorist attacks like those of September 11, 2001.

The unfinished pyramid and the eye depicted in the logo were
taken directly from the reverse side of the Great Seal of the United
States of America.[31]

The DARPA IAO logo was a poorly considered design decision and an
inappropriate use of these venerable old symbols, and the public didn't stand for
it. Consider the difference in their interpretation of the eye and the Founding
Fathers' interpretation of the eye. The founders called it Divine Providence—
that was their power. The DARPA people called it "information collected by
spying"—that was their power. The hubris was outstanding even in their symbolism. The W. Bush administration has focused on restricting freedoms, claiming to do so to make the world safer. But the world that is protected is just their
own small version of it and available only to a privileged few. What is coming
will be the great leveler. Unprecedented earth changes are in our future, and by
ignoring them and denying the need to prepare for them, the current administration is taking America down a road far from the course laid out for us by our
founders. America is supposed to be the leading example of how liberty and
freedom foster enlightenment and the betterment of humanity. It takes enlightened leadership to acknowledge that we must change our wasteful and non-
sustainable habits or our planet will become uninhabitable. Because our current

administration is stuck in the old paradigm of conquer and control, America is not leading the way, but rather digging in its heels.

The Great Seal in the New Paradigm

Paradigm shifts are always uncomfortable, as many cling desperately to the old and familiar despite the obvious need for change. The civil rights movement is an excellent example of how painful a paradigm shift can be for many people. The new paradigm currently struggling to be born puts its emphasis on partnership, conservation, and cooperation, and stresses whole brain knowing. The key characteristic is transformation, which is a state that allows for multiple levels of interpretations to any symbol.

The radiant eye over the pyramid is a symbol of positive power and growth that can be seen in many examples in Christian iconography, such as this image of the Star of Bethlehem over the Holy Manger.

When we are allowed to chose and have the freedom to make our own interpretations rather than being dictated to, our creative collective unconscious will be able to make such transcendent correlations as the ones I'm proposing, and use and appreciate this symbol for what it really is: one of positive power and growth. This union of opposites to create a new whole (male/female, celestial/terrestrial, spiritual/material) can be depicted in hundreds of ways, including many examples in Christian iconography. One of my favorite books for illustrating numerous examples from nature and science resembling the reverse of the Great Seal is called *Inner Wealth*. It provides hundreds of illustrations to show how the radiant eye in the triangle over the pyramid can be used to discover your inner wisdom, comparing the reverse of the Great Seal to the Star of Bethlehem over the Holy Manger, the Christmas tree crowned by a star, the Milky Way Galaxy, and Mendeleyev's Periodic Table. The theory even extends the archetypal secrets of the reverse of the Great Seal to exploring the nature of the unified field, the mastery of which will be the next paradigm shift in science.

The next time you see the reverse of the Great Seal relegated to a report on the financial news, or parodied in a cartoon of George W. Bush spying on Americans, or compared to corporate logos and an "Illuminati" plot, remember some of these more enlightened comparisons that can also be drawn from this noble symbol. Remember, too, how many of the great minds of our Founding Fathers deliberated over a national coat of arms before accepting this design as symbolic of their mission statement.

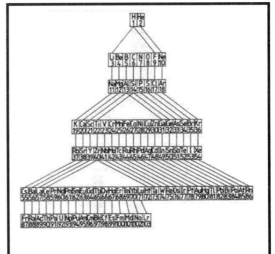

Mendeleyev's Periodic Table can also be compared to the eye in the triangle over the pyramid and is just one of hundreds of examples of how this American symbol is reflected in positive ways throughout culture.

It wasn't the Freemasons or the Illuminati that influenced their decision, but rather the Enlightenment and an appreciation for classical imagery that was much deeper than is common today. They chose this symbol because it said to them: Providence is smiling upon our undertaking, and we intend to live up to that trust by creating a nation of independence and liberty that is strong and enduring. Both our nation and the individuals in it are unfinished without the cosmic consciousness element of the soul or Divine Providence with which we should all be striving to connect.

CHAPTER 3

THE AMERICAN FLAG: AN AMERICAN BEAUTY, A NEW CONSTELLATION

ach time we gear up for another presidential election, we must brace ourselves for the endless parade of patriotic symbols. Many of you will groan as you see them rolled out again and again, and perhaps you have observed a change in your own "gut reactions" to the overuse of one symbol in particular: the American flag. It is sad that so many Americans today have reactions far from love and respect when they see this beautiful combination of red, white, and blue colors and shapes. It really is a beautiful flag, if you can just step out of the associations that we have tagged to it, and try to see it anew. We are so used to seeing it draped over the coffins of soldiers, or waving in the hands of politicians on the pro-war ticket, or decorating phony election campaign debates, that appreciating it without these frames can be a challenge.

The preeminent symbol of our nation is going through an identity crisis. The American flag is now viewed by many around the world as a symbol of tyranny, oppression, and corporate values, the absolute reverse of the ideals it was designed to embody. I know this firsthand too well from the angry and sometimes explicit comments aimed my way after I painted American flags all over my car. I've been called a fascist and a war-sympathizer by ill-educated Americans whose knees jerk when they see red, white, and blue. They see our flag as symbolizing the lies that were wrapped up in her, dragging us into a war we can't seem to get out of. And these reactions are mild compared to what the young "freedom-fighting" rebels in the Middle East and elsewhere must feel when they see the American flag, having only ever known the United States as the Evil Empire.

As I will demonstrate in this chapter, a symbolic rendering of the "Stars and Stripes" describes ideals and a vision quite at odds with the actions of the George W. Bush administration. Furthermore, I believe that at least some of the symbolic interpretations we will examine were intended and understood by the Founding Fathers and Mothers, although there is no written documentation to back up this conclusion. It was not simply for aesthetic reasons that they chose the colors, numbers, symbols, and patterns that they did. The design was at least partially plotted out to inspire the bold new sentiment of the Great Experiment.

America was the first country to succeed in "forming a new nation" that was "of the people," and in that way the flag we chose to represent us is the first *national* flag in history. Flags had always been associated with individual sovereigns rather than with the *people* of a country, and flag expert Whitney Smith uses this idea to argue that the American flag (followed soon thereafter by the flag of France born out of the French Revolution) is the first national flag "of a country."[1] Our colonial leaders knew the important power of symbols, and I believe they devised a flag with intentions for it to inspire the individuals who gazed upon it with the belief that the people could govern themselves. How sad and ironic that today, millions of people—from peace-loving, war protestors in America to martyrdom-loving radicals around the world—see the American flag as a symbol of both tyranny and corporate imperialism.

When those governing a nation reject the very essence of their own symbols or distort their meaning, the symbols are at risk of being deflated. It is not yet too late for our flag to bounce back and become associated in our minds and hearts once again as a symbol of unity, liberty, and rebirth—but it's close. A new leadership can still change the course of our domestic and foreign policies that are counterproductive to our sustainability, and uphold the higher ideals envisioned by our ancestors. When that happens we will all be proud to fly the American flag again and see in it what our forefathers saw: the wonderful hope that is America. Abraham Lincoln said, as he raised the new 34-star flag on Washington's birthday in 1861, "[S]omething in the Declaration [gives] liberty, not alone to the people of this country, but, hope to the world for all future time. It was that which gave promise that in due time the weights should be lifted from the shoulders of all men."[2] As we will attempt to show in this chapter, the American flag is a symbol of hope for the individual, the nation, and the world.

Unless we the people manifest a radical shift in leadership in 2008, however, it's possible this beautiful symbol could die. It took only a few short years for Adolf Hitler to subvert a millennia-old symbol for goodwill into one that is essentially taboo today. The swastika or hooked cross was a sacred symbol for Hindus, Buddhists, northern Europeans, and even Native Americans. Variously, these cultures used the swastika to symbolize rotation, the sun, spirit, or the spiritual fire of revelation, the kundalini force found in all human beings. Most of these cultures venerated a hooked cross with the arms pointing to the left, but when Hitler co-opted the sign as a symbol of the Aryan "master race," he reversed the arms and pointed them to the right. So now, despite its use and veneration in thousands of temples and carvings around the world, today the swastika is associated primarily with Nazism and white supremacy, and the cruelty of that administration. Let's not allow that to happen to the American

Painting the Roses Red: In 1986 and 1987 I painted a series of watercolors called *The American Beauty,* different perspectives on American flags where the seven red stripes were composed of as many as 16 intertwined red roses. We all know that the red rose stands for love, respect, and courage, and these are ideals I would like to reconnect to our flag. I chose the number 16 for the first few versions in this series as deliberately as the roses. For me, it conjures the 16th president of the United States, Abraham Lincoln, who gave his life to perpetuate the American experiment. In numerology, 16 is an expression of happiness, good wishes, and hopes. In the mystical *I Ching,* the 16th hexagram is "enthusiasm," which assists one "to install helpers and to set armies marching." Following numerological procedure, 16 = 1 + 6 = 7. Seven in the mystical Hebrew Kabbalah is "victory." Adding 16 roses to the American flag projects a balance of strength, courage, and honor with love, beauty, perfection, and achievement. This *American Beauty* presents a more complete picture of the American experience inspiring both patriotism and higher ideals. Photo by Stuart Zolotorow.

flag. Use your political will and get involved in shaping the leaders of this country. We all face the same mission in this lifetime: to elevate our physical, material selves to the divine, spiritual level. This necessary step for human evolution is best supported by a form of representational government where freedom of religion, thought, arms, assembly, and so forth are inalienable. I believe it is America's destiny to lead the way with this example of representational government and "liberty to all the inhabitants thereof," as it says on the Liberty Bell. To that end, a new interpretation of our American flag could not be more timely.

Instead what we get is meaningless discussions about legislating against the individual's rights to burn the flag. These arguments are trotted out for electioneering every few years because this symbol is tied viscerally to our national identity, making it painful for many of us to see an American flag being burned. Any proposed legislation to "protect" the flag from desecration, however, is actually aimed at suppressing the freedom of expression of those with opinions different from the current administration. By providing a deeper meaning for the symbolism of the flag, we are reminded that the American flag does not stand for the current administration alone or its decisions to involve America in an unpopular war. It stands for the higher values of unity and rebirth and evolution to a higher state of consciousness on both an individual and a national level.

A New Age for Flags

Though it took decades to catch on as a symbol popularly recognized by the common people, the starred American flag was important to our developing sense of self-identity and oneness as a nation. Our flag was first designed as the Naval Flag of the United States, understandably, because flags had always played a more essential role on water than on land, allowing ships of differing nations to identify each other over vast distances. In fact, Washington's army did not get official flags until 1783, after most of the major Revolutionary War battles were over. As late as 1779, Washington was still in correspondence with the War Board settling on a design for a flag for the army. He preferred one with red and white stripes all the way across, with no blue canton, and a square right in the middle of the stripes with some kind of design on the square, suggesting a "don't tread on me" serpent.[3]

The first American flag was known as the Continental Colors, and, although it's not the Stars and Stripes we know today, it is recognizable as its antecedent. It became the unofficial flag of the revolution when General Washington gave the orders for a striped design of the flag to be raised in January 1776. It was intended as a display of continued defiance to the British troops after the Colonists' first defeat at Breed's Hill. Rather than the traditional all-red flag of rebellion, it was composed of 13 red and white stripes, just as we know them today with red at the top and bottom, and in the top left corner or canton was probably the British royal banner known as the Union Jack. A flag with 13 red and white stripes (just stripes, no canton) was already being flown as a flag by the semi-organized secret society of militant instigators known as the Sons of Liberty. They called it the "union" flag, and it flew over the Liberty Tree in Boston and probably over the Boston Tea Party. By connecting himself with the Sons of Liberty, Washington was attempting to send a message to the British Navy off Boston harbor. Americans who viewed it immediately saw the symbolism of these stripes as a need for the 13 colonies to *unite as one*. The Continental Colors stirred in some a celebration that they were separating from Britain. At the same time, some of the British were confused by the Union Jack in the canton and reported that the raising of this flag said we were capitulating to King George's latest demands. This confusion is probably what led to the eventual redesign of the canton to feature what they called the "New Constellation" of 13 stars.

Another theory regarding the change was advanced in 1937, showing that the Continental Colors greatly resembled the flag flown by the British East India Company, the very company against which the Boston Tea Party rebelled. Most vexillologists stress that this flag was never flown outside of the Indian Ocean, making it highly unlikely that it was a source of inspiration for the Sons of Liberty in Massachusetts. Though it is possible the Sons of Liberty created a red-and-white-striped flag because they were copying the East India Company flag, it is not documented anywhere. More importantly, the Continental Colors were soon replaced by the official American flag when the entirely different canton with the New Constellation was resolved.

Leading up to this time, there had been many flags of widely various designs representing the Colonials and the burgeoning revolutionary movement. Flying the Union Jack or using parts of it in new designs for Colonial flags had been popular from the earliest days of settlement in the 1600s. Using it as a canton in the upper left of what was essentially the Sons of Liberty union flag indicates how much the Colonists still viewed themselves as British, even then in January 1776. It was the use of the 13 stripes that gave the immediate message: This was no longer the fight of just the men of Massachusetts, or any single colony, but of all 13 united in a single cause. This flag called for union so strongly that it became better known by its nickname of the Grand Union Flag.

The Sons of Liberty were the patriots and instigators of the American rebellion. They had chapters in all the Colonies, but were most famously active in New England, where the organized resistance movement started. Massachusetts members included Paul Revere, John Adams, Samuel Adams, and John Hancock. Many Freemasons were members, it's true, but it was not a Freemasonic organization, or even much of an official organization at all. The Sons of Liberty was more of an identifying phrase for those opposed to the British attempts to control the Colonists. They organized the resistance to the Stamp Act in 1765 using public demonstrations, legislative resolutions, threats, and sometimes violence, resulting in its repeal the following year. In December 1773, the Sons of Liberty staged the Boston Tea Party, their best-known act of defiance. The British authorities called them the "Sons of Violence" or the "Sons of Iniquity." To poorly paraphrase John Adams, they were responsible for the revolution that took place in the minds long before the War of Independence broke out.

Snakes on Flags

Even after the debut of the Grand Union Flag outside Boston on New Year's Day 1776, American flags continued to vary from battlefield to battlefield. Some regiments, including Washington's own, used combinations of flags, troop banners, and homemade flags. Many of the earlier flags had mottoes written on them—for example, "Liberty and Union," "An Appeal to Heaven," and "Don't Tread on Me." There were blue flags, green flags, red flags, striped flags, and many with depictions of flora and fauna. One of the most popular was the series of rattlesnake flags implying that the American Colonists, like this dangerous indigenous snake, were coiled and ready to strike if provoked. Ben Franklin had used a snake in his early campaign for union in 1754 when he issued a political cartoon showing a divided snake and the motto "Join or Die." At the time, Franklin had recently been inspired by the peace conferences in Albany with the League of the Iroquois Indians, where the Indian wisemen taught Franklin and the other colonial delegates what their long experience had shown them about the importance of unifying the smaller tribes into a larger "league." (See Chapter 6 for a lengthier discussion of the Native Americans' inestimable influences on the founders.)

Franklin wrote a piece for the *Pennsylvania Journal* in 1775 in which he ruminated on the popularity of the rattlesnake as a symbol for America. In it he said he first consulted a man learned in heraldry to determine that animals were chosen as national symbols on the basis of their estimable qualities only, disregarding any negative traits. He then set out to list as many estimable qualities of the rattlesnake as he could, and in so doing realized how well they matched with the American fight for independence. The only animal without eyelids, the snake was ever watchful on defense. Its primary weapon was kept hidden in its mouth, and it appeared defenseless to the unwise. It never attacked unless provoked, and then only after giving fair warning with its rattles. When the "don't tread on me" warning was ignored, its attacks were usually fatal. The rattlesnake was indigenous to America, so it was a new symbol, not one borrowed from European heraldry.

Depicting the snake with 13 rattles reinforced the call for unity among the Colonies, but Franklin also observed that the snake would grow new rattles, just as America would one day grow new states. In a final propagandistic stroke, he associated the rattles with the lesson of many other symbols used to remind the revolutionary generation of their strength in numbers: "'Tis curious and amazing to observe how distinct and independent of each other the rattles of this animal are, and yet how firmly they are united together, so as never to be separated but by breaking them to pieces. One of those rattles singly, is incapable of producing sound, but the ringing of thirteen together, is sufficient to alarm the boldest man living."[4]

The Evolution of the American Flag Design

It may have been a Native American man who prompted the infant Congress to settle upon an official design for the American flag. This was a full year and a half after the Grand Union flag was ordered flown over Prospect Hill by George Washington. In June 1777, a Native American possibly named Thomas Green requested a token of recognition to present to his tribe. This was an established custom between the natives and the British, and uniforms, medals, and flags were exchanged as a gesture of soliciting favor from the tribes, and to secure safe passage through one another's territories. By 1777 it had grown apparent to all Americans that nothing but a complete separation from the Mother Country would be the result of the current conflict, and therefore the presence of the Union Jack on the Continental Colors was no longer meaningful. On June 14, 1777, Congress resolved, in one rather non-descriptive sentence, the future Stars and Stripes. This resolution resulted in what most of us recognize as our first flag, which we have erroneously (as we will see later) nicknamed "the Betsy Ross flag." The lack of detail in the description implies that the design was already familiar to them, and it is very likely that the need to replace the Union Jack in the canton was acted upon long before June 1777.

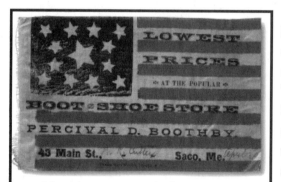

Advertising messages on the flag were common in the mid-nineteenth century as in this handbill, until citizen groups lobbied for a code of flag etiquette. (Illustration from Hinrichs and Hirasuna's *Long May She Wave*.) Used with permission.

The only interpretation we have for the design of the first official American flag reads shortly and sweetly: "*Resolved, That the flag of the thirteen United States be thirteen stripes alternate red and white; that the union be thirteen stars, white in a blue field, representing a New Constellation.*" Beyond this one sentence, all other interpretations of this red, white, and blue combination of symbols and colors cannot be proven to have been the original intention of the founders, and must be considered conjecture. Note especially that the resolution does not call for the stars to be displayed in a circle, nor how many points should be on the stars. In fact, knowing who was the artist behind this design leads to the conclusion that the stars were six-pointed rather than five, and arranged randomly rather than in a circle. That artist was Francis Hopkinson, whom we mentioned in the last chapter in reference to his work on the Great Seal. I would argue that Hopkinson, well educated in the fields of heraldry and regalia, knew exactly what he was doing when he proposed retaining the red and white stripes and replacing the Union Jack with the New Constellation.

Francis Hopkinson: America's Unknown, Unpaid Artist

Artist Francis Hopkinson designed our first Stars and Stripes flag, several pieces of currency, several official seals, and contributed to the U.S. Great Seal. He was also a signer of both the Declaration of Independence and the Constitution. But he was most popular among his contemporaries for penning stinging satires and popular songs that helped sway the average man toward independence. From a 1785 portrait in Patterson and Dougall, *The Eagle and the Shield.*

Maybe if Francis Hopkinson had draped a flag over his knee and posed for a painting of himself working on it, his name would be as popular today as that of Betsy Ross, and little children would dress up as *him* in the school pageants. As it was, Hopkinson was too aware of the fact that the Congress had more pressing issues of concern in the early days of the Revolution than to pay the modest invoices of the graphic designers of the day. Several years later, in 1780, however, he did submit a petition for payment for his time and effort in conceiving of this, and several other designs, for the new country, wondering if a quarter cask of the public wine might not be sufficient remuneration. His petitions for payment were ultimately denied, but not before leaving a telling, and rather pitiful, paper trail that has convinced most flag historians that Hopkinson was the true designer of our first Stars and Stripes.

Many authors have read between the lines of the bureaucratic runaround to which the Board of Treasury subjected Hopkinson, finding it noteworthy that in none of the denials of his petitions was there any dispute that *Hopkinson had, in fact, designed the American flag.* His contemporaries must have accepted that Francis Hopkinson designed the first American flag as described in the resolution with the New Constellation in the canton. It appears he had an enemy on the Board of Treasury, however, and his invoices were repeatedly returned to him, first requiring vouchers, then itemization, and then quibbling over the amounts in hard money versus Continental currency. The itemization he provided allows for an interesting observation: He asked only £9 for the design of the American flag, but he wanted £600 for the time he'd spent on the design of the Great Seal. Hopkinson had apparently spent a great deal of time and deliberation on his Great Seal work, probably working over different sketches or renderings of the committee's ideas, and he valued this time at £600. Asking for only £9 for designing the American flag indicates to me that the idea to replace the Union Jack in the canton with the New Constellation of stars came to him rather quickly, in a burst of inspiration, rather than throughout a long course of laboring, sketching and resketching different drafts and changes.

By this low figure, he may also have been acknowledging that other people had contributed to this design of the flag—namely, the red and white stripes were already in use. It was this collaborative effort that the Board of Treasury ultimately used as their best excuse for why they declined his petition for reimbursement. Not only was the design not exclusively his idea, but also somehow the public was entitled to these extra services from men in public office. Most telling, however, is that no one disputed his assertion that he designed the first American flag. As Rear Admiral William Furlong and Commodore Byron McCandless concluded in their Smithsonian publication, *So Proudly We Hail*: "The journals of the Continental Congress clearly show that he designed the flag."[5]

Francis Hopkinson was a signer of the Declaration of Independence and a ratifier of the Constitution. He was a New Jersey delegate to the Continental Congress and head of the Marine Committee, which directed most naval matters during the war. He served as treasurer of the Continental Loan Office, judge of the Admiralty Court of Pennsylvania, and judge of the U.S. District Court. He was an artist, musician, lawyer, and author. His popular songs, poems, and pamphlets were compared at the time to the writings of Tom Paine. He was an avid "fancier" of official seals and emblems, and known to doodle them in his spare time. We know from Hopkinson's library and his correspondence that he was familiar with heraldry and art. He collaborated with du Simitière on the design of the state seal of New Jersey, and is officially recognized as the single designer of the seals of the U.S. Navy and Treasury Department, and several pieces of Colonial paper currency. From his position on the Navy Board he would have been one of the first to hear of the confusion being caused by the presence of the Union Jack on the Continental Colors, and we can easily see Hopkinson in between his board meetings, doodling over ideas for how to re-place it. His idea for white stars on a blue field equating this new country to a "New Constellation" was his way of showing the world that this upstart America would become something permanent. He saw America appearing as a new constellation in the sky.

The Circle of Eternity

It is probable that Hopkinson left his stars in a random pattern on his flag, rather than in a circle. This was the accepted heraldic placement of stars, first of all, as well as how the stars were originally placed on the 1782 design for the Great Seal, which Charles Thomson acknowledged was modeled after the American flag. There is no evidence that the circle of stars was used on *any flag* until the 1800s, though in 1782 the artist for the third committee of the Great Seal, William Barton, suggested that the stars in the Seal be placed into a circle.[6] Maybe flag makers were also placing them in a circle as early as then, too. Barton's handwritten description gives us the best documentation for why the circle was seen as an ideal symbol for early Americans. The stars repre-sented "a new Constellation," said Barton, alluding to, "the new Empire, formed in the World by the Confederation of those States," symbolized by the stars. Their disposition in the form of a circle, he said, "denotes the Perpetuity of its Continuance, the Ring being the Symbol of Eternity."[7]

There was no official standardization for the flag until 1912, so throughout the 18th and 19th centuries the details fluctuated wildly from flag maker to flag maker, including the layout placement of the stars, the colors of the stripes (some-times blue!), and the number of points on the stars. There are many colorful and probably fictional accounts for how the stars on the flag came to be placed in a circle, but we believe the most likely is that the circle is an ingrained archetype for eternity and unity, and flag makers responded to this natural inclination. Symbologists compare the circle to the ancient Ouroboros, or the serpent biting its tail, a symbol used to depict the cyclical nature of life, especially in terms of con-stant renewal or elemental unity. There are some grand, patriotic quotes attrib-uted to George Washington that did not appear until a hundred years later, in which he is claimed to have compared the circle of stars to King Arthur's round

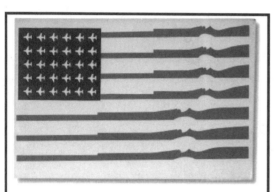

table where none of the colonies could be considered more prominent than the others. Dave Martucci, past president of the North American Vexillological Association, told us, "Washington never said any such things. These quotes surfaced in the 1870s when the history of the flag became more interesting to Americans, and they appear in dozens of little patriotic flag books at that time."[8]

This Anti-War Placard, circa 1968, was produced on the campus of the University of California at Berkeley for an anti-war protest. (Illustration from Hinrichs and Hirasuna's *Long May She Wave*.) Used with permission.

Another popular legend is perpetuated to remind us of the important contributions of our Jewish Founding Fathers. A famous Jewish merchant and personal friend of George Washington, Chaim Solomon, is alleged to have asked Washington to display the stars on the American flag in the shape of a six-pointed Star of David. Washington agreed to do this in gratitude for the Jewish bankers and merchants who had helped fund the war. When Christians allegedly objected to this plan, however, the circular placement of the stars on the flag was the resulting compromise.

The hexagram layout pattern of the stars did end up on the Great Seal, of course, but I believe that this pattern was chosen to reflect the balance and unity of two interlocking triangles rather than an acknowledgement to any one group or religion that might use this symbol. The eagle side of the Great Seal is all about balance. The eagle is holding both the arrows of war and the olive branch of peace, which can be interpreted to mean the United States will retain our independence only as long as we use war to maintain peace. This difficult equilibrium requires great wisdom, which can be boosted by placing the 13 stars over the eagle's head in the pattern called the Seal of Solomon. This ancient symbol for wisdom is made up of the heaven-pointing triangle representing spirit and the earth-pointing triangle representing matter: It is the wisdom of balance. Our founders saw a future where wisdom would infuse all our national decisions.

How Francis Morphed Into Betsy

The design we all "know so well" of the first American flag showing five-pointed stars displayed in a circle is something that evolved throughout several years after much trial and error. It was decades before the Stars and Stripes became a popular icon among the common folk. It would be almost a hundred years before anyone outside her family heard the name of Elizabeth Griscom Ross Ashburn Claypoole. Thanks to a compelling piece of oral history first recorded by her grandson, however, for the past 100-plus years the American pantheon has included a "Founding Mother." Betsy Ross's grandson, William Canby, claimed that Betsy had told the family how in 1776 she and George Washington together had designed the Stars and Stripes with five-pointed stars placed in a circle. Canby presented his paper to the Historical Society of Pennsylvania in 1870, at a time when the country was in dire need of healing from the Civil War, and the hype was beginning to build in preparation for the centennial of the Declaration of Independence. Corroboration for his story was obtained through notarized affidavits from one of Betsy Ross's daughters, as well as a niece and a granddaughter, two of whom had worked together with the widow Ross in her upholstery and flag business.

Though there are several holes in the Ross family legend, it is possible that some elements of truth lie within it to indicate that Betsy Ross *did* play a valuable role in the early life of the flag. Along with Rebecca Young (mother of Mary Young Pickersgill, who sewed the Ft. McHenry flag, which inspired Francis Scott Key to write "The Star-Spangled Banner"), Betsy Ross is among at least three women who claimed to have sewn the first flag. Ross may have actually sewn one of the first flags ever to contain stars, and it is also highly believable that she contributed to the change from a six-pointed to a five-pointed star, though she may not have been the only one to initiate that change. The only documentary evidence that connects Betsy Ross to one of the first flags stems from the minutes recorded for the State Navy Board of Pennsylvania, commissioning her to sew several flags for Navy vessels. On May 29, 1777, there is recorded, "An order on William Webb to Elizabeth Ross for fourteen pounds twelve shillings, and two pence, for making ship's colours, &c, put into William Richards store."[9] Martucci significantly points out that "she was issued far more blue fabric than red or white, and this makes sense if you know what the flag of the Pennsylvania Navy looked like, which was all blue except for a small canton composed of 13 red and white stripes."[10] Betsy Ross was certainly a flag *maker* and a staunch supporter of the war, despite her Quaker upbringing. She also worshiped at the same church as Washington when he was in Philadelphia, and there is no reason to doubt her claim that she did tailoring work for the great man. According to the 1871 affidavit of her daughter, Rachel Fletcher, "Washington…had often been in her house in friendly visits, as well as on business. That she had embroidered ruffles for his shirt bosoms and cuffs."[11]

The most disputable part of their account is the presence of George Washington in her house in 1776. Nowhere in his copious diaries and letters did Washington ever mention a pivotal meeting in the back room of a seamstress's house where he and she together knocked out the final design for the new national standard. And as late at 1779, Washington was still corresponding with the War Board about the design for the "Standard of the United States," something he was unlikely to do had he already approved of the final design back in '76.

The Mother Myth and Betsy Ross

The author of one of the first complete histories of the American flag, George Preble, disputed Canby's claim as early as 1872, and historians have been battling Betsyites over this very popular legend ever since. Whitney Smith proposed several scenarios for how the family could have misinterpreted Ross's claims, and pulled together other bits of truth to reach the wrong conclusion. Historians are unanimous at least in their complete dismissal of the time line Canby presented, which claimed that Betsy Ross's flag was flying to great popular acclaim in time for the Declaration of Independence on July 4, 1776.

So why did our national psyche so completely embrace her story despite the lack of foundation? Part of the reason is the timing was right. The Betsy Ross story came along just when the country needed a collective boost to the ego, immediately after the Civil War and preparing for the first Centennial. Further, there was a PR campaign launched by the Betsy Ross Memorial Association in 1909, which reproduced a painting that eventually made its way into schoolbooks and impressed itself into our collective unconscious. In it we see a composite Betsy Ross based on portraits of her descendants, with the flag across her knee and surrounded by the alleged committee of Congress in her parlor.

In addition to it being just the right patriotic (matriotic?) story for the time, the legend of Betsy Ross also helped fill a void in our history with the much-needed mother-figure archetype. Similar to the Pietá, with the Mother Mary holding the body of Christ across her lap, the image of Betsy Ross cradling the flag inspires a sense of motherly care and affection that had been lacking in our national identity since the intervention of the white man. For countless centuries before Columbus, this land had been populated by a tribal culture, a great many of whom operated on a matriarchal basis. Though Franklin, Jefferson, Paine, and others wrote about adopting the governing practices of the natives, the one tradition of the League of the Iroquois Indians that was *not* adopted by the Founding Fathers was their high regard for women. As we'll see in Chapter 6, women played an important role in Native American society. We have only recently begun to allow women the legal rights and privileges that were commonly afforded by some of these ancient American cultures. In the inner world, our need for a mother figure asserted itself much sooner. A subconscious craving for a Founding Mother could help explain why Betsy Ross's legend was accepted so readily.

The Betsy Ross of legend gave birth to the form, in this case a flag, from the modest surrounds of her own home, the castle within. She nurtures and protects. She gives hope to every individual, and particularly to every woman that her contributions are valued. She reminds us that it is the heart and the simple deeds of each one of us that ultimately affirm the human spirit. Betsy Ross's story represents the world mother camouflaged in heraldry. That we chose a young widow to be the personage behind our flag, instead of an accomplished man in charge of the Continental Navy Board, is revealing of our unconscious needs. As so often happens with "history," the greater Meta-need overrules the factual evidence. In the perpetuity of the Betsy Ross legend, the Meta-need for wholeness, for accepting our female qualities and treating women with equal regard, was more vital than recounting what was historically accurate.

Our Flag as Cosmic Drama

One reason we did not inherit lengthy explanations of the symbols in the flag is because the Revolutionary generation had a far greater level of familiarity with heraldry, symbols, and art than is commonplace today. Minute interpretations seemed unnecessary to most of them to whom reading symbols and designs would have been as simple as reading in a foreign language. There are obvious practical reasons why they chose the colors and designs that they did, but our founders were also aware of some of the ancient correspondences attached to these colors, numbers, and shapes. Symbols that express fundamental, archetypal truths can transmit the same message generation after generation without guidebooks.

The design for the Great Seal (1782) and the design for the American flag (1777) are interrelated, having been created and approved by many of the same people. Unlike the Great Seal, however, the flag was very casually described, and continued to significantly transform in design long after the 1777 resolution. Because of their similarities, many of the interpretations we all take for granted about the flag were actually written to describe the symbols in the Great Seal, and are only *assumed* to apply also to the flag.

Ginny Holmes modeling a version of the flag in 1967. Painting bodies was a fad in the late 1960s and early '70s, and I enjoyed this opportunity to paint on another type of moving canvas—a startling and new way to send art and symbolic messages out into the world. With painted bodies, there are obvious distractions to the art, and thus I always painted in symbols to speak directly to the subconscious. See a photo of my biodiesel Founding Fathers Artcar on page 33 for another moving canvas.

Vexillologists mostly say that the colors red, white, and blue were chosen for the American flag because they were the most available, and because they were the same colors used in the Union Jack of the Mother Country. Whitney Smith points out that "in heraldry, there were only the basic colors of red, blue, green, and black. There was also yellow, gold, silver, and white, but they were used mostly to separate the other colors…. There weren't any good green dyes in those days….

The symbolism of black was negative, and yellow was the color of quarantine.... So there just weren't many choices, and since red, white, and blue were the British colors, it made sense." [12] Although this practical explanation is compelling, it does not address the soul-stirring power this arrangement of colors and shapes has over us at certain times. Assessing our flag from an archetypal and symbolic perspective, we can reveal a deeper meaning and an entirely new appreciation for "Old Glory."

There is a common prejudice that only the physical, material world with documentary evidence should be considered. A higher state of awareness reveals that man is more than just a physical body. Though we have no documents from the Founding Fathers giving us their symbolic interpretations of the flag, if we accept a "Divine Providence" overshadowing their decisions, an archetypal rendering of these symbols can be most revealing. It is my hope that a deeper appreciation of these symbols will lead Americans once again to recognize themselves as a nation of one people, and our diversity can be our strength when we rally around the flag of unity.

The Rectangle Is a Temple

The blue canton of the flag, and the entire flag itself when viewed as a whole, are both rectangular in form. To the ancients, rectangles symbolized temples, probably because most ancient temples were constructed in this shape. The stars within the blue canton represent the stars in the heavens, meaning the temple of our flag is related to the universe. The founders acknowledged this when they called the stars a New Constellation in the June 14th resolution. The white in the stars is linked to silver and thus to the moon representing the perfected personality, the perfection of the physical body in alignment with the spiritual temple.

3 Colors: A Trinity

Three colors were chosen for the design of our flag. Not two, not four, but three. The powerful three of the trinity is also the three of the triangle, as the tetrahedron is the basic building block of the universe. These three colors could symbolize the trinity of Father (blue), Son (red), and Holy Spirit (white). In *A Dictionary of Symbols,* the triangle is "the geometric image of the ternary, and in symbolism of numbers, equivalent to the number three.... [W]ith the apex uppermost it also symbolizes fire and the aspiration of all things towards the origin or the irradiating point."[13]

When I last counted, nearly 30 countries used the same three colors of red, white, and blue in their flags, and another 20 used predominantly these three. Examples include: Cuba, Costa Rica, Chile, Norway, France, Ukraine, Nepal, Thailand, South Korea, and Australia. Why so many flags carrying the same colors? Is there some kind of unrecognized law at work here, or maybe a karmic relationship between these countries? Or are there just too few colors to choose from?

Red

According to Charles Thomson's description of the Great Seal, red stands for "hardiness and valour."[14] The color red is traditionally linked to the planet Mars, which symbolizes more or less a masculine energy, though it is also associated with the blood of fertility. The red rose is the symbol of love and fidelity. Red is frequently used to symbolize blood. Blood is the element that flows within all of us carrying the genetic structure of the energy of the seven bodies, where all is interconnected from the physical to the divine. Red is an agitating heat-giving color. In the Greek mysteries the irrational sphere was always considered as red, for it represented that condition in which consciousness is enslaved by the lusts and passions of the lower nature.

White

The color white in the Seal "signifies purity and innocence."[15] But in heraldry, white is also used to symbolize silver, which is linked to the moon, and therefore to the feminine. White is symbolically the combination of all colors, or the rainbow. We have unity expressed in at least two places in the canton. First, in the early versions of the flag, all 13 states were placed equally in a circle. Unity is also expressed in making the stars white. It says, "out of many, one." All the states are equal to each other, and all the people within each state are equal to each other. We are all one.

Blue

In heraldry blue has always been used to represent the heavens, where one looks for wisdom. Blue is also related to the planet Jupiter, standing for justice, knowledge, honor, and nobility. Jupiter is the symbol for expansiveness, all-inclusiveness, and a breaking down of barriers and limitations. Thomson said the color blue signified "vigilance, perseverance and justice."[16] We can also read into the symbols to see white stars on a field of blue, suggesting that our country is designed to be in line with the spiritual elements of the heaven worlds, as above, so below. It depicts a place where the spiritual world and the physical world are in alignment, and therefore a state of perfection.

Triskaidekaphobia Is Not the American Way

If ever a number has been misunderstood, it's 13. The fear of this number is a relatively recent phenomenon, and, when examined as to its source, it appears to be a strange leftover from superstitions of the Dark Ages. When the church was clamping down on pagan folk healers and persecuting women, the number 13 was associated with followers of the Goddess and the way this culture marked time, based on the annual menstruation cycle of the average woman. The current administration of those days spread the word that 13 and symbols associated with 13 were evil, and they began burning the folk healers as witches. Some fundamentalist-conspiratorialists explain that 13 is unlucky because it is the number in the room after Judas arrived at the Last Supper to betray Jesus. They fail to mention that 13 is also the number of the group of 12 disciples together with Jesus during all the years of his ministry. Some have gone back even further to the first time 13 is used in the Bible. It appears in Genesis 14:4 in the list of a litany of wars between kings surrounding the story of Abram and Lot. "Twelve years they had served Chedorlaomer, but the thirteenth year they rebelled" is the phrase, and from this they have concluded that the number 13 is associated with rebellion. Some say that the reason we fear Friday the 13th is that it's the date on which the Knights Templar were arrested in October 1307, linking the date to bad luck ever since.

Before all of these theories, however, in many ancient cultures, 13 was seen as a number of transformation, symbolizing renewal, rebirth, and regeneration. This interpretation may have resulted from the fact that 13 follows the nice, round, complete number of a dozen. Thirteen is the number of the Zodiac when you include the sun as it travels through them in the year. Thirteen is the initiate, the one regenerating himself. Often associated with the number 13 is the zodiacal sign of Scorpio, the sign that is also linked to themes of regeneration and rebirth. One could conclude that in order for America as a nation to reflect the 13 in our flag, many trials and errors throughout many lifetimes, many rebirths and regenerations will be required for the ultimate success. When we add together the numbers one and three to assess the number 13 numerologically, we arrive at the number four. Four can refer to the four elements of the physical world: air, earth, fire, and water. It is in the physical world where rebirth and regeneration must take place to be reborn in spirit or attain spiritual vision. In the *I Ching,* the 13th hexagram is T'ung Jen, or "fellowship with men" that "must be based upon a concern that is universal."[17]

As classically trained scholars, some of the Founding Fathers were probably aware of the association of 13 with rebirth. The number of colonies uniting in 1776 as 13 was fortuitous, when an attempt to coerce Canada into becoming a 14th state failed miserably early on. But once they were the Thirteen Colonies the founders really played up that number in their propaganda and symbolism. By doing so, they very well may have been consciously emphasizing rebirth and renewal as much as the number of united colonies. When the artists depicted them as stripes, or stars, or tiers on the pyramid, or arrows in the eagle's claw, or berries on the olive branch, it meant the *13 individual states were united as one* in their effort of renewal.

6 White and 7 Red

The number 13 in the fly of the flag is achieved by combining six white and seven red stripes. Six symbolizes beauty, balance, symmetry, harmony of opposites, equilibrium, and reciprocity. Six combined with the white (Holy Spirit) stripes could symbolize that the Holy Spirit manifests through beauty and harmony (6).

Seven is a very popular biblical number. It appears many times in the book of Revelation (for example, in the seven sealed scrolls, the seven golden lampstands, and the seven-horned lamb). In the Kabbalah seven symbolizes victory of spirit over matter. It took seven days for the creation. On the seventh day God rested. He was victorious over matter. Seven combined with the red (Son) stripes could symbolize the Son's victory of spirit over matter, of consciousness over unconsciousness. Seven is considered a holy number, but is also related to time, expressing the rhythm of evolution in the changing positions of the sun, creating a seven-day week.

The ageless wisdom teachings suggest that the human is not one body, but seven, ranging from the lowest, the physical body, to the highest, or divine body. Six has often been related to Venus, meaning harmony and balance. When you add six and seven, you could be indicating that all seven bodies are aligned harmoniously, as in a perfected human, so that the fly of 13 stripes is relating not just to America, but to all humans in all nations.

Red for Mars stands for activity and masculine energy. It is the color of power and ambition. The color white is astrologically linked to the moon, or the feminine energies. White symbolizes purity without and within. External and internal, above and below. Once again we have a demonstration of symbolic balance on the American flag. Linking the number 6 with the color white (the feminine side of the human), and the number 7 with the color red (the masculine aspect), we have an alchemical combination known as the hermaphrodite. The word *hermaphrodite* is itself a balance between the names of Hermes (Mercury or the messenger) with Aphrodite (Venus or the higher mind) and the hermaphrodite is a balance between masculine and feminine energies. It is the natural evolution of spirit. The red and white stripes could thus be translated: Victory (7) is assured through the Son (red) by the balance and harmony (6) of the Holy Spirit, or power of God (white).

Clipping a Point Off the Stars

George Washington seems to have preferred a six-pointed star, carrying it on his banner while leading the Continental Army. He appeared in the Betsy Ross legend with a drawing of the proposed flag using six-pointed stars, and she allegedly demonstrated for him how much easier it was for a seamstress to clip a five-pointed star than a six. Francis Hopkinson also seems to have preferred the six-pointed star. His family coat of arms featured three six-pointed stars, and he used the six-pointed star in his design for the Great Seal. Both Hopkinson's Great Seal stars and Washington's Headquarters flag stars more closely resembled three intersecting tapered lines (or six-pointed flowers) than interlocking triangles or stars.

There is no existing documentation that explains why or when the five-pointed star came into use on the American flag. It was possibly influenced by the 1841 new steel die for the Great Seal cut by John Peter Van Ness Throop. The original 1782 die had become worn, which may explain why Throop mistakenly gave the eagle only six arrows and the stars only five points.[18] Many of the earliest depictions of the Stars and Stripes flag show it with six-pointed stars, though seven-, eight-, and five-pointed stars also make appearances early on. The explanation may be as simple as the practical decision of seamstresses in upholstery shops around the Union (or perhaps one in particular in Philadelphia) that it was easier to cut out five-pointed stars.[19] The symbolic difference is significant, but it does not appear that anyone was giving it that much thought.

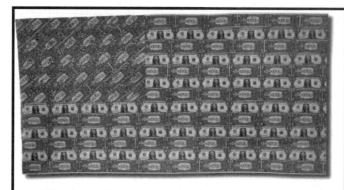

By stitching together $157 worth of dollar bills into this familiar shape, artist Ray Beldner made the statement in 1997 that America is built on the almighty dollar. (Illustration from Hinrichs and Hirasuna's *Long May She Wave*.) Used with permission.

The 5-Pointed Star

The five-pointed star was almost unheard of in flags before this time. In heraldry, stars of the sky would usually be depicted with six, seven, or eight points, and a five-pointed star would sometimes refer to starfish or flowers. Hexagrams, or the intersection of two triangles, represent the union of male and female energies, or fire and water, or spirit and matter, and would have symbolically reinforced balance and unity. Sometimes called the star of man, the five-pointed star can be likened to the head above the torso with two arms and two legs (think of DaVinci's *Vetruvian Man*), or even to man's five physical senses. The five-pointed star has many mystical meanings. Paul Foster Case said five is "the sign of absolute universal synthesis," symbolizing the small world or the microcosm.[20]

Today, through long identification, the five-pointed star is strongly associated with the U.S. military, which began using it based on its use in the American flag. A pentagram is a five-pointed star made by drawing intersecting lines in one stroke with equal angles at all five points. It is thought to have first been deemed sacred by the ancients tracing the path that Venus makes as it traverses the Zodiac. The pentagram has a long history as a magical symbol for many cultures and religions, including the Babylonians, Egyptians, early Christians, and Freemasons. In the last century the pentagram became associated with Satanism, possibly due to a misunderstanding of ceremonial magic. Even if Satanists do use a pentagram, that is just one possible level of interpretation for this popular symbol. Magical historian Eliphas Lévi was responsible in the 19th century for incorrectly identifying the difference between an inverted pentagram, calling it negative, and an upright pentagram, calling it positive. Before Lévi's ideas were published the pentagram was used by early Christians and everyone else with the points facing both up and down without any distinction.

50 Stars and the Meaning for Today

The number of stars has increased as our country expanded, symbolically demonstrating the evolution of America. Today we have 50 stars on our flag, meaning we are at a stage where the number 50 has some meaning to us. Following a numerological procedure of adding the two digits 5 + 0 gives us a total of 5, meaning the earlier translation also relates to the contemporary version of 50 stars on our flag. Five is translated by Paul Foster Case as "the dynamic law proceeding from abstract order.... [It is] mediation..., adaptation, means, agency, activity, process, and the like."[21] In the *I Ching,* the fifth hexagram is Hsü, or waiting. It is not the waiting of empty hope, but with the inner certainty of reaching the goal. The 50th hexagram is Ting, the Cauldron. According to Richard Wilhelm, the cauldron "presents a transformation.... Ting shows the correct way of going about a social reorganization."[22] The cauldron also means taking up the new—as in the "New Order of the Ages," one of the mottoes on the reverse of the Great Seal. The cauldron can be likened to the "melting pot" philosophy of this nation.

Much more could be said of the deeper levels of interpretation surrounding our flag and the mythologies behind these colors and numbers. With even this small code, however, anyone familiar with the language of symbols can form a deeper appreciation for our flag. Overly sophisticated academics will probably scorn this symbolic approach, because there is no written documentation to indicate that any of the founders considered any of these correlations. Deliberate or not, however, I believe that it is on these esoteric levels that the true meaning of our flag may be revealed.

CHAPTER 4

THE STATUE OF LIBERTY: IN AMERICA, IT'S GODDESSES WE TRUST

ver wondered why there is a 150-foot pagan statue in the New York Harbor? Of course, I'm using the term *pagan* here not as an insult, but rather as a literal descriptive to point out how much the Statue of Liberty is based on a Greco-Roman goddess. If you've ever wondered why, you may have already discovered that this goddess is by no means unique in the iconography of America. The Statue of Liberty, or "Liberty Enlightening the World" as she is formerly called, follows *centuries of tradition in this country of representing America as an allegorical female,* with popular emphasis on the neoclassical goddess as in the American "Liberty." Through the time of colonization and beyond the Revolution, various female forms symbolized this new land, and when it came time to inspire the call for independence, the Americanized goddess of Liberty surged in popularity for many decades.

Before "America" became a toga-clad goddess called "Liberty," or her other common name, "Columbia," this country was depicted in the form of a beautiful, half-naked Indian Princess. Even earlier, in the maps of the first European discovery, the Western Hemisphere was depicted as a voluptuous but savage Indian Queen riding an alligator or an armadillo. The War of Independence coincided with an evolution from the Indian Princess to the more enduring, robed figure with her Liberty Pole and Cap, influenced by the neo-classical school of art. Very often overshadowing this American goddess of Liberty we see Minerva, the goddess of wisdom, and Mercury, the god of commerce and communication.

Why would the men of the Revolutionary era pick symbols for us from so-called "pagan" iconography? Where is all the Christian symbolism if this country was "founded as a Christian nation," as the evangelicals are so fond of saying today? Though it's true most of the Founding Fathers were devout Christians, none of them was interested in founding a "Christian nation." The consensus was to found a nation of religious tolerance. Though sometimes influenced by the Bible, their choices of symbols followed the current trend of the time: the neoclassical. Classical Greek and Roman mythology is also the accepted and expected tradition in heraldic and medallic art, and all the founders agreed that they wanted to look acceptable. They wanted to be taken seriously in the eyes of Europe, and they tried to strictly observe all the rules of protocol in their official documents and designs.

One of many examples of Revolutionary era artwork depicting America as a goddess. This engraving, entitled *America Trampling on Oppression,* was used as the frontispiece to Samuel Cooper's *History of North America,* published in England and America between 1789 and 1793. America is wearing Minerva's helmet plumed with ostrich feathers. In her left hand is a liberty pole and cap; her right hand points to heaven. By her right foot is a cornucopia and her left foot tramples the British lion. The symbols over her head include the caduceus, symbol of Mercury for commerce and communication. Print Collection, Miriam and Ira D. Wallach Division of Art, Prints and Photographs, the New York Public Library, Astor, Lenox and Tilden Foundations.

Before considering her symbolism, it's important to look at the Statue of Liberty in context by first examining the multitude of images like her that appeared in early American art. Differing versions appeared on coins, medallions, pamphlets, seals, etchings, and so on., effectually *nurturing the revolutionaries with the concept of Liberty like a mother.* You could even say it comforted them enough to embolden the break from their former Mother Country, also depicted in many of these scenes as a woman: the goddess Britannia. After the 1820s the visual personification of the United States began to transform into more masculine characters such as Yankee Doodle and Uncle Sam, but the image of Liberty as an American goddess did not fade out entirely. She was seen on our coins until 1947 and has reappeared recently on the new one dollar coins. Liberty or her counterparts appear on many state seals, flags, and capitol domes including New York (goddesses of Liberty and Justice); New Jersey (Liberty and Agriculture); Virginia (Virtue); Alabama (Liberty); Hawaii (Liberty); Arkansas (Liberty); and California (Minerva). Her counterpart "Columbia," always more popular in prose than in pictures, lives on through the names given to countless rivers, cities, and corporations—not to mention the capital of our nation.

Today the Statue of Liberty is immediately recognizable to almost anyone in the world; possibly considered right behind the American flag as the premiere symbol for this country. Most Americans may not consciously recognize her as a goddess, but understanding that she is not unique in that classification is the first step in deflating the fundamentalist-conspiratorialist claims that the Statue of Liberty is somehow Satanic. We will examine the leaps in logic that lead them to this conclusion later in this chapter, but first we will trace the classical inspirations behind the Statue of Liberty and give a symbolic rendering meant to *unite* Americans in the spirit of "Out of Many, One." To begin our investigation and determine what influences may be behind the Statue of Liberty, we need to examine the life and inspirations of her creator.

The Biography of a Statue: Meeting its Maker

The Statue of Liberty was conceived and designed by a Frenchman of Italian descent named Frédéric-Auguste Bartholdi (1834–1904). In 1856 Bartholdi was a 22-year-old art student who had just completed his first city monument in his hometown of Colmar, France. He was beginning to realize the challenges of working in his chosen profession of monumental sculpture: namely, the need for a sponsor before any expensive materials could be obtained. Often there were years to wait between the inspiration and the making of a statue. His desire was to work big, a desire made only grander when he visited the Egyptian monuments and temples that would affect him for the rest of his life. For eight months, he and his friends toured the ancient and gigantic works of art, and Bartholdi made copious drawings and notes. He particularly fell in love with the grand temple of Abu Simbel, writing that he admired the way the clean lines and the monumental size of the structures added to their physical strength in duration

Designer of the Statue of Liberty, or "Liberty Enlightening the World," Frédéric-Auguste Bartholdi (1834–1904). Photo credit: National Park Service.

as well as their ability to transmit ideas across centuries of time. "Their kindly and impassive glance seems to ignore the present and to be fixed upon an unlimited future," he said.[1]

It was during his trip to Egypt that Bartholdi met another of the key players in the birth of the Statue of Liberty. Ferdinand Marie Vicomte de Lesseps was the organizer of the Suez Canal project, and Bartholdi was captivated by the formidable undertaking de Lesseps was proposing to link the Black Sea to the Mediterranean with a canal all the way across Egypt. Proponents said it would herald a breakthrough in communication and commerce between the worlds of the West and the East, because it would allow ships from Europe directly through to Asia without having to circumnavigate Africa. Bartholdi's imagination fired with the idea for a gigantic lighthouse monument at the entry of the canal to symbolize the West shining its light on the East, likening it to the legendary Pharos lighthouse of Alexandria, one of the Seven Wonders of the Ancient World. He was never able to find a sponsor to fund it, but he tried several times to sell his idea of a lighthouse in the form of a woman holding a torch, which he called *Egypt (or Progress) Carrying the Light to Asia.* The Egyptian Khediev Ismail Pasha was receptive to the idea, but rejected it for economic reasons both of the times it was presented to him in 1867 and 1869. Bartholdi remembered the 1865 dinner party with French intellectuals as the place when he first had the idea for the Statue of Liberty, but many believe that it was this never-commissioned Suez Canal statue that eventually moved, in his mind, to America. In his book, Bartholdi denied any association between "Progress" and the final design for the Statue of Liberty.

Bartholdi's surviving clay maquettes of the proposed Suez Canal lighthouse, *Egypt Carrying the Light to Asia.* Despite its similarity to the Statue of Liberty, Bartholdi denied this never-completed statue was related in any conscious way. On display at the Statue of Liberty Exhibit on Liberty Island in New York. Photo courtesy of Barry Moreno.

After returning from Egypt, Bartholdi built his reputation as a monumental sculptor with publicly and privately commissioned fountains, statues, and other large-scale works benefiting by the late-19th-century popular trend for public artwork. He was befriended by a circle of intellectuals headed by Edouard René Lefèvre de Laboulaye, who had commissioned Bartholdi in 1865 to do his bust. Laboulaye was a professor and expert on America as well as a political activist for the cause of the French Republic. Whenever he and his intellectual friends gathered they usually extolled America as an ideal model for what they wanted to see in their own revised government. Most of France was ready for an end to the monarchical system under Napoleon III and was yearning for a form of constitutional republic. The 100th anniversary of the American Declaration of Independence was approaching, and supporters of a French Republic took every opportunity of remembering the instrumental support given by France to aid the success of the American Revolution. As usual, they focused on the good parts, such as how Louis the XVI gave crucial monetary support, and how Lafayette and others gave strategic military support, and how much the French had adored Ben Franklin. Before their own bloody revolution took hold, France and the brand new United States had developed a strong "sister-republic" relationship. In 1780 and 1781 the bells of Philadelphia were rung in honor of the birthday of the King of France, probably including the bell that would later become known as the Liberty Bell.[2] Conveniently forgotten was how narrowly our two countries avoided a declared war in the years immediately following the War of Independence.

Years later, Bartholdi recounted these conversations during that 1865 dinner party as the seed for the great idea. Laboulaye suggested that France make a grand gesture in honor of America's 100th birthday as a means of strengthening the memory of the sister republic relationship and inspire in France the American ideals of liberty and independence. Laboulaye, Bartholdi, and friends knew they had a daunting fundraising task ahead of them, and that it would require extraordinary efforts to gain permission and approval from both countries to manifest their vision. They decided to put the whole project on hold for a few years, until the timing was deemed more appropriate. Soon after, France found itself at war again, invaded this time by Germany. Bartholdi immediately enlisted in the army, with personal motivations to fight for his own liberty. His native Alsace region right there on the border was one of the first taken by the Germans, much to his embarrassment.

In 1871 when Paris fell, a dejected Bartholdi decided it was time to visit America and seek inspiration to further his ideas for building a monument to Liberty. Laboulaye sent him off with words of encouragement and letters of introduction, many to very influential people. With just five years left, they were still optimistic that they might launch the massive fundraising campaign and get their present ready in time to be part of America's Centennial celebration in 1876. In the end, it would take them quite a bit longer.

As soon as Bartholdi's ship sailed into New York Harbor that spring in 1871, he knew immediately it was the perfect location for the statue. Bedloe's Island was the home of an abandoned star-shaped military post called Fort Wood, and it ended up making a perfect base for the pedestal. He took his sketches and enthusiasm, along with this new idea for where to locate it, to his meetings around the country. Everywhere he went he was warmly received, recounting his inspiration to create "a work of profound moral worth,"[3] to inspire people with the ideals of the American Revolution. But first he had to convince the Americans to pay for their share of the "gift."

Bartholdi held meetings on the proposed joint-nation venture with President Ulysses S. Grant, Henry Wadsworth Longfellow, numerous veterans of the Civil War, and many other esteemed notables. Everyone thought the idea was grand and the gesture magnanimous, but they all objected to the idea of having to pay for half of it. If the statue would be in New York, then let New York pay for it, some said. It would be several more years before the idea fully took off in America, thanks to fundraising campaigns organized by some of the biggest names of the era, including Joseph Pulitzer and Henry Spaulding. American fundraising would lag well behind the activity in France, and there it did not really begin in earnest until 1875, after the Third Republic took control of the government.

Enough money was raised to begin work on the statue later that year, but they soon realized they would never have it done in time for the Centennial Exposition in Philadelphia the following July. Bartholdi made his new goal to complete the 42-foot right arm and torch for the Expo display. He missed the July 4th goal by only a month, and it arrived before the Expo closed in August. Visitors flocked to climb inside the arm and marvel at the first statue designed to welcome public visitors on the inside.

Hired to construct the interior frame of Liberty was Alexandre-Gustave Eiffel, who would not become famous for his own iron tower in Paris until 1887. On Eiffel's frame were hung great sheets of hammered copper. Imagine how she must have looked brand new when she still gleamed coppery bright, reflect-

"Liberty Enlightening the World." Photo credit: National Park Service.

ing the dazzling sun! Fundraising and enthusiasm for the project peaked and waned in both countries for several years until the statue was finally completed in France in 1884. By 1883, crowds of French people were gathering on Sundays to watch the enormous statue taking shape and to listen to speeches about liberty and the need for a permanent republic in France. "Liberty Enlightening the World" was dedicated in a ceremony in Paris on July 4, 1884. Early the next year it was disassembled, packed into crates, and shipped to New York, where it took six months to put it back together after another delay because the pedestal was not yet completed. It was officially unveiled in New York to much pomp and ceremony on October 28, 1886. Just three years later, France would declare its Third Republic official and permanent.

The Freemasons and the Statue of Liberty, Part I

The main contributors and fundraisers for the Statue of Liberty in France had always been the intellectuals and politicians surrounding Laboulaye. Many of them were Freemasons, who recognized a statue honoring liberty as a worthy cause to support. As a group the Masons contributed a considerable sum of money, but so did thousands of citizens of Paris, and other cities and businesses across France. It was the Franco-American Union established in 1874 that was responsible for raising the necessary funds. The effort was not initiated, nor solely financed, by the Masons, and therefore it is not accurate to say that the Statue of Liberty was a gift from the Freemasons of France to the Freemasons of the United States, as so many fundamentalist-conspiratorialists like to claim.

That said, people attracted to Freemasonry are generally the kinds of people who are moved by projects that inspire positive ideals for future generations. For the same reasons, Freemasons in America also got behind the fundraising efforts for the pedestal, as well as the building of the pedestal—a job *for masons,* after all. Contemporary accounts of the time do not contain any complaints or accusations of the statue being a Freemasonic conspiracy for nefarious mind-control purposes, as her critics do today. These ideas have been put forth just in the last few years with the growing mania to attach American symbols to the Illuminati conspiracy. In fact, it was the small contributions from the little people that turned the tide for the fundraising efforts in America. Joseph Pulitzer, publisher of *The World* newspaper in New York, adopted the project and editorialized his readers to send in all their spare change: "Let us not wait for the millionaires to give this money. It is not a gift from the millionaires of France to the millionaires of America, but a gift of the whole people of France to the whole people of America."[4] We will return to the question of a Masonic influence on the Statue of Liberty later in this chapter, but, for now, suffice it to say that the number of prominent people involved in the project who happened to be Masons does not prove a Masonic conspiracy.

Emma Lazarus Helps the Statue Find Its Purpose

In 1883, as Bartholdi neared completion of the statue in France, the campaign for funds to build the pedestal in America hit a snag. The pedestal needed to be almost as large as the statue itself, and as time ran out committee members began looking for new methods to raise cash. Former Secretary of State William Evarts organized a charity auction of manuscripts by several leading writers of the day, including Mark Twain and Walt Whitman. Evarts requested a poem from a popular poet named Emma Lazarus (1849–87), but she turned him down. Even though she loved the idea that liberty was the symbol for education or enlightenment for the world, she was afraid nothing in her collection was suitable for the occasion. Being a sensitive poetess, she was appalled when he asked her to write something to order, even though the auction was just a week away. Lazarus was from a wealthy family prominent since Colonial times, and she had led a sheltered life. Her poetry tended toward the transcendental, similar to that of one of her mentors, Ralph Waldo Emerson.

Lazarus believed quite strongly that she could not command her poetic muse, and must wait for it to work through her. The sketches that Evarts had shown her that day, along with his rousing proclamations about liberty dispelling ignorance and prejudice, must have been just the thing to inspire Lazarus's muse, however. She sat down that very afternoon and wrote a sonnet called "The New Colossus" in a few hours. It was destined to outlive her, and eventually become just as famous as the statue itself.

"The New Colossus" was the big hit of the night for the charity auction, and once again the money started pouring in. Critics applauded the poem for giving the statue a voice and, with it, a plausible reason for its existence, generally believed to have been lacking until then. Bartholdi and Laboulaye had not intended their "Liberty Enlightening the World" to be a beacon for immigrants, but many refugees seeking liberty from oppression were obviously seeking that liberty in America. And with a huge copper homage to liberty gleaming in the harbor as their first impression of their new home, it would not be long before the concept of immigration became entwined with the Statue of Liberty. In 1903, long after her death, Lazarus's poem was pulled out of the files and attached to a plaque in the lobby of the monument, as if it were intended to be there all along.

A few years before writing this poem, Emma Lazarus had been shaken out of her comfortable existence by the cause of her fellow Jewish immigrants being slaughtered in the pogroms of Eastern Europe. All America was horrified at the violence that seemed so counter to the spirit of the age, and many prominent Americans helped organize assistance for these immigrants. Through her volunteer work, Lazarus found herself speaking for the first time with men and women who had a firsthand appreciation for the precious commodity of liberty that so many Americans take for granted. She continued working with Jewish refugees until her death and is credited as one of the pioneers of the modern Zionist movement. The fundamentalist-conspiratorialists who attack the Statue of Liberty as Satanic often reveal their anti-Semitic streak when they focus on the poet's interest in helping Jewish immigrants and the need for developing a homeland for the Jews.[5] They decipher this connection as proof that the Statue of Liberty is meant to symbolize a Jewish woman calling all Jews to move here and take over the country and banish Christianity.

For the majority of rational people, however, ever since the poem was affixed to the pedestal, the Statue of Liberty has been welcoming all immigrants to the land of the free. At the same time she became a reminder that not so long ago all of our ancestors were immigrants, and we must fight the tendency to take for granted these precious liberties and freedoms. Remembering why a steady stream of immigrants continues to move here helps us stay united under this common idea. As presidents Cleveland, Roosevelt, and Reagan all similarly mentioned at their addresses from the foot of the statue (at its inauguration in 1886, its 50th in 1936, and its 100th in 1986) the Statue of Liberty symbolizes the strongest unifying factor about America: our freedom.

In 1924 the Statue of Liberty became a National Monument under the control of the Park Service. Her image has been seen on U.S. postage stamps more than 15 times, and her torch alone on two others. She has appeared on commemorative coins, on license plates of cars in both New York and New Jersey, and in countless films. Who could ever forget her significance in the final scene of *Planet of the Apes*? The Statue of Liberty has so completely embodied the archetypal ideal of freedom that people all over the world have created replicas of her for their own towns. In the 1950s, the Boy Scouts of America distributed more than 200 8-1/2-foot-tall replicas of the Statue of Liberty to cities across America in commemoration of their 40th anniversary theme, "Strengthen the Arm of Liberty."

The most famous replica of the Statue of Liberty is one of Bartholdi's test models, a 40-foot-high version in the River Seine, just down the river from the Eiffel Tower. There are also replicas in other cities in France, as well as in Austria, Germany, Italy, Japan, China, and Vietnam. The Western world was especially moved by the symbolism of the "Goddess of Democracy" raised by students during their violent uprising against the repressive Chinese government in the Tiananmen Square massacres of 1989. In order to not appear too pro-American, the sculptor remembered trying to make his lady with a torch deliberately unlike the Statue of Liberty, but the similarity was still obvious. As such a familiar image, we all pretty much take her for granted today. But who is she, really?

Liberty Was a Goddess Long Before She Moved to America

Most of us in America today are so poorly trained in history that when we see a provocative comparison between the Statue of Liberty and the Roman and Greek goddesses who inspired her, we gasp in astonishment! Just a little digging into American history, however, will reveal that "Liberty Enlightening the World" follows a long tradition of identifying America as an assortment of female goddesses. Both Bartholdi's time and the time period that he was saluting with his monument were influenced by the recurring waves of neoclassicism in the arts. Americans were identifying themselves with the goddess of Liberty long before there was a split between those loyal to Britain and those advocating independence. Liberty was

> **"The New Colossus"**
> by Emma Lazarus
>
> Not like the brazen giant of Greek fame,
> with conquering limbs astride from land to land;
> Here at our sea-washed, sunset gates shall stand
> a mighty woman with a torch, whose flame
> is the imprisoned lightning, and her name
> Mother of Exiles. From her beacon-hand
> Glows world-wide welcome; her mild eyes command
> The air-bridged harbor that twin cities frame,
> "Keep, ancient lands, your storied pomp!" cries she
> with silent lips. "Give me your tired, your poor,
> Your huddled masses yearning to breathe free,
> The wretched refuse of your teeming shore,
> Send these, the homeless, tempest-tost to me,
> I lift my lamp beside the golden door!"

a moral ideal held passionately by a large, articulate segment of Colonial society. Americans had come to think of their entire way of life as the pursuit of liberty, in religion, property-holding, business, social advancement, newspaper decision-making, expression of criticism, and self-determination. Franklin popularized a declaration made earlier by James Otis, that "where Liberty dwells, there is my country."

Indeed liberals on both sides of the Atlantic regarded English America as the critical front in the crusade for liberty. Men interested in the advancement of mankind everywhere projected this ideal to the young nation-in-the-making with what amounted to religious fervor.

Beginning in the 1500s, European map-makers depicted the Western Hemisphere as a voluptuous Indian Queen astride an armadillo or an alligator, carrying a club and wearing eagle feathers in her headdress. Images drawn from eyewitness accounts of the Native or First Peoples made a strong impression in Europe, where even most *women* still believed that the female sex was the evil temptress in Man's downfall and was appropriately subjugated by her father or husband. Reports and images of a matrilineal culture and women in leading roles were puzzling, and it would be several hundred more years before significant legal changes were made for white women to enjoy a similar sense of equality as our First People already had.

From the earliest days of discovery of the new world, America was depicted in the female form. This savage Indian Queen first evolved into a paler Indian Princess before donning a toga. Cartouche from Sheet 17 of Henry Popple's 1733 "Map of the British Empire in America with the French and Spanish Settlements adjacent thereto" (London, 1733). Library of Congress, Geography and Map Division.

The Status of Women Among the First People

Females in America held positions of political power and influence for hundreds of years before Columbus landed. Don Grinde and Bruce Johansen's

Exemplar of Liberty details well the life of women in the societies of the First People:

> Iroquois women, for example, nominated men for positions of leadership and could "dehorn" or impeach these leaders for misconduct. Women's approval was usually a necessary precondition for conducting war. In a matrilineal society—and nearly all the confederacies that bordered the colonies were matrilineal—women owned all household goods except the men's clothes, weapons, and hunting implements. They were the primary conduits for culture from generation to generation. In the Cherokee home, for example, the woman was supreme. An eighteenth-century observer reported that the "women rule the rost [*sic*], and weres [*sic*] the britches and sometimes will beat thire [*sic*] husbands within an inch of thire life."[6]

It wasn't long after colonization began in earnest that the image of the untamed Indian Queen evolved into the more manageable Indian Princess to represent the British Colonies in America. In light of the later atrocities inflicted on the First Peoples by the white men, it is interesting that when they first settled here, they chose the symbol of an Indian woman to represent them. Sometimes the Indian Princess is seen receiving homage from the goddess of Liberty, to show that America was the home of the free.

"America" Evolves Into a European-Looking Goddess

The Indian Princess was the symbol for America in the arts until at least 1790, by which time the neoclassical movement had firmly taken root. The Indian Princess had been paler and thinner than her predecessor, but she was always seen carrying a tomahawk or bow and arrows. She wore a feathered headdress and was often scantily clad. Even with her more European features she was still earthy and real, and the rugged frontiersmen in America easily identified with her. She was most assuredly based on a real race of women.

Around the time of the War of Independence we see "America" beginning to evolve into a European-looking goddess. In his excellent essay, "From Indian Princess to Greek Goddess," E. McClung Fleming says, "Part of the new classical spirit was a fresh taste for allegory and symbol making. Gentlemen on both sides of the Atlantic set to work borrowing from Greek and Roman mythology to adapt old figures or create new ones to represent the United States."[7] Gradually the buckskin changed to a toga and sandals, the arrows and tomahawks to a sword and shield, and the eagle feathers in her hair changed to ostrich plumes. There was almost always another classical symbol placed nearby this new American goddess, either a pyramid, an altar, a temple, or an obelisk, all meant to associate America with the idealized republics of Greece and Rome. Both the buckskin-clad America and the robed America were supported by Roman and Greek gods and heroes such as Athena/Minerva, Hercules, and Libertas. Whereas Minerva and Hercules were usually seen in supporting roles, Libertas found herself crossing all the way over the ocean and eventually merging with the female form of "America." Originally a Roman goddess of both personal freedom and the freedom of the state, Libertas has become so closely linked with America that we made her one of our own.

This engraving shows the goddess America holding the shield and surrounded by symbols and gods from the neoclassical period mixed with American symbols. The "Genius of America" is being counseled by Minerva, Goddess of Wisdom. To the left is Mercury standing beside bales of goods, and gesturing toward three ships in the harbor. He is pointing out why navigation must be protected to Ceres, the Goddess of Agriculture, who is leaning against a beehive. John J. Barralet, "America Guided by Wisdom." Philadelphia, ca. 1815. Engraving by Benjamin Tanner. Courtesy Winterthur Museum.

Libertas appears on many Roman coins and medallions indicating how important the concept of liberty was as both a political issue to the many emperors and as an ideal to the citizens. Libertas was originally linked to slaves who had won their freedom, and she was frequently depicted with a pole and a cap, the props used in the ceremony of giving a slave his freedom in ancient Rome. The cap was called the pileus or the Phrygian cap, and was brimless and slightly pointed and flopped over at the top.

With so many Colonists coming to America in search of liberty of one sort or another, it wasn't long before they were recalling the Roman goddess Libertas to personify that freedom that was becoming the most essential element in their new lives. The Liberty Cap and the Liberty Pole, as her props came to be called in this country, remained with Liberty's costume when she moved to America. The Sons of Liberty and other organizers of the rebellion would erect enormous poles, sometimes called Liberty Trees, around which they would declaim the British king and call for independence. British troops would cut them down, and angry Colonists would put them back up.

This 1804 engraving from Boston shows Columbia wearing a tiara, holding a laurel branch and the American flag, and supporting a shield emblazoned with the American eagle. The border consists of the popular motif of the linked chain of the American states, here numbering 15. Samuel Harris, *Emblem of the United States of America.*" Courtesy Winterthur Museum.

As the image of America evolved, a third allegorical female emerged as a sort of transitional character in between the Indian Princess and the American goddess of Liberty. She was named Columbia, a feminized name for Christopher Columbus. Although later scholarship would prove otherwise, the legend of Columbus as the first one to "sail across the ocean blue" was so popular among early Americans that they even named a goddess after him. Unlike Liberty, Columbia was never depicted with feathers or ostrich plumes in her hair. She was either bareheaded, or crowned by radiant stars, or sometimes wearing a Liberty Cap. William Barton included a type of Columbia in his second draft for the Great Seal of the U.S., calling her "the Genius of the American Confederated Republic." He described her as a maiden with flowing hair, and on her head was, "a radiated Crown of Gold, encircled with an Azure Fillet spangled with Silver Stars."[8] Another amalgamated goddess featuring symbols from both the Indian Princess and the classic period is seen today atop the Capitol Dome in Washington, D.C. Known as the Statue of Freedom, this goddess was designed by American Thomas Crawford about 20 years before Bartholdi's Statue of Liberty. (We discuss her further in Chapter 7.)

The Origin of America's Name

The first time the name "America" appeared on a world map was 1507. Most of us learned in school that America was named after Amerigo Vespucci, an Italian cartographer and explorer, but this theory is not at all as solid as we might have believed. In recent years, as the archeological paradigm shifted to include evidence of intelligent civilizations indigenous to the Western Hemisphere, more critical investigations have been made to determine why we call this land "America." How many other continents or new countries are named after a person's *first name*, anyway? The discrepancies in the 1507 mapmaker's story, that the land was named "America" in honor of Vespucci, have spurred many investigators to put forth alternative theories. One suggestion is that America derives its name from the gold-rich mountainous district of *Amer-rique* in Nicaragua, which both Columbus and Vespucci allegedly visited. A closer look at Vespucci's original first name reveals it was actually Alberigo, and he changed it to reflect the importance of the discovery of the gold-rich *Amer-rique*. Another claim is that the name came from Richard Amerike, the English merchant who financed John Cabot's voyage to the New World in 1497. A third possibility stems from the 11th-century legends that Moorish Moslems organized oceanic expeditions to the "Westlands." These expeditions were led by military leaders named Wadha El-*Ameri* and Zohair Al-*Americ*.

Frank Joseph's *The Atlantis Encyclopedia* presents yet another theory that I find even more plausible. What if the 16th-century Spaniards first arriving on these continents were told by the indigenous "Indians" that they called this "the Land of A-Mu-Ra-Ca," a reference to the flood hero from Atlantis? Joseph lays out a compelling case for the use of the name America among the natives, as recorded even in the logs of Christopher Columbus. On his third voyage to the New World, Columbus recorded meeting Indian natives who introduced themselves as "Americos," a tribe that was also identified by the later explorer Alonso de Ojeda. The Carib Indians of Venezuela tell of a deluge hero named Amaicaca who escaped in a big canoe. Colombian native traditions speak of A-Mu-Ra-Ca, a hero who escaped the catastrophe from the great ocean kingdom and led his followers to South America. He was described as a bearded white man who taught the natives about agriculture, medicine, and religion, and built their stone cities. Joseph concludes that "A-Mu-Ra-Ca's resemblance to the 'Plumed Serpent,' known by the identical name to the northerly Mayas and Aztecs, means that the same set of Old World culture-bearers arrived throughout the Americas."[9]

As it happens, however, the colonizing countries of the 16th century did not have a custom of adopting the names given by the natives to their own countries, preferring instead to assign new names related to their conquest. If Joseph is correct, the Vespucci explanation for the name "America" may have been manufactured simply to appear more politically correct for the times.

"[T]he names 'Minerva,' 'Liberty,' 'Columbia,' and 'America' were often used interchangeably," notes E. McClung Fleming.[10] As Americans grew to appreciate liberty as the one ethic above all others that unites us, the other female depictions of America eventually merged with the goddess of Liberty. Fleming says, "It is obvious that the impulse to represent the United States was strong, the vocabulary of meaningful symbols was rich, the resulting image was various," and then goes on to wonder if "the uncertainty of the image reflects a measure of uncertainty of self-interpretation by the young nation in a period of ambitious and turbulent self-identification in the family of nations."[11]

This transitional "America" from 1804 shows her with ostrich plumes instead of eagle feathers, the liberty pole and cap, the shield with the American eagle, and the curious amalgamated character of the Negro-Indian boy. *America,* London, 1804. Courtesy Winterthur Museum.

Consistent among all her early incarnations, the goddess of Liberty was always surrounded by several other symbols or figures to assure her association with America. In the earliest days these symbols included the cornucopia, feathers, arrows, and the tomahawk. Later they would be the new American flag, the eagle, the Constitution, portraits of the revolutionary leaders such as Washington or Franklin (sometimes wearing togas), or the date July 4, 1776. According to Fleming four especially American symbols were the rattlesnake (an indigenous American cousin to the serpent of wisdom), tobacco, Niagara Falls, and a curious character, also evolving, that represented a large portion of the population of this wild country. As the Indian Princess was replaced by the Roman goddess, her Native American attributes were sometimes transferred to a companion in the figure of a dark-skinned boy who wore feathers in his hair. Sometimes he appeared more African and other times more native. I find it synchronistic to note that both the subjugated classes, the Negro and the Native, were merged together into one symbol.

This is also the time period that the United States began the organized displacement and later massacre of the Native Americans, as the two cultures began to clash in their approaches to the land. The Natives' concept of liberty was to roam freely and hunt anywhere, versus the Colonists, who saw liberty as owning a plot of land. With the passage of time, the new American leaders stopped seeking the wisdom of the sachems as our Founding Fathers had, and artists sometimes displayed the Native Americans and the Negro slaves as one and the same: a crouching representative of the disenfranchised yet integral parts of the American identity.

To design the Statue of Liberty, the sculptor Bartholdi made an intensive study of all these allegorical females representing America dating back to her earliest days of colonization. His Lady Liberty borrows a little bit from all of them to become something new, and as we shall see, adds in elements of even earlier goddesses.

Yes, the Statue of Liberty Is a Goddess

After reading the preceding section, I hope you will no longer be afraid to use the word *goddess*. It should be apparent that our ancestors of the late 1700s/early 1800s were not afraid of it, and I think it's time to remind ourselves to be tolerant of pre-Christian men and women who worshipped the goddess and those who continue to do so today. This is a land of religious liberty, and anyone should be allowed to worship in any way they believe best. Christ was tolerant of everyone except the moneymakers in the temple, and we should follow his example. Now that we have presented the historical background for the statue, and the evolution of the goddess imagery, we will try to provide a more archetypal interpretation of the symbolism of the Statue of Liberty.

To look at the Statue of Liberty from this perspective, we will base our reading on the companion symbols depicted with her as well as her overall impact when the symbols are combined. For example, why is she wearing a crown of rays, and why are there seven rays coming from it? Why is she cradling a book in her left arm, and why is the torch in her right? Why is she trampling on chains, and why is her pedestal in the shape of an 11-pointed star? That last one's easy: because Fort Wood was already shaped that way and the pedestal for the statue was built directly on top of this fort. Star forts were devised as a means of protection against siege when the development of cannon fire made flat walls more vulnerable. Why this particular star fort was constructed with 11 points I don't know, so we won't add it to our symbolic assessment of the Statue of Liberty. Bartholdi's original sketches for the statue show it on a much grander pedestal in the shape of a stepped pyramid. The more tapered column built instead was preferred by the American architect who was chosen for the job, and slightly resembles the shape of the Pharos Lighthouse of Alexandria.

To examine something symbolically, we use sources for correspondence systems derived from ancient wisdom teachings and divination arts not considered by mainstream academics. They usually lack the formal requirements for standard documentation, but, as long as they don't conflict with historical data, I believe they are worthy of consideration. Most esotericists, and that includes the fundamentalist-conspiratorialists, pay too little attention to the authentic historical data. This allows for connections that can easily be invalidated by reading a little history, as we will see especially in the chapter on the Liberty Bell. If we examine some of the facts laid out by our fundamentalist-conspiratorialist friends on the Statue of Liberty, however, we find some of them do check out historically. Where I disagree is how these historical links are interpreted on only one level and used as further "proof" for their preconceived idea that anything pre-Christian or touched by a Freemason is necessarily proof of an Illuminati conspiracy.

How Much Isis Is There in the Statue of Liberty?

Bartholdi never said that "Liberty Enlightening the World" was symbolic of the Egyptian mother goddess Isis. Nor can we find anywhere that he said his earlier idea for a lighthouse statue at the Suez Canal was symbolic of Isis. He also denied the Suez Canal statue was the inspiration for his statue in New York.[12] It is likely that he downplayed the suggestion that "Liberty Enlightening the World" was a recycled idea, feeling that might diminish the perceived value and originality of the gift to America. But even if the Suez Canal statue was not intended to represent Isis, or if the two statues *were* completely unrelated in his mind, it would still be valuable to examine Isis in our discussion of the symbolic interpretation of the Statue of Liberty. As two female goddesses, Liberty and Isis share the idea of the archetypal female.

It was commonly believed by Bartholdi's contemporaries that the face of the Statue of Liberty was modeled after his own austere and domineering mother, Charlotte. Photo credit: National Park Service.

Isis is a Greek word for the Egyptian goddess of the throne, and it is not really known how the Egyptians would have pronounced her name. The hieroglyphics for it are usually written *jst,* and Egyptologists like to pronounce that as *ee-set,* but it's just a guess. Originally she was always depicted in the company of her husband, Osiris, and son, Horus, and she was considered the goddess of creation, mothers, and fertility. She was seen in the sky as the star Sirius, which follows the constellation Orion, which was identified as Osiris. Gradually, Isis grew more popular and took on the attributes of other mother goddesses and, by assuming their natures, took on their symbols as well. Worship of Isis as an individual became widespread only in the Roman times and remained popular until the sixth century CE when the Christians outlawed it. The Greeks compared Isis to Demeter, and the Romans compared her to Ceres.

The Roman goddess Libertas is not traditionally associated with motherhood as Isis is, but the Statue of Liberty has a couple of mother connections. Emma Lazarus identified the mother image in Bartholdi's statue by naming her the "Mother of Exiles." This Liberty is like a mother who loves all her children equally, including all the poor refugees; she impartially gives liberty to all. Bartholdi may also have seen a mother in his design for the Statue of Liberty, more specifically than anyone else, in fact. It was commonly believed at the time that the face of the Statue of Liberty was modeled after his own austere and domineering mother, Charlotte.[13] A comparison of a photograph of Charlotte Bartholdi with the face of the Statue of Liberty reveals why it is easy to believe this rumor.

The Roman goddess Libertas is not traditionally associated with light, either, as Isis is. Perhaps when Bartholdi added the elements of light to his Liberty he was subconsciously adding something of Isis to his statue, but it's more likely that his symbolism was to demonstrate the concept of liberty as a precursor to enlightenment. Graham Hancock and Robert Bauval have connected the dots to show that Bartholdi may have been thinking about Isis when he designed his Suez canal lighthouse and therefore, by extension, the Statue of Liberty. Bartholdi himself had compared his earlier proposed statue to the great Alexandrian Pharos Lighthouse, which, though not in the shape of a woman, had been dedicated to the goddess Isis.

The Freemasons and the Statue of Liberty, Part II

As another connection between the Statue of Liberty and Isis, Hancock and Bauval emphasize the importance of the Egyptian strain of Freemasonry that was especially prevalent in France during Bartholdi's time. One of Bartholdi's heroes, Guiseppi Garibaldi, under whom he served briefly during the Franco-Prussian War, later joined the Masonic Order of Memphis-Misraim,[14] which also counted as members the Egyptian Khedive, whom Bartholdi had solicited about his Suez Canal statue. Bartholdi did not become a Freemason until five years after they started the Statue of Liberty project, and long after he came in contact with Garibaldi. He was initiated in the Alsace-Lorraine Lodge of the Grand Orient of France in 1875.[15] An argument can be made that some of the symbolism he emphasized in the design was influenced by the ideals celebrated by Masons, such as truth, justice, and enlightenment. The connection to Egypt, however, comes from his trip there as a young man when he recorded how much he admired the simplicity and grandeur of their ancient monumental sculpture. Another possible connection to Isis is the date chosen for the cornerstone-laying ceremony for the pedestal by the Grand Lodge of New York. Bauval contends that someone intentionally chose the date of August 5th because on that day in 1884, Sirius, the star sacred to Isis, was making its famous rising before the sun at dawn, which in the old days would have signaled to the ancient Egyptians that the Nile was about to flood, and their fertile growing season would begin.

In the latter part of the 19th century, Freemasons were much more romantic in tracing the origins of their brotherhood, and there was a wide belief that Freemasonry originated in the Egyptian mystery traditions. There are indeed similarities enough to make connections, but not enough for historical documentation by current standards. Modern freemasonry today does not accept the conclusions of Mackey, Pike, and others from the 19th century that their Craft originated in any distant source. Sticklers for documentary evidence, can reliably trace their origins only to the late 16th century, thus contradicting many of the Freemasonic writings that are used by the anti-Masons to prove that Masons are pagans or somehow linked to an ancient conspiracy of elitists.

It is possible that some people involved in the Statue of Liberty project were reminded by her of Isis, but there is no documentation to attest to this claim. Nor is there any contemporary record that anyone complained about the Masons' involvement or suggested that they were part of a conspiracy. I believe it is unnecessary to document how many Freemasons were involved in this project. Of course, they were involved, and they did not try to hide it. It is also unnecessary, to some degree, to compare the Statue of Liberty to Isis in order to associate her with an aura of ancient goddess power. She is already quite straightforwardly a powerful ancient goddess. Recognizing her as what she was intended to be is phenomenal enough: the Americanized goddess of Liberty using freedom and wisdom to enlighten the world.

As with the construction of Washington, D.C., and with the American Revolution itself, as it happens, a lot of the people involved in the Statue of Liberty project were Freemasons. For one reason, Freemasons enjoy celebrating the American ideals of liberty, union, and peace, and as a result they are the ones organizing the ceremonies, laying the cornerstones, designing the architecture, and funding the sculptures. They want this country to succeed, just as many other civic-minded organizations do. Public sentiment about the Freemasons tends to fluctuate over time, and we are currently in a period of high suspicion and fear. Let's just remember that in another time, conspiracy-minded people will be examining the names on the historical record to add up how many Jews were involved, or how many Catholics, or whatever is the current scapegoat. Right now, it's the Freemasons being blamed for secretly controlling the world, and thus anything connected with them is going to be scrutinized.

The Crown of Light

There are many ways of interpreting a radiant crown, a symbol used by many cultures across history. The Christian symbol of the halo comes immediately to mind. For centuries, artists have depicted a shimmering light around the heads of holy men and women who were supposed to have had a special connection to the divine. Carl Jung concluded that the radiant crown is the symbol *par excellence* of reaching the highest goal in evolution: "for he who conquers himself wins the crown of eternal life."[16] The crown symbolizes the victory of the higher aspirations of man over the lower baser nature of instincts. The crown of rays of light has always been a symbol for spiritual enlightenment, which can be gained through the transmutation of ignorance into knowledge. Bernard Weisberger's beautiful book, *Statue of Liberty: The First Hundred Years,* includes several photos of other statues of female forms called "Faith," "Liberty," and "Religion" from the 1780s through the 1880s who are all wearing rayed crowns very similar to Bartholdi's "Liberty."

In Kabbalah, the oral tradition of the Hebrew mysteries, the crown is Keter, the top sephirot, or vessel in the Tree of Life. Keter is said to hold the light of illumination and the source of all life. We may experience this emanation as the glow that occurs in moments of mental, emotional, and spiritual oneness. It is the light of the Creator that flows to us through our body, mind, and soul. It is also called the limitless light (or En Soph).[17]

A luminous crown could also be a symbol for a stimulated kundalini spirit fire from the root chakra to illuminate the crown chakra. In the Eastern traditions, there are seven chakras corresponding to seven energy centers in the body through which one learns how to raise the kundalini energy. The kundalini energy is related to the fire of the Holy Spirit and mastering its flow leads to an ecstatic union with God or cosmic consciousness. The process through which humans can enter the spiritual world is through Prana, or the breath of life. "Brahman... is the prana, the breath of life that pervades both the universe and the human body," said Paul Deussen in his *Philosophy of the Upanishads.*[18] A glowing crown chakra would imply that Liberty has gained her highest spiritual potential.

7 Rays in the Crown

Lucky number 7, why is it so lucky? Seven is the combination of 3 and 4, and may have been deemed holy or lucky by early man just by playing with fundamental geometric shapes. Seven is the result when you draw a triangle around a square, which was done to symbolize the sky over the earth, or by inscribing a triangle within a square, which was done to symbolize spirit within matter, the soul within man. Seven stands for a complete period or cycle of time, such as seven days in a week. Cirlot catalogues that seven "corresponds to the seven Directions of Space (that is, the six essential dimensions plus the centre), and to the seven-pointed star. It is the number forming the basic series of musical notes, of colors and of the planetary spheres, as well as of the gods corresponding to them; and also of the capital sins and their opposing virtues."[19]

In the Hebrew Kabbalah, the seventh sephirot is Netzach, which stands for victory and eternity. Netzach is our ability to put a plan into action and follow it through. It is the way the willpower of a person is applied to life and leads to victory. Netzach shows us the Creator's tireless participation in the world and how our devotion to Him in any undertaking is what makes it manifest in the world of action.[20]

Thus we have the light of illumination and the source of all life flowing from the crown to all human beings in the world. The light of Liberty is the limitless light that manifests through the symbol of perfection for a complete period or cycle (in the number 7).

Hancock and Bauval found two other ancient goddesses who wore seven pointed crowns. One was the Egyptian Sechat, wife or daughter of Thoth, who is depicted with a seven-pointed star over her head. The star is thought to have originally been a papyrus plant to acknowledge the material that was sacred to this goddess of writing. There is also the seven-pointed star crowning the head of the woman on the 16th card of the Tarot, "the Star."

The National Park Service tells us that the seven rays in the crown symbolize the Seven Seas, or possibly the seven continents, but they also acknowledge that these interpretations did not originate until the 20th century. According to Barry Moreno, librarian and historian at the Statue of Liberty National Monument, and author of *The Statue of Liberty Encyclopedia,* Bartholdi is not known to have ever stated any symbolic interpretations of his statue.[21] Though he was obviously interested in symbols, he would have also known that there is always more than one way of interpreting them, and he preferred for the viewer to define them individually. He also made it a point to keep his monumental sculptures simple in detail, knowing that from a distance suggestion rather than precision worked best. Seven rays may have been simply what fit the size and proportion of the crown without becoming too complicated.

The Torch Is in Her Right Hand

Starting with the interpretation of the National Park Service: The torch is obviously meant to symbolize the "light" in Bartholdi's title for the statue ("Liberty Enlightening the World"). Emma Lazarus was moved by the connection of the light to education, which she believed could dispel all the darkness of ignorance that caused prejudice. Laboulaye explained the torch in a speech in 1876 as "not the torch that sets afire, but the flambeau, the candle-flame that enlightens."[22] The torch is not being brandished, but held aloft as a giver of light. The ancient wisdom teachings all say that opening the eye of light, or the third eye, is emblematic of the attainment of divine knowledge. After creating the heavens and the earth, "let there be light" was the first thing God said as He separated the light from the darkness. The two symbols of light from both Liberty's torch and crown can be interpreted as her having an elevated awareness opened up to the spiritual worlds. She has accomplished spiritual vision, and the Holy Spirit is shining through her. Liberty's torch is a symbol of purification through illumination or truth.

The Better Business Bureau is one of countless organizations using the torch in their logo, demonstrating illumination through knowledge. Used with permission of the Council of Better Business Bureaus, Inc., 4200 Wilson Blvd., Arlington, VA 22203, www.us.bbb.org.

The torch is held in her right hand. Bartholdi's original models show the statue holding the torch in her left hand. Why did he change it? Probably for aesthetic reasons, but it's also worth pointing out that the right hand is considered the more favored position in heraldry, and in esoteric symbology the right hand is the hand of activation. The left hand is the symbol for more passive, contemplative features.

The Tablet Is in Her Left Hand

The Statue of Liberty is cradling in her left hand a book or a tablet. Carved with the date July 4, 1776, the tablet is meant to symbolize the birth of our independence as a nation, and at the same time the Law on which this republican experiment was founded. Holding something in the left hand is indicative of nurturing or meditation, passive energies. Bartholdi included the date of the Declaration of Independence as a clear indication that this goddess was the *American* Liberty. She is cradling or protecting our independence.

What is a book? Cirlot tells us that "a book is one of the eight Chinese common emblems, symbolizing the power to ward off evil spirits."[23] He goes on to trace broadly how the book is also linked to the symbolism of weaving and from there it is compared to the universe, where all characters, thoughts, and actions are inscribed and woven together. In symbolic terminology, a book can be used to represent "the book of life," or the record of all things, commonly called the Akashic Record. Many cultures around the world speak of a book or hall of records, which can be accessed from a spiritual plane or altered state to reveal past events, probable futures, and individual soul or life records. The word *Akashic* comes from the Sanskrit word for the sky or ether, on which all this information is said to be recorded.

The book of life is mentioned repeatedly in the Bible in Psalm 69:28 and Philippians 4:3, and many times in the book of Revelation, where it is described as the record that God keeps of your sins. Many of the most famous Western mystics in the last hundred years have spoken about accessing the Akashic Record, including Max Heindel, Rudolph Steiner, and Edgar Cayce. Cayce (1877–1945), a devout Christian, is probably the one most commonly associated with the term, as he described it in several of his psychic readings. When asked about the source for his remarkable diagnoses and cures that he gave to thousands of sick people, he called it the book of life. With a symbolic goal of "Enlightening the World," it would make sense that Lady Liberty holds such a book.

The Chains of Oppression

The chains beneath her feet show that Liberty has thrown off the chains of tyranny. Bartholdi's earlier models had her holding these chains in her hand, a classical image, and possibly he moved them to underfoot to better demonstrate how liberty tramples oppression. He was also encouraged by Laboulaye and friends to include the tablet or book of Law in her hand, as a tribute to the American success with republican democracy based in the law.[24] Interestingly, chains are also used as a symbol for linking things, and a 13-link chain was a popular symbol used by Ben Franklin and others to symbolize the unity of the Colonies. In this case they stand simply for the bondage of religious and political oppression. In America, Liberty ensures that we have the freedom to choose our ways of worship and governance. Liberty allows for freedom not only in the physical world, but mentally and spiritually as well.

Nurturing the World

In sum, here is one way of putting together the symbols in the Statue of Liberty: We have the crown of seven rays that could refer to the seven seas or continents, but in esoteric symbolism we see seven as the symbol of the victory of spirit over matter. The torch raised in Liberty's right hand is wisdom (the torch) activated (right hand) by our recognition of the feminine principle within each of us. The tablet or book can be compared to the book of divine law or the Akashic Record, which not only notes the thoughts and actions of all living things from inception, but also interacts with our present and affects our future. The broken chain symbolizes both a people winning their freedom and the ability to break our bondage to the physical world and control our personal destiny.

The New Tories

Despite the fact that the Statue of Liberty is revered by the vast majority of Americans as a symbol of liberty and compassion and providing refuge for the poor and homeless, the fundamentalist-conspiratorialists have attacked her as a symbol to fear and despise. Because there is a strong Masonic connection to this monument, anti-Masons have dissected her, looking for clues to secret symbols and messages. The most often repeated claims in their attack are that the Statue of Liberty was a gift from French Freemasons to the American Freemasons and that, because she is a symbol of light, she is making a statement that the Illuminati control this country. This theory takes for granted, of course, the idea that the Freemasons are controlled by Satan-worshipping Illuminati and intent on world control. (I will cover this nonsense again in Chapter 8.) The torch she holds is defamed as a crude joke that we are controlled by "the illuminated ones," but most of us are too stupid to see it. Once again we see how one singular interpretation of a symbol can result in an absolute contradiction to its intended meanings or what can be gathered from the multi-leveled approach. By attacking our American symbols, the fundamentalist-conspiratorialists have taken on the role of the new Tories. Back in the days of the Revolution, they would have been the loyalists who were afraid of the concept of men governing themselves. They would much prefer a strict monarchical, patriarchal system of government where a single male authority tells them what to do and what to believe. To them, freedom is a dangerous thing.

Lucifer Is Really the Planet Venus

Many of the Mother Goddesses around the world are associated with either the constellation Virgo or the planet Venus. Venus is the brightest object in the sky and is called both the Morning Star and Evening Star, as it can be seen at both times variously during the year. Rising just before the Sun, Venus took on the name "bringer of light," a nickname that translates in Latin as "Lucifer." The name Lucifer—meaning Venus and the "Morning Star"—is used only once in the King James Version of the Bible: in Chapter 14 of Isaiah, where it is quite obviously referring to a man, not a fallen angel or Satan. Most probably that man is the king of Babylon, who had been nicknamed the "Day Star, son of the Dawn" for his vainglory. During his lifetime he had persecuted the children of Israel. The King James Version of the Bible was not translated into English from the Hebrew texts, but rather from the Catholic Vulgate Bible produced largely by St. Jerome in the fourth century, which is where the mistranslation of the metaphor into "Lucifer" originated. A few decades after the King James Version came Milton's *Paradise Lost,* where the name "Lucifer" was assigned to the character of a fallen angel, and ever since then Christians have misappropriated this name for their concept of the Devil. Literally translated, Lucifer means "bringer of light," and for all of recorded history, until the last 300 years, it meant the planet Venus.

According to these theories, those of us who see Liberty's crown as a symbol of enlightenment and her torch as a symbol of purification through illumination, are in league with Satan (or, in David Icke's version, with reptilian aliens). Fundamentalist-conspiratorialists identify anything symbolizing light as a message from their fabricated construct of "the Illuminati." The torch held by the Statue of Liberty gives them added ammunition by its being a pretty good phallic symbol, too. Jordan Maxwell uses the torch symbol to link the word *alumni,* used to describe graduates of universities, to "Illuminati." According to Maxwell, universities are havens of liberal intellectuals who are really Illuminati, as evidenced by their frequent use of the torch to symbolize themselves as centers of enlightenment and learning. Because *alumni* uses some of the same letters as "Illuminati," he says when you are given the title "alumni," it actually means you've become indoctrinated as one of the "Illuminati."[25] Needless to say, *alumni* is Latin for pupils, not illuminated ones, but who needs Latin when "sounds like" is close enough? Maxwell also tried to imply the control of the Illuminati by demonstrating the prevalence of the torch symbol on everything from the American dime to the symbol for the Olympics. Their fear of light is also related to their fear of the mistranslated word *Lucifer,* meaning "bringer of light" and standing for the planet Venus (though commonly accepted today as another name for the Devil). I'm not sure how they reconcile the many references to a symbolic light in the New Testament, including John 8:12 (when Jesus himself says, "I am the Light of the world; he who follows Me will not walk in the darkness, but will have the Light of life."); Luke 11:36 ("If therefore your whole body is full of light, with no dark part in it, it will be wholly illumined, as when the lamp illumines you with its rays."); and John 1:7 ("He came as a witness, to testify about the Light, so that all might believe through him.").

Fundamentalist-conspiratorialists are happy with any connections that can be made between the Statue of Liberty and Isis, judging her as they do as being from a pagan culture, and therefore of Satan. We have already established that the link to Isis is more symbolic than historical, so the fundamentalist-conspiratorialists have added their fabulously inaccurate way of twisting words to suit their interpretations. They will tell you with an exclamation mark that the ship that carried the crates of the dismantled Statue of Liberty from France to New York was named *Isère.* Noticing the first two letters are the same as in Isis, they make another grand connection, saying *Isère* is derived from *Isis,* another obvious "clue" that the secret cabal of Satan-worshippers was behind the whole deal.[26] We did a little digging and found the name of the ship *Isère* does not derive from Isis, but rather from a region in the east of France named after the Isère River. As far as the French Embassy could tell, the Isère River derived its name from the Celtic word *isar,* which means iron ore, apparently very abundant on the bank of the river in proto-historic time.[27]

Fundamentalist-conspiratorialists zero in on one interpretation and ignore all others. They are fond of saying that the real name for the Statue of Liberty is the "statue of *libertines.*" In their fabricated construct of Illuminati-Satanists ruling the world, licentiousness and immorality would be the cabal's ultimate goal, meaning the elites secretly constructed a statue of *libertines* and are laughing behind our backs because we naïvely interpret it as *liberty*. They define the rays around her crown as the sun, because numerous pagan cultures depict sun gods wearing similar crowns with rays of light coming from them. With this connection they can conclude that the Statue of Liberty's rayed crown is a reference to a sun-worshipping culture such as Egypt or Babylon. Rather than the goddess of Liberty, fundamentatlist-conspiratorialists have decided this statue is actually based on an older goddess such as Ishtar or Semiramis.

The fundamentalist-conspiratorialist fear of Semiramis, who historians believe was a real person, possibly a Queen of Nimrod, originated in Alexander Hislop's *The Two Babylons: or the Papal Worship,* an anti-Catholic tract published in 1858. Hislop's anti-Catholic theories have been picked up and repeated in modern times by the evangelical comic book series by Jack Chick in an attempt to prove that Protestantism is the only true faith, and that Catholicism is secretly based on old pagan Mother Goddess cults. Hislop decided the legends about Queen Semiramis were the origin for all Mother Goddesses to follow, including Isis and the Catholic version of the Virgin Mary.

Liberty as a Symbol That Can Unify Us

What I recommend to everyone worried about a "New World Order" either run by the Illuminati or the Vatican or the global corporations, is to get out there in your neighborhood and volunteer your service to your fellow man. Your best weapon in any situation is a heart filled with compassion. We are living in a moment in time where a distinct paradigm shift is necessary, as our way of dominating the earth is speeding to a complete environmental crisis. We the people of America have the ability to convince our leaders to shift out of the old mindset and learn to live in harmony with nature.

One thing to inspire hope is the increasing number of women taking positions of leadership in government and industry. As this trend continues, I believe our world will become a better, more compassionate place to live. Women have proven abilities in nurturing, and we must allow them to nurture our planet back to wholeness now. Women's rights in this country symbolically followed on the heels of the birth of the Statue of Liberty, the Betsy Ross legend, and the discovery of the reverse of the Great Seal, all three of which are related to the feminine archetype. May they continue to inspire in our collective unconscious the values of the enlightenment that emphasized partnership, conservation, and cooperation.

The American Civil Liberties Union is one of many companies adopting the Statue of Liberty into their logo. Courtesy of the ACLU.

At the end of the film *Ghostbusters II,* the protagonists decide they need to raise a tremendous amount of good will among the native New Yorkers in order to defeat the bad spirits that have taken over the city. To motivate citizens into feeling more positive about each other the heroes say, "We need a symbol…that appeals to the best in each and every one of us. Something everyone can get behind. Something good, something decent, something pure." They were, of course, talking about the Statue of Liberty, who then helps them save New York. Despite all her many challenges, "Liberty Enlightening the World" continues to shine and inspire people all over the world that true liberty and independence are the clearest paths to gaining knowledge and the light that allows for evolution. It's okay, America. Go ahead and trust the goddess.

CHAPTER 5

THE LIBERTY BELL: FROM EVERY MOUNTAINSIDE, LET FREEDOM RING!

When people are happy, they sing and shout. They ring bells, they honk horns, and they lift up their voices to the Lord. It is understandable that a bell would become famous for doing its duty when that duty was to help the new nation celebrate its new nationhood. Unlike the other symbols in this book the Liberty Bell was not chosen or designed or deliberated upon as a symbol, but rather, it became famous *because of its participation* in the Revolution. Created several decades before the Revolution, the Liberty Bell was rung to announce the noteworthy passages leading up to the Revolution and then throughout the early formation of the new government that followed. It was not until long after the Revolution that the Liberty Bell received its familiar crack and, around the same time, its new nickname. When we ponder how the old State House bell in Philadelphia became "the Liberty Bell," we realize how closely tied together are bell-ringing, celebrations, and announcements about freedom. So much so that *freedom* itself would soon be described as "ringing" from every mountainside in this "sweet land of liberty."

My country, 'tis of thee,
Sweet land of liberty,
Of thee I sing;
Land where my fathers died,
Land of the pilgrims' pride,
From every mountainside
Let freedom ring!
—Samuel Francis Smith, 1831

As with so many of our traditional American icons, the history of the Liberty Bell is somewhat sketchy, though the colorful legends have become firmly established in our collective consciousness. We will examine how one grew into the other, and why the bell is such a perfect symbol for liberty and freedom in the American ideal. We will also look at how this particular bell was recognized and used as an energizing totem for rousing Americans' pride, patriotism, and collective spirits. It was a natural choice as a symbol for both the abolitionist and women's suffrage movements, and many, many other groups, causes, and products since then.

Throughout history, bells have been used to gather people for announcements, help with emergencies, celebrate public holidays, and aid in worship services. The sounds and the vibrations they make, especially as they slowly reverberate into silence, can be useful in altering the human brain waves to enter a more relaxed state of consciousness, where one can attain union with their God. We will examine the Liberty Bell on this level as well, as on the level of a functional object designed to create sound. Our fundamentalist-conspiratorialist friends have had a hard time finding reasons to criticize this American symbol, but, by employing semantic skullduggery, they found a way, as we'll see at the end of this chapter.

The Beginnings of the Liberty Bell

Until the early 1800s, the Liberty Bell was known as the State House bell of Pennsylvania, or its first nickname, the Old Independence Bell. It was originally commissioned in 1751 to replace the bell hanging in the steeple of the Pennsylvania State House, which had just been built in 1746. Today we know this building as

The Liberty Bell with Independence Hall in the background at dusk. The inscription includes the names of the Americans who recast the bell the second and third time, "Pass and Stow." © iStockphoto.com/drbueller

Independence Hall. The Pennsylvania Assembly discovered that the original bell was not loud enough to be heard all over Philadelphia, and in 1750 a committee was formed to see about getting a new bell.

Pennsylvania was always ahead of its time, thanks to the determination and values of its founder,

William Penn. One of the first Quakers, Penn was interested in protecting religious freedoms of all kinds in his new territory, and people from other persecuted religious sects moved there in droves. Penn's revolutionary Charter of Privileges of 1701 is considered a precursor to the U.S. Constitution because, with it, Penn gave up his family's rights of absolute power, and granted them to the people instead. Pennsylvanians were among the first in the country to proclaim the need for independence from Great Britain, and yet their pacifistic streaks were so strong that the delegates from Pennsylvania nearly kept the Declaration of Independence from passing in an attempt to avoid armed conflict. They were also advanced in their beliefs on slavery, and from the beginning many Pennsylvanians worked hard to abolish it in their neighboring states.

Some historians have supposed that William Penn's Charter of Privileges for Pennsylvania that passed in 1701 was the event described in the Bible quote inscribed on the Liberty Bell. It reads: "Proclaim Liberty thro' all the Land to all the Inhabitants thereof." Decades after the bell was installed, someone with a flair for a colorful story looked at the complete verse from Leviticus 25:10 that surrounds the excerpt inscribed on the bell. All together it reads, "And ye shall hallow the fiftieth year, and *proclaim liberty throughout all the Land unto all the Inhabitants thereof*: it shall be a jubilee unto you; and ye shall return every man unto his possession, and ye shall return every man unto his family" (King James Version). They looked back approximately 50 years from the date on the bell and discovered William Penn's significant charter was dated 1701. They matched that up with the year that the Liberty Bell was commissioned, 1751, and decided that "hallow the fiftieth year" from the earlier part of the verse must tie the inscription to the Charter.

Doesn't it sound great to learn that the origins of the Liberty Bell reveal something of Americans' spunkiness for independence dating all the way back to 1701? Unfortunately, this conclusion is probably wishful thinking. The origins of the Liberty Bell are most likely nothing more than a utilitarian need for a bigger bell that could be heard all over the capital city when it was time to be summoned to a meeting.[1] Many of the State House records still exist, and there is no indication that the bell committee formed in 1750 was marking any kind of anniversary, 50th or otherwise. All the records talk about replacing the smaller bell with the intended purpose of getting a larger sound. Also, they directed the original inscription on the bell to read 1752, not 1751. 1752 was the year they thought they would install the bell, though, as we shall see, that didn't happen.

History and Legend

Townsfolk are generally proud of their steeple bells to begin with, but this one in Philadelphia became an object of admiration even more than most, due to the sheer fact of its location in time. The State House in Philadelphia was a center of power for the early Revolution, and the signal bell in its steeple announced events significant to all the Colonies. From 1790 to 1800 Philadelphia was the temporary capital of the entire nation, and, as the new national government took shape, the State House bell in Philadelphia rang out time after time to mark new advancements. Long before the war, the bell was ringing to mark the steps toward independence. When Ben Franklin was sent on his first negotiation trip to England in 1757, the State House bell rang. When Philadelphians were summoned to oppose the Stamp Act or the Tea Tax, or to learn of the battles of Lexington and Concord or the blockade of Boston, it was from the ringing of the State House bell.

Although the State House bell in Philadelphia was originally created to call the Pennsylvania council members to Assembly, in this eventful time it was ringing so often that in 1772 the citizens of the neighboring streets petitioned the Assembly for more peace; the frequent tolling was disrupting their lives. In 1777, as the British advanced on Philadelphia, the bell was evacuated, along with all other metal sources of potential cannon fodder for the British. It waited out the war in the basement of a church in the nearby Allentown, returning in time to be rung for the signing of the Constitution in 1787. It rang every year after that to mark the visits or the deaths of important people, the 4th of July, and the 22nd of February for Washington's Birthday, until it cracked beyond repair in 1846.

Despite one of its more popular legends, however, the State House bell did *not* ring to mark the signing of the Declaration of Independence on the 4th of July 1776. In fact, no bells or other celebration occurred to mark that date, as nothing much happened, other than this hugely important document was signed by its first two official signatories and sent to the printer. The historic voting had occurred on July 2nd, which is the day the bell ringer would have been ringing the bell in joy if the 1847 fictional romance tale by George Lippard were true.

Lippard's tale, fully disclosed as fictional, also had the bell receiving its famous crack on the 4th of July 1776, and, because his colorful story was mistakenly repeated elsewhere as fact, for a long time this legend was believed as truth.

The State House bell *might* have rung four days later on the *8th* of July 1776, to summon Philadelphians for the first public reading of the Declaration of Independence. There is no official documentation to indicate that it did *not* ring on the 8th of July, but recent historians have also called into question the participation of the State House bell in this equally historic moment. Philadelphians were definitely summoned by bells on July 8th to hear a reading of Thomas Jefferson's finest, but we're not absolutely sure that the State House bell was among the bells doing the summoning.[2] The records of the Pennsylvania Assembly as early as 1774 indicated that the steeple housing the bell was rotting and in serious need of repair. It has not been proven, however, that the State House bell was out of commission on July 8, 1776. All of the diaries and letters written about that momentous day were similar to that of John Adams, saying, "the bells rang all day and almost all night."[3] No one said, "All the bells except the State House bell."

The Crack

There are many other legends explaining the famous crack, but there's only one unquestionably true story about a crack in what was soon to be called the Liberty Bell. The first State House bell really did crack on the very first strike of the clapper upon its arrival in this country in 1752. The bell we know today is actually the third version of itself after having been twice melted down and recast. The bell was originally ordered from the Whitechapel Foundry in England and it took almost a year to arrive. Before it was installed in the steeple in late 1752, the head of the bell-ordering committee, Isaac Norris, hung it temporarily in the square to test its tone. He wrote that he was mortified when upon the first swing, the bell cracked.

They immediately set about making a new bell, and decided to contract two local foundry workers, John Pass and John Stow, to completely melt down the bell and recast it. Pass and Stow added more copper in an attempt to strengthen it, and this may have affected the tone. When they hung it back up to test it again, no one liked the sound it made. The townspeople complained so much, in fact, that Pass and Stow agreed to try again. A third time they melted the bell down and fiddled with the balance of the metals before recasting it. They also added their names to the inscription and the year that it was by then: 1753. Everyone agreed the tone was not greatly improved, but they hung it up in the steeple anyway.[4] Thanks to the World Wide Web you can listen right now to how this bell probably sounded before it cracked by clicking on the audio clip at *www.ushistory.org.* The Normandy Liberty Bell, cast in 2004 as an exact replica of the Pass and Stow bell, was made in honor of the 60th anniversary of the storming of Normandy in World War II.

The earliest contemporary written record referring to the trademark crack is from 1846 when it cracked beyond repair. The *Philadelphia Public Ledger* reported on February 26, 1846, that on Washington's Birthday a few days earlier, "The old Independence Bell rang its last clear note on Monday last in honor of the birthday of Washington."[5] They added that the irreparable crack was an extension of an earlier hairline crack that had been sustained at an unknown previous date:

> It had been cracked before but was set in order of that day by having the edges of the fracture filed so as not to vibrate against each other....It gave out clear notes and loud, and appeared to be in excellent condition until noon, when it received a sort of compound fracture in a zig-zag direction through one of its sides which put it completely out of tune and left it a mere wreck of what it was.[6]

Through the years, many different eyewitnesses claimed to have been present when the first hairline fracture appeared. Unfortunately, all were reported decades after the fact, and none are supported by contemporary written accounts. It is possible that one or more of the eyewitnesses are telling the truth, as the crack likely worsened with subsequent uses. For a long time it was popular to believe the Liberty Bell first cracked during the funeral of Supreme Court Justice John Marshall in 1835. Earlier claims have dated it, however, to Lafayette's return visit to Philadelphia in 1824, or the passage of the Catholic Emancipation Act in 1828, or Washington's Birthday in 1835. The only one that made the newspaper was the one that put it out of commission in February 1846. As that report mentioned, the large "crack"with which we are all so familiar is actually what was drilled out in an attempt to keep the two sides of the earlier crack from reverberating against each other.

Historical Symbolism

The Liberty Bell is still rung today, or rather, it is symbolically tapped, on every 4th of July. The honor is given to children who are descendants of signers of the Declaration of Independence. By the time of its retirement, the bell was becoming linked in the public mind with the Revolution and independence. After languishing in limbo for a few years, the bell was lowered and given a place of honor. Its national popularity surged after the Civil War when it was trotted out as a symbol for Americans to rally around in an attempt to *unify them as one people in one country* in time for the centennial celebrations.

In 1885 the Liberty Bell left on the first of several trips to cities around the country to attend pep rallies and expos. It returned to Philadelphia for good in 1915 when it was determined that the traveling was worsening the crack. On all its cross-country rail tours, the Liberty Bell excited huge crowds of cheering spectators and sold many a war bond. Traveling by rail to as far away as San Francisco, the Liberty Bell stopped at hundreds of cities along the

Photograph taken during a trip of the Liberty Bell from Philadelphia to Charleston, South Carolina, in January 1902, to be exhibited at the Interstate and West Indian Exposition. All three gentlemen in the photograph are wearing Liberty Bell badges. Courtesy of Independence National Historical Park.

way to be seen and kissed by millions of Americans. Instrumental in getting the bell to make each of its several trips outside of Philadelphia were petitions from thousands of schoolchildren. It energized and aroused Americans' pride and collective spirit, and its role as a national symbol has never slackened since. Replicas were made during the Cold War to send to Berlin, Israel, and Japan as gestures of unity, and it continues to serve as a focal point for demonstrators both for and against America's policies. Civil rights demonstrators hold sit-ins at the Liberty Bell, and foreign dignitaries today make pilgrimages to lay wreaths. It has been seen on at least six postage stamps, including the 2007 Forever stamp, on numerous coins, and as a logo or name for countless companies. It has even become an

The Liberty Bell has been featured on at least six postage stamps, including the first Forever stamp launched in 2007. © 2007 United States Postal Service. All Rights Reserved. Used with permission.

integral point in the baseball stadium for the Philadelphia Phillies, with a giant neon replica swinging back and forth over right field whenever a home run is hit.[7] The Liberty Bell is an All-American, made in America, "one of us" kind of symbol.

In 1976 the Liberty Bell was moved to a pavilion across the street from Independence Hall in anticipation of the increase in visitors celebrating America's Bicentennial. In 2003 a new multi-million-dollar Liberty Bell Center was opened at 6th and Chestnut streets. To this day, the Liberty Bell continues to fire the debate over that hard-won phrase, "Liberty to ALL inhabitants thereof." When it was discovered that the entranceway to the new Liberty Bell Center was only a few feet from the slave quarters built by George Washington for the President's House during his term there, protestors organized a request for a plaque noting this proximity. I think the crack in the Liberty Bell and the way our nation embraced a "cracked symbol" are both tied up with the issue of slavery in this country, and how we allowed it to devolve into a bloody civil war instead of abolishing it peacefully.

The Symbolism of the Crack

It is partly *because* of its crack that the Liberty Bell became the beloved national symbol that it did. If it had not been cracked and retired, it might never have left on its cross-country tours that added so much to its renown. The crack also made it more "human" in a way, as people identified with it as imperfect, or worn out from long, hard work. As the centennial approached in 1876, many people petitioned the city of Philadelphia to repair the crack so it could be rung in honor of the celebration, but the city council rejected these ideas partially on the grounds that the crack was now an important part of the history of the bell.[8] Percussionist Mickey Hart of the Grateful Dead seems to have a particular fondness for the Liberty Bell and has written about it many times. On his blog he wrote, "Its crack is a reminder that liberty is imperfect, hopefully evolving to include those who have been denied full participation in a democratic society. So vote, or else liberty is meaningless."[9]

> From every mountainside, let freedom ring. And when this happens, when we let freedom ring, when we let it ring from every village and every hamlet, from every state and every city, we will be able to speed up that day when all of God's children, black men and white men, Jews and Gentiles, Protestants and Catholics, will be able to join hands and sing in the words of the old Negro spiritual, 'Free at last! Free at last! Thank God Almighty, we are free at last!'
>
> —Martin Luther King, 1963

Abolitionists and the Liberty Bell

It was this power of the bell as a symbol that was spotted by the leaders of the abolitionist movement as early as 1835. In 1837, the New York Anti-Slavery Society printed a stylized (still uncracked) reproduction of the bell on the frontispiece of their publication, using it to point out how hypocritical was its inscription ("liberty to all the inhabitants") when black people were still being bought and sold as slaves. The abolitionists also pointed to the entire verse from Leviticus, interpreting "ye shall return every man unto his possession, and ye shall return every man unto his family" as an instruction to free the slaves. In 1839, *The Liberty Bell* tracts were first published for a Boston abolitionist organization. William Lloyd Garrison reprinted a poem about the bell in his nationally known *The Liberator* in 1839, and this has long been acknowledged as the first nationally published use of the nickname "The Liberty Bell." More recent research has unearthed an even earlier use, however. The Museum

An early use of the Liberty Bell as a symbolic device. From R.A. Smith's *Philadelphia As It Is In 1852* (Lindsay and Blakeston, 1852). Courtesy of Independence National Historical Park.

Curator of Independence Historical Park at Philadelphia, Pennsylvania Robert Giannini told us of the discovery of the term "The Liberty Bell" in an 1835 publication of the American Anti-Slavery Society, which he found in the Library of Congress. In this tract, Ransom G. Williams, probably a former slave, wrote of his moving experience when he saw "the Liberty Bell" firsthand. Entitling this section in his *Anti-Slavery Record,* vol. 1, no. 2, "The Liberty Bell," indicates that the name was already in common usage by this time. Rev. Williams describes why the Liberty Bell and its inscription were symbolically inspiring to all Americans, and indeed to all humans who yearn to be free:

The Liberty Bell

> Being in Philadelphia a few days since…we did not fail to examine the celebrated Bell. It is remarkable that the following inscription was on the bell when it was cast. It was considered a sort of prophecy: "PROCLAIM LIBERTY THROUGHOUT ALL THE LAND, AND TO ALL THE INHABITANTS THEREOF." May not the emancipationists in Philadelphia, hope to live to hear the same bell rung, when liberty shall in fact be proclaimed to all the inhabitants of this favored land? Hitherto, the bell has not obeyed the inscription; and its peals have been a mockery, while one sixth of "all inhabitants" are in abject slavery."[10]

The crack in the bell helped heal the rift in the nation from the Civil War. After the centennial, a request was sent from New Orleans for the bell to travel to the opening of their World Industrial and Cotton Centennial Exposition. Acknowledging that the nation was still healing from the war, their letter said the bell was dear to the common history of the North and the South, and that they believed themselves to be "co-inheritors of its glories."[11] The mayor of Philadelphia wrote in support of sending the bell to the South, saying it would demand "the setting aside of any sectional or partisan views."[12] He was willing to take the risk, "if the presence of the Old Bell which rang out the birth of a great republic can be the means, by its presence at New Orleans, in restoring or cementing the same patriotic spirit in the entire nation at this time…."[13] It turned out he was right and that indeed the people of the south were just as "affectionate to the traditions of Our Country," as were their brethren in the

North.[14] When Jefferson Davis, ex-president of the Confederacy, came out to salute the bell as it passed through Mississippi, his demonstration of respect permitted others to pay homage to the Liberty Bell as a symbol of unity for all America.

The abolitionist movement gradually led to the women's suffrage movement, and, in 1915, leaders in the fight to gain women the right to vote also adopted the Liberty Bell as their symbol. A wealthy Pennsylvania woman from nearby Philadelphia paid for the forging of a 2,000-pound replica of the Liberty Bell, which they called the Justice Bell. This bell traveled all over the state on a campaign to win the right to vote for women. Demonstrators chained the clapper of the Justice Bell to its side to symbolize the silenced voices of women, which they hoped to unchain through their efforts. Later it traveled to rallies all over the country in support of the 19th amendment to the Constitution. In 1920 it was rung in Independence Hall in Philadelphia in celebration of the ratification of the amendment. Today it hangs in the Washington Memorial Chapel in Valley Forge, Pennsylvania.

Other countries with causes to celebrate have also been drawn to the symbol of a bell as an effective unifier. There are hundreds of replica Liberty Bells and "peace bells" around the world that attest to the connection between a ringing sound of a bell and spreading the message of peace and freedom. People want peace, and the freedom and liberty to practice peace, and they want it to spread gently and thoroughly across their lands in the manner of tones reverberating from a bell.

History and Use of Bells

What's in a bell? Well, to be exact, it's about 77 percent copper and 23 percent tin, making a bronze known as "bell metal." Variations in the percentage of the metals cause the fluctuations in tone. It's not known for certain where bells originated, but they were perfected first in Asia. According to bell historian and carillonneur Wendell Westcott, in China's Hubei Province a group of bronze bells was discovered dating from the fifth century BCE. The craftsmanship of these particular bells is remarkable in that they are perfectly attuned to each other, a skill not mastered in Europe until a few centuries ago.[15] In China bells are generally made without clappers inside. Designed to be stationary, their bells are struck with mallets on the outside or with swinging rods in the case of very large bells. Asian bells tend to be barrel-shaped, whereas Western bells tend to resemble an upside-down tulip, flared on the bottom. Primitive European bells consisted of two flat sheets of hammered metal fastened together down the sides, but in the 1600s Western belldom took a huge stride forward when the Hemony brothers perfected the art of bell-making in the Netherlands. Unfortunately, many of their bells were destroyed in subsequent wars and revolutions, melted down to make cannons.[16] What a strange corollary, indeed, as so often happens in the life of great bells. Bells that ring peace and joy into the hearts of their hearers are too often turned into cannons aimed at ripping apart these same hearts.

Large forged bells have been made since the Bronze Age, but smaller bells have been discovered from pre-historic times made from all kinds of hollow materials including bones, wood, jade, or other semi-precious stones. Because of their transcendent ability to affect consciousness through vibration, bells are connected with religious ceremonies of many different faiths. They are also used in everyday life by people all over the world. They are tied to the collars of animals to help us find them; they are tied to doors to alert us of visitors; they are grouped together and played as musical instruments for creative expression. Bigger bells belonging to the town are rung to call for justice, to mark deaths and births of important people, to gather folks together, and to keep time. In fact, the Latin word for bell is *cloca,* meaning clock.

In heraldry, bells were used to indicate a link to church authority. More rarely seen are falconry bells indicating a royal connection.[17] From the world of mathematics and statistics we have the interestingly shaped phenomena of the bell curve, something you may remember from helpful high school grading systems. The bell curve is the graphical representation of Gaussian or normal distribution. It demonstrates how the mathematical mean of a number of random variables will be approximately normally distributed. Normal distribution has been applied effectively in many fields, particularly statistics, finance, and astronomy, but it may be a far more spiritual effect than any of these scientists realize.

Bells Around the World

Bells for peace and freedom similar to the Liberty Bell have been created all over the world. We will list just a few of the more recent and meaningful ones here. In 1950, to honor the bicentennial of the Liberty Bell, uncracked replicas were commissioned and delivered to all the states in the union. Some states painted cracks on their replicas to more closely honor the original. In honor of America's Bicentennial in 1976, Queen Elizabeth II presented an exact replica of the Liberty Bell to the United States. Forged in the still extant Whitechapel Foundry in England, this "Bicentennial Bell" now hangs in the new steeple next to Independence Hall.

The Peace Bell in Hiroshima Peace Memorial Park, dedicated in 1964, is decorated with a map of the world showing no national boundaries. Visitors are invited to ring the bell as a testament to their wish for peace. The inscription expresses the hope of the donors for an end to all nuclear armaments and all wars. The tolling of this one-ton bell is determined to spread the hope for peace across the world.[18]

The Mental Health Bell was chosen as a symbol of freedom in the 1950s after a revolution in the care for patients with mental illnesses. Through centuries of poor understanding, it had been common to restrain mentally disturbed individuals in chains and often subject them to cruel treatments. In 1953 the National Mental Health Association (NMHA) gathered the discarded shackles and chains from asylums around the country, melted them down, and forged a bell. This 300-pound bell is currently on display at the National Mental Health Association headquarters in Alexandria, Virginia. Its image is used in the NMHA literature as a reminder of the transformation from the chains of ignorance to a more humane understanding of mental illness.[19]

An example of the Liberty Bell appearing in a corporate logo as a symbol of trust. The Pennzoil logo is a registered trademark of Pennzoil-Quaker State Company, Houston, Texas, 2008. Used with permission.

Big Bells

Weighing just a little more than 2,000 pounds the Liberty Bell is by no means the largest bell in the world. Originally recorded at 2,080 pounds, the Pass and Stow bell was thoroughly analyzed in 1960 by the DuPont Company and the City of Philadelphia, which says today it weighs 2,050 pounds. A shocking 25–30 pounds have been chiseled off by souvenir collectors. The largest bell in the United States today is in Newport, Kentucky, called the World Peace Bell. It weighs 66,000 pounds, which increases to almost 90,000 pounds when the weight of the clapper and the supports are included.[20] Installed as part of a millennium monument in 1999, the inscription on this large bell reads, in part, "The World Peace Bell is a Symbol of Freedom and Peace." The largest bell ever created is believed to have been the Great Bell of Dhammazedi in Burma at a reported 300 tons. This bell was lost in a river by the Portuguese navy in 1608 as they attempted to remove it from the temple.[21] The largest existing bell is the Tsar Kolokol bell in Moscow, weighing about 200 tons. A huge chunk of this bell (11.5 tons) broke off in a fire in 1737, before the bell was even removed from the forge. The two pieces are on display today in Moscow's Red Square, where they are a popular tourist attraction.

The Tsar Kolokol Bell in Moscow's Red Square is thought to be the largest bell in existence. With a huge chunk missing, it is hardly identical to the Liberty Bell, as conspiracy advocates have claimed.

Because it is Russian, and because it is a big bell with a chunk missing (a chasm, mind you, not a thin crack), Jordan Maxwell has declared that it is "identical" to the Liberty Bell in a lame attempt to show a secret Communist (Satanic) connection to our Founding Fathers through the Liberty Bell. A hundred and fifty times larger with a huge chunk missing is hardly "identical" to the Liberty Bell. This is what Maxwell says about our Liberty Bell in his *Matrix of Power*:

Our liberty is threatened. Look at the liberty bell, the symbol of liberty. An equal identical bell was found, with the same crack, in Moscow. It has become known as a symbol, the symbol of the

Brotherhood of the Bell. Bell, being Bel, the ancient God in the Mesopotamian Valley, being the one that we call Beelzebub, or Yahweh.[22]

Just after this inflammatory and factually erroneous claim, Maxwell captions an illustration of the Liberty Bell as "Symbol of Freedom and Liberty, another Masonic Symbol." Always good to stick the Masons in there somewhere when attacking American patriotic symbols, though how a bell is linked to Freemasonry is left unexplained.

How Even the Liberty Bell Has Been Deciphered as a Symbol of the Illuminati

It is a very long stretch for the fundamentalist-conspiratorialists to find what they consider a Satanic link to the Liberty Bell—but they managed. They played their "sounds like" semantics game and decided the evil Founding Fathers picked a *bell* as a symbol because they secretly intended for Americans to venerate the ancient Babylonian god known as *Bel,* or *Ba'al,* or the derivative name *Beelzebub (Ba'al Zebub)*. As usual, their argument completely ignores the etymological history of both words, *bell* and *Bel.* The word *bell* in English traces its origins back to Old English as influenced by the Middle Dutch and Middle German words *belle,* meaning a bellowing or rutting sound as a deer or dog would make. Further back it can be traced to the Proto-Indo-European base *behl,* meaning the same sound.[23] *Bel* or *Ba'al,* on the other hand, translates to "lord" or "master," and *"Baal Zebub"* to *Lord of the Flies. Ba'al* was a popular name for several deities among the Semitic peoples and is mentioned several times in the Bible as a "false god." When Milton described *"Beelzebub"* in *Paradise Lost* as one of the original fallen angels, the name was picked up by Christians as another way of referring to Satan, similar to what happened with the name Lucifer (discussed earlier).

David Icke is ready with an explanation for the differing etymological roots of *Bel* and *bell.* He says that the Phoenician language was not so much about spelling as it was about sounding, and sounds alike means alike. The antagonists in Icke's version of the conspiracy are a hybrid mixture of reptile aliens with the current ruling elite who are allegedly blood descendents from the early desert peoples, the evil Babylonians or Egyptians. The way he spins it, a disguised hybrid race is sending coded messages to its members using a sound-alike game spoken through logos and symbols. According to this theory, coded messages appear daily in plain sight in the entertainment media, corporate logos, public statutes, architecture, and art. It's easy to find connections when you open up the whole world to your field of comparison. Here is Icke on the Liberty Bell in his book, *The Biggest Secret*: "Where was the American War of 'Independence' orchestrated from? Philadelphia and there you will still find the Liberty Bell—symbol of Bel, the Sun god of the Phoenicians and the Aryans. The Phoenician language is about sound, not spelling, and integral to the secret, symbolic language of the reptile-Aryans is the sound of a word."[24]

The clinching proof for the fundamentalist-conspiratorialists in establishing a reason to fear the Liberty Bell is a fictional 1960s made-for-TV movie starring Glenn Ford called *The Brotherhood of the Bell*. Ford plays an unsuspecting member of a secret society (apparently based on the very real Skull and Bones at Yale) who tries to expose them when he decides they don't play fair. The brotherhood, of course, turns on him, and an action movie ensues. The fundamentalist-conspiratorialists have decided that this television movie about a fictional secret society is a deliberate clue to their idea of an Illuminati conspiracy, and they cite it as proof of a Satanic connection to the Liberty Bell.

The fundamentalist-conspiratorialists have taken a fictional movie title, added the word *lord* from the ancient Semitic peoples, and decided that references to bells today are coded messages of the Satanic conspiracy regarding the takeover of the world. The following example from a UK chat forum shows how these connection theories are enlarged and spread on the Internet. Notice the extreme use of semantic skullduggery used to prove the point:

Baal - Bel - Belial – Bell

The bell, as in the American Liberty Bell, is symbolic of Bel, Bil, or Baal, the Aryan Sun god of the ancient world.

Bell Correlation: An interesting set of circumstances? The picture is the Bell (Baal) County Courthouse in Texas, located in Belton (Baal-Town). The dome or bell tower (Tower of Baal or Ba-bel) on the courthouse was recently restored by Campbellville Industries (Camp Baal?). Near the Baal County courthouse is the Bail (Baal) Bondsman. Baal Town is the county seat and one city in a triune city metroplex; [its] sister city is Temple (Temple of Baal County). The other member of the triune is Killeen (Killing?); site of the Infamous Killeen Massacre, where a crazed (Baal mind controlled) man murdered 24 persons in a cafeteria on a Killeen spree. Baal Killeen is home to the mind-control facility known as Fort Hood. This area of Texas is approximately 30 miles from Waco (hueco— the hole or depression) which is the site another massacre, performed by the Liberty Bell Choir or ATF against David Koresh and the Branch Davidians. Waco is also the home of Baylor Illuminati Training University. The prophets of Baal certainly won in Texas over its Elijahs.[25]

If the fundamentalist-conspiratorial school of semantics were to apply, then the Liberty Bell could just as easily be a coded conspiracy message about Belgians (also abbreviated as "Bel") trying to take over the world. And if they are going to condemn the Liberty Bell on the strength of the word *bell* sounding like the name of an ancient Phoenician, Babylonian, Philistine, Semitic god, then shouldn't they necessarily condemn all bells including those rung so prominently in Christian churches?

Bells have played very important roles in the worship services of many religions, most notably Buddhism and Christianity. In fact, it was not until the advent of Christianity that the concept of a swinging bell in a steeple tower became popular. Almost all major religions place strong emphasis on the sound of bells to create a contemplative atmosphere for their religious services, though in the desert life of the early Jewish people, the trumpet and shofar, or ram's horn, were more prominent. By the time of the foundation of Islam, bells were already so strongly associated with Christianity that Mohammed decided against using them for his ritual.[26]

Mystical Interpretations of Bells

As we said before, the Liberty Bell was not consciously and deliberately constructed, selected, or designed as an image to represent America. Its reputation as a symbol grew gradually, and only after years of utilitarian service had endeared it to the hearts of the public. There are no other practical objects (famous quill pens, illustrious saddles, noteworthy washtubs, for example) that faithfully served the founding of this great nation and then turned into American symbols. From this I conclude there must be something about the *bellness* of the Liberty Bell that is responsible for the strong reaction in our emotional bodies, making us identify with it as a symbol.

It was not until after performing its functional duty for almost a hundred years, and after the bell broke, that its secondary personality as an American symbol was fully born. When its "injury" forced it into retirement, I think the public embraced it all the more. Plans for the centennial brought it to life again, and the crowds coming to see it have grown incrementally ever since. Today more than a million people a year make a pilgrimage to the Liberty Bell. They come to touch it, and to stand in its aura, to be inspired.

Our attraction to the Liberty Bell derives in part from the sense of unity we experience while listening to the ringing of a bell. The tones of a bell vibrate through the clothes, skin, blood, and molecules of its listeners simultaneously. It is a collective experience that subconsciously draws us together. The Liberty Bell helped unify the Colonists on a vibrational level down to their very molecules, and, according to some sound/healing researchers, down to the level of creation. Creation stories from around the world include passages metaphorically describing sound or vibration as a creative force. When we create sound here on Earth, we are honoring that first creation.

What exactly is in a sound? A better question might be: What *isn't*?

Sound began the universe according to our religious texts: "In the beginning was the Word, and the Word was with God, and the Word was God" (John 1:1, New American Standard Bible). Sound researcher Carlisle Bergquist explains that the earliest translations of the word *Logos* (Greek for "word") in this phrase implies the concept of movement or vibration between a projective and receptive element of Creation. In the oral tradition of the Hebrew people, God created the world through the 22 sacred Hebrew letters. "For when the world was created it was the supernal letters that brought into being all the works of the lower world, literally after their own pattern. Hence, whoever has a knowledge of them and is observant of them is beloved both on high and below."[27] The Kabbalah teaches that with sound added to thought or intention we are instructed to repair the world as co-creators with God. In Sufism, the mystical tradition of Islam, they teach of a sound called "Hu" that is an aspect or direct pointing to the God Allah that pervades all creation. Chanting Hu is said to lead to transcendence with God. As the sacred name of God, Hu is within the sound of every musical instrument (especially bells) and in the babble of every running brook, the wind in the trees, and the buzz of an insect.[28] The Hindus and Buddhists consider everything to be contained in the word *Om*. The past, present, and future are "Om"; it is the generative creative principle behind their entire cosmology, and it is thought to put the chanter into a state of attunement with the Creator by aligning his or her chakras and creating a bridge to the spiritual dimensions. The Kybalion, thought to be a collection of the wisdom of the sage Hermes Trismegistus, teaches that spirit and matter differ only by a degree of vibration. According to most of our world religions, sound and vibration are believed to be both the beginning force and the sustaining power for all life.

Religions all around the world use the ringing of bells to achieve mystic, contemplative states of consciousness among their adherents. Early man worked out a long time ago that certain tones, chants, or beats on a drum produced certain states of consciousness from meditative to ecstatic. The Chinese in particular intuited how sound can alter consciousness, and placed great thought and ritual into the implementation of the temple bell in their services. Seeing the bell as a symbol of primeval sound, they invented many different kinds of bells that they use throughout their services. Striking the bell puts your mind into a prayerful state, and is believed by many different religions to sanctify a holy place. In India, the innermost part of the temple is called the Garbha grha or the womb, and it is believed that the temple bell rung from here aligns the seven chakras to an awakened state. Ultimately, temples are symbols for the temple inside you, and the bells used in religious services are symbolic of finding the silence inside you. In Christian services, in addition to being rung to call people to worship, bells took on added significance in the Roman Catholic liturgy with the development of the sacring bells. These bells are rung at the moment that the bread and wine are consecrated during Holy Communion, and the tone of the bell is said to mark the moment that the transubstantiation takes place.

Bells are also symbolic of creative energies because of their shape. J.E. Cirlot points out that because a bell is "in a hanging position, it partakes of the mystic

NATIONAL ASSOCIATION OF
RADIO TALK SHOW HOSTS

A Liberty Bell logo for the National Association for Radio Talk Show Hosts (NARTSH) designed by Bob Hieronimus.

significance of all objects which are suspended between heaven and earth. It is related by its shape, to the vault and consequently to the heavens."[29] The bell is therefore a symbol for the belief that within us is a spark of the Diety. It is through the practice of meditation and prayer that we can "be still, and know that I am God" (Psalm46:10). Going within oneself to experience the silence can be metaphorical for entering the womb to be reborn.

Sound and Healing

As science catches up with religion, quantum physics is providing further understanding for our rational minds to grasp why the sound of bells has been so revered. Bell tones have a particular way of vibrating and hanging in the air, slowly and noticeably dimming away. This can be compared to the field of quantum physics, taking us further and further into the smallness of what composes all matter. Current theories involve a vibrating sea of energy beneath all matter connecting everything.[30] Healing and psychic phenomena can occur by tapping into this life stream. Consciousness itself is a vibration. By learning to increase this vibration, one can elevate consciousness into the spiritual worlds. Some researchers, such as those at the Robert Monroe Center, believe that brainwave entrainment can be manipulated by alternating tones, accompanied by lights.

Music therapy is based in the understanding that sound, whether it is musical or a mere single tone, reverberates in the cellular makeup. The body is composed mostly of water, an ideal conductor of sound. Tribal cultures have long used healing songs and musical instruments in their medicine. Mantras have also been used for hundreds of years to distract the brain from mind-centered thoughts. Chanting creates a resonance within the group and a harmonious field around the chanters. Exploring various wavelengths made by sound, scientists are hoping to match the exact sounds to the exact illnesses to stimulate recovery. We are only beginning to understand the potential of healing through sound and vibration, and for more on this subject we recommend Richard Gerber's *Vibrational Medicine* and Don Campbell's *The Mozart Effect*. Campbell has shown that the younger a child is introduced to music, the better it is for brain development.

International research teams are studying why sound therapies work. Sound researcher Silvia Nakkach summarizes the bodily functions determined to be directly affected by sound therapy, including "pulse rate, brainwaves, heart rate, respiration, EMG papillary dilation, EEG, body temperature, and endocrinal functions."[31] Calling sound "energy medicine," Nakkach concludes, "Sound is nutrient for the brain and can either charge or discharge the nervous system."[32]

Sound researcher Jeffrey Thompson reports that "specific states of consciousness are associated with specific brainwave frequency patterns.... [R]esearch dating back as far as the 1940s has indicated the ability to influence these brainwave patterns."[33] Bergquist echoes these sentiments, concluding:

> All instruments have the capacity to affect us, however, certain of them consistently produce changes in consciousness states. These include the drum, rattle, gong, *bell* [emphasis added], singing bowl, bullroarer, didgeridoo, and droning string instruments like the sitar. Harner (1980), Kalweit (1992), Rogers (1982), Dialo and Hall (1989), Khan (1983), Roseman (1991), and Heinze (1991) all note the use of such instruments to change consciousness. Maxfield (1994) confirmed the drum's effect on the EEG demonstrating a shift in brain wave frequencies downward into theta dominated

states (4–7 Hz.) with several minutes of exposure.... Clearly on every continent, in culture after culture, instruments are part of a consciousness technology.[34]

Not all sound research is being conducted with the best of intentions, however. Sound and light are also being studied for use in "non-lethal" warfare because of their ability to affect consciousness through focused intent. Mid-frequency sonar equipment used by the U.S. Navy is criticized for causing disorientation among marine mammals, leading to an epidemic of whale beachings. The recently leaked report on nonlethal weapons terms and references published for the Air Force in 1997 described many weapons still in the proposal stage, though some have been used since the 1970s. These include acoustic bullets, a curdler unit, infrasound, and a squawk box, all of which use sound to incapacitate enemies or rioting crowds by causing severe pain or nausea.

Humans and animals are not the only life forms that have been exposed to lab tests with sound. When Cleve Backster first hooked his polygraph machine to a plant, as reported in *The Secret Life of Plants* by Chris Bird and Peter Tompkins, he realized that plants responded to human thoughts and intentions. This led to further research showing that plants also grew better when played soothing music, and died when listening to heavy metal music or other harsh and jarring sounds. Dan Carlson has discovered certain frequencies related to the sounds of birds that will open the stoma of crop plants and allow them to receive more nutrients and grow more abundantly. He calls his treatment "Sonic Bloom," and some of his huge vegetables grown with it hold Guinness Book world records. Austrian mystic Rudolf Steiner emphasized resonance and tone throughout all the multiple disciplines he studied. His farming system called biodynamic agriculture is based on the theory that certain plants and insects resonate on the same frequency channels, which can be effective in supplying nutrients to the plants and protecting them from pests.

On one level of interpretation, therefore, the Liberty Bell is the symbol of the creative power. Each time it rang marking another step toward the ideal inscribed on its side, a mass of people shared a unifying moment. The sound waves of Liberty penetrated everyone's consciousness simultaneously. A reverberating bell connects our consciousnesses with realms beyond the physical. When the Liberty Bell became the distinctive creator of sounds heralding events significant to our nation, it naturally transformed into an archetypal symbol of American liberty.

Chapter 6

The Eagle: The Price of Peace Is Eternal Vigilance

T he eagle was a "national bird" in this country long before the white men arrived. Most historians show the derivation of America's national bird from early European and Middle Eastern influences, but none of them places enough emphasis on the high status of the eagle as a symbol among the Native Americans. As evidenced in the totem poles and petroglyphs found across the continent, the First Peoples had already entrained this land to the spirit of the eagle through their centuries of sympathetic emulation, making the eagle a natural choice for the white men when it came time for them to pick their own symbols. Though it may not have been conscious, and it certainly wasn't documented in writing, the fact that both the native peoples and the European settlers elevated the eagle to be the bird above all birds was more than a coincidence.

The Native American connection to the Great Seal eagle is made through Charles Thomson, the Founding Father most responsible for the selection of the eagle as the new symbol for the United States. As a young man, Thomson was adopted into the Delaware Indian tribe (Lenapi). In recognition of his fairness and integrity they gave him an Indian name meaning "man who tells the truth." His upright honesty was a quality also admired by his colleagues of European descent, who had a saying: "It's as true as if Charles Thomson had said it." Though he was never an elected delegate to the Continental Congress, he served as its secretary for all 15 years of its existence, earning great renown for the unbiased and careful minutes that he recorded of the proceedings, debates, and decisions of these momentous years. As secretary, Charles Thomson was the only person (with John Hancock, president) who signed the Declaration of Independence on the 4th of July 1776.

As we detail further in *Founding Fathers, Secret Societies,* Thomson is among many of the principal Founding Fathers who recorded in writing their admiration of the *noble savages,* as Thomas Jefferson called them. John Adams wrote his observations of the native form of government in his influential *Defence of the Constitution* in 1787, saying, "[G]reat philosophers and politicians of the age [are attempting to] set up governments of...modern Indians."[1] Thomas Paine said in 1797, "There is not, in that state [the Indians of North America], any of those spectacles of human misery which poverty and want present to our eyes in all the towns and streets of Europe."[2] But most importantly to this chapter, Charles Thomson, the principle designer of the obverse of the Great Seal, said in March of 1788, "The Iroquois...[are] like the old Romans in the time of Gaul."[3]

It is likely that Thomson had some idea that Native Americans all over the country revered the eagle as a symbol of strength and majesty and far-sightedness. One of the most esteemed honors among many tribes was to be awarded the feather of an eagle in recognition for a valiant accomplishment. Those so honored considered the feather a sacred object requiring eternal protection from profanity or disregard. Little shrines were built for their display, as it was believed that the possession of an eagle feather brings the attention of the Great Spirit. Because the eagle flew so high he was considered to have a special relationship with the Creator in the heavens. The eagle is also compared to the Thunderbird, the legendary gigantic bird of the First Peoples, which crosses the continent in their mythologies. The Thunderbird is related to the Great Spirit itself, and is responsible for making thunder with its wings and lightning with its beak. It is usually described as a cross between an eagle and a vulture, and is also sometimes compared to the symbol of the phoenix.

Particular to the founding of this nation, however, we must make a study of the union of five and later six tribes centered in the New York area called the League of the Iroquois (the Mohawk, Cayuga, Onondaga, Seneca, and Oneida, later joined by the Tuscarora). Examining their use of the eagle as a symbol in their concept of the Great Tree of Peace can provide new insight into Charles Thomson's decision to make the eagle the central focus of the

U.S. Great Seal. The Great Tree of Peace is called the Iroquois' symbolic constitution, because, for a people without a written language, symbolic constructs were the means of transmitting complex ideas down through the generations. The Iroquois were proud to share with the Colonial leaders their oral tradition, which included the legend of the prophet Deganawidah and his spokesperson, Hiawatha, and their Great Tree of Peace.

The Great Tree of Peace. In this painting, one of the Haudenosaunee (what the League of the Iroquois called them-selves) meets with Benjamin Franklin underneath the Iroquois Great Tree of Peace. Notice the war club and hatchet buried under the tree, and the bundle of five arrows symbolizing unity. The eagle soars above the tree to remain vigilant and protect the peace. Courtesy of John Kahoinhes Fadden.

The Great Tree of Peace

The Iroquois wanted the Colonials to know their history. Many hundreds of years ago, as long ago as 1142 CE by some accounts, their five original tribes were constantly at war with each other. Then, a prophet was born, Deganawidah, who determined how to unite the five tribes and create a lasting, peaceful union. The rules set for their coexistence maintained a peace among the tribes for several hundred years before the American Revolution. As early as 1744, Ben Franklin was eagerly taking notes on everything he learned from the Iroquois chiefs when he attended tribal councils or served as printer for their treaties. The white men learned how Deganawidah and Hiawatha,[4] a skilled orator and politician, traveled between the warring clans and described to them this vision. It started with a great white pine tree. The white pine was a common tree that all the tribesmen saw throughout the course of every day and served as a perpetual reminder of their compact. Deganawidah called this the Great Tree of Peace and said the roots stretched out to the four corners of the earth and all inhabitants. The branches of this great tree symbolized the shelter, security, and protection provided by the great law of peace. In the vision, Deganawidah lifted up the great tree and under-neath showed that there was a great cavern and running water. The warring braves threw down all their implements of war into this cavern, and symbolically buried them under the Great Tree of Peace. They buried the hatchet.

Writers on Native American mythology say it is difficult to translate into English words the Native American concept of peace. It is far more than the opposite or the cessation of war. It is also distinct from an unattainable utopia of perfection. Peace was considered the fundamental element to right living, and their ideal state of existence. Bruce Johansen points out that the all-important Northwest Ordinance of 1787, which laid out the plans for acquiring new states into the union after the War of Independence, was probably authored by Charles Thomson, and likely modeled after the Great Law of Peace.[5] The Iroquois provided for expansion of their territory when they detailed the roots of the Great Tree of Peace extending to the four corners of the Earth. Similarly, peace was the motivating factor in the Northwest Ordinance, which called for no slavery in the new territory and just treatment of the Native Americans. Both ideals proved problematic to enforce, but the point is that, though the Founding Fathers were very worried about how to maintain a republic over such a huge expanse of land, peace was the goal.

Deganawidah's vision included an eagle perched on top of the Great Tree of Peace. To the Native Americans, the eagle stood for watchfulness, far sight, and a close relationship with the Great Spirit. The eagle was there, said Deganawidah, as a symbol to remind them that the price of peace is eternal vigilance.[6] "The eagle shall have your power" meant that the people were responsible to maintain a peaceful existence. Just because the laws or branches would shelter them, they couldn't shirk their duty to keep watch. They needed to watch over their Great Tree of Peace as an eagle would, and cry alert for any advancing dangers from the outside. As Donald Grinde put it, "the best political contrivance that the wit of man can devise is impotent to keep the peace unless a watchful people stands always on guard to defend it."[7] The law of the League of the Iroquois included the power to impeach leaders who were judged incompetent. This and many other political powers were reserved for the women in the tribes, who were also relied upon for their prodigious memories, preserving hundreds of years of oral history. The Iroquois believed in protecting the rights of the individual from a centralized authority, disallowed slavery, elected representatives from each of the tribes to serve, and were tolerant of differing religions. It's no wonder our founders were in awe of them.

The Arrows: Another Native American Influence on the Great Seal

One of the preliminary designs of the second Seal committee included a shield being supported on one side by an Indian figure carrying arrows. The other side was supported by a classically robed female figure representing Peace. The Indian was changed to a sword-carrying warrior before this design was submitted to Congress, however. Because the artist, Francis Hopkinson, was the first to propose arrows for our Great Seal, historians who count such things give him the credit for the arrows that ended up in the talon of the eagle. Another Native

(left) The Statue of Freedom by Thomas Crawford is located atop the dome of the United States Capitol. Just as in the Iroquois Great Tree of Peace, Freedom is crowned by the eagle. The eagle is standing vigilant at the very summit of Congress, ever watchful and far-seeing for threats to our liberty. Photo credit: Architect of the Capitol. (right) Detail of the great eagle plumage cresting the helmet of the goddess of Freedom on top of the Capitol Dome. This photograph depicts a 9-inch authorized reproduction sculpture in the author's personal collection.

American influence is seen in du Simitière's first design for the Great Seal, which included an American soldier as one of the supporters of the shield (standing opposite a classically robed female figure representing Liberty). This American soldier was outfitted partially as an Indian in Native garb of buckskin complete with tomahawk. These designs for the Great Seal show that the early Americans had already adopted some of the symbols of the Native Americans and considered them integral to the composition of their own unique national identity. It set them apart from the Europeans.

For the first 200 years, the white man's history of the founding of this nation routinely discounted the influence of the First Peoples on the early Americans. Yet, their very proximity, interaction, and population made their influence on the Colonists inevitable and indisputable. In 1744 Franklin attended the treaty council in Lancaster, Pennsylvania, when Canassatego, an Iroquois chief, counseled the Colonial leaders about their concept of unity for peace. In the symbolic way of the Indians, he demonstrated how simple it was to break one single arrow, and yet how difficult it was to break five or six arrows when they were bound together. "Our wise forefathers established Union and Amity between the Five Nations," he told them, saying unification had, "made us formidable; this has given us great Weight and Authority with our neighboring Nations. We are a powerful Confederacy and by your observing the same methods our wise forefathers have taken, you will acquire such Strength and power. Therefore, whatever befalls you, never fall out with one another."[8] Ben Franklin wrote in 1751 to publisher James Parker, "It would be a very strange thing if Six Nations of Ignorant Savages should be capable of forming a Scheme for such an Union and be able to execute it in such a manner, as that it has subsisted Ages, and appears indissoluble, and yet a like union should be impracticable for ten or a dozen English colonies."[9]

In 1754, Ben Franklin published what is considered the first political cartoon, his famous "Join or Die" serpent. This showed a snake cut into eight sections, labeled with the names of eight Colonies in an attempt to rouse support for his Albany Plan of Union. The state legislatures at that time, however, were not yet ready to give up their identification as separate units, and Franklin's early suggestion for a federal system did not pass for another 20 years, when many of its proposals and concepts resurfaced in the Articles of Confederation.

Toward the end of his life Franklin began publicly advocating the rights of Native Americans. He compared their civility in government with the European tradition:

> Having frequent Occasions to hold public Councils, they have acquired great Order and Decency in conducting them. The old Men sit in the foremost ranks, the Warriors in the next, and the Women and Children in the hindmost. The business of the Women is to take exact notice of what passes, imprint it in their memories, for they have no Writing, and communicate it to their children. They are the Records of the Council, and they preserve the Stipulations in Treaties a hundred Years back, which when we compare with our Writings we always find exact.[10]

Now, more than 200 years later, as we Americans have finally begun to recognize the important role of women as political leaders in our own society, it's time we also exercise some of the responsibilities we inherited from the League of the Iroquois system. I'm talking about defending ourselves and our environmental future from the neglect and abuse our leaders are allowing to happen. We can look to the eagle to motivate our citizens' rights to protect the environment—which is, after all, essential to protecting our liberty.

Environmental Symbolism of the Eagle

The American bald eagle has quite recently become a new kind of symbol for the repairable relationship between humans and the environment. Because of its status as our national bird, people really responded to the news that the bald eagle had been placed on the endangered species list. At their lowest point in 1967, fewer than 500 eagle pairs were counted in the lower 48 states. Today there are close to 10,000.[11] There are many theories about what made the biggest difference, but, because their only real enemy is man, one of the most effective measures must have been the strict enforcement of no hunting laws. The banning of DDT also played a role. Bald eagles had begun laying eggs with very soft shells that broke before they were hatched, believed to have been a result of DDT and other chemicals, such as mercury, dioxin, and PCBs, in their environment. The main threats to the bald eagle continue to be illegal hunting, power lines, loss of habitat from over-development, and loss of nutrients in their environment.

Bald eagle enthusiasts celebrated in 2007, however, as the birds were finally removed from the endangered list and had their status lowered to "threatened." It is still illegal to buy, sell, or trade in bald or golden eagle feathers, which has resulted in protests from the Native Americans trying to maintain the sacredness of this object in their traditions. Today, tribes must apply for a permit in order to acquire one of the processed dead eagles that are collected and tracked at the National Eagle Repository in Colorado.

Charles Thomson knew that the bald eagle was native exclusively to this continent, and wanted to show an *American* symbol. The natural habitat of a bald eagle ranges literally all over North America. The bald eagle has adapted to live in environments from sea to shining sea, including the hot arid deserts of the West, the cool pine forests of the North, and the humid swamps of the South. It's an all-over-America bird as well as an all-American bird, though the great majority of bald eagles live in Alaska and Canada due to the habitat of abundant fishing grounds.

The Choice of the Eagle for the U.S. Great Seal

Charles Thomson specifically changed the eagle on the U.S. Great Seal to the American or bald eagle. The golden eagle (which looks very similar to the bald eagle except for a brown head and tail feathers) is a species common worldwide and would have been the likely choice if the intention was to follow the heraldic practices in Europe and Asia.

Thomson was confidently following the tradition of using the eagle to portray majesty, independence, and far-seeing, and all its other estimable qualities. There is no doubt that Thomson had European and Middle Eastern traditions in mind when he chose the eagle as the central focus of the new Great Seal, though we cannot discount his obvious admiration of the Native Americans as another possible inspiration. From Thomson's own writings, it is clear that the sense of American independence was what he most wanted to convey with his choice of the bald eagle as America's national bird.

To find out how he reached that conclusion, we must return to the years 1776–1782, the same years when the Continental Congress was otherwise occupied with keeping the suffering army supplied, evacuating the capital, and winning the Revolutionary War. The debate over what to put on our new coat of arms must have seemed less important to some in light of these other pressing concerns. And yet they rejected three proposals in a row, showing that the Congress agreed on at least one thing: The Great Seal had to be something strong, distinguished, and outstanding. They knew it would symbolically represent the new United States of America and affect their reputation with all other countries in the world. They wanted it to pictorially proclaim the uniqueness of the American vision of independence, freedom, and liberty for (most of) the common men. There were enough learned men in Congress to know that, so far, all of the designs proposed were too derivative of other countries' seals, or not strikingly simple enough. Even the suggestions by such imaginative minds as Jefferson, Franklin, and Adams, all of whom served on the first committee, were tabled as not quite right. Many of the earlier committees made good suggestions that were retained in the end, but the various combinations of the symbolic elements we know today were never pleasing enough to excite a "this is it!" moment.

After the designs of the third committee were rejected in May 1782, Secretary of Congress Charles Thomson, who had overseen the work of all three committees since 1776, was charged with synthesizing all of the best ideas. It is not accurate, however, to say that he merely rearranged selected symbols from the three earlier proposals. Although it is true that most of the symbols in his final version of the Great Seal had already been proposed in different combinations, Thomson's arrangements clearly resulted from unique insights and other outside influences. Patterson and Dougall have demonstrated convincingly that Thomson had access to images that predate the Great Seal that show an eagle supporting a shield, and other images showing an eagle holding symbols of peace in one talon and war in the other.[12] Because no historical proof exists that he actually did see either of these sources, however, it also remains possible that Thomson had his own epiphany to depict an eagle supporting a shield while holding an olive branch and a bundle of arrows.

The *E Pluribus Unum* banner, the radiant eye in the triangle, a shield, and a tiny Imperial eagle were in the designs from the first committee. The cloud with 13 stars (the glory), the olive branch, and the arrows were in the designs from the second committee. A small white eagle, and the unfinished pyramid together with the eye were in the designs for the third committee. The white eagle in the third design was explained by William Barton as symbolizing "the supreme Power & Authority, and signifies Congress."[13] So the eagle had appeared in two earlier rejected designs, but both times it was small and served only as a fraction of the meaning of much more complicated designs. It was Thomson's decision to make the eagle the center focus of the Seal, but his large bald eagle was intended to signify independence rather than Congress.

(left) The most likely source of inspiration for the eagle holding symbols of peace and war was Joachim Camerarius's emblem book, originally published in 1597. Ben Franklin owned an edition of this book and might have shared it with his friend Charles Thomson. (right) The obverse of the Great Seal of the United States designed mostly by Thomson. The shield was supported solely by the eagle because the United States of America ought to rely on their own virtue. Department of State pamphlet 8868, July 1976.

Emblem Books

The most likely source of inspiration for the eagle holding peace and war was the 1702 edition of Joachim Camerarius's collection of emblems and mottoes owned by Thomson's friend Ben Franklin. A comparison of them side by side, in fact, implies a relationship (see the illustration on this page), but we are lacking any written documentation from Thomson stating that this image influenced him. Records of Franklin's library establish that he owned the Camerarius book, but Thomson might also have seen an eagle holding symbols of peace and war from a series of coins from the Two Sicilies in 1551 that may have been in the large collection of Pierre Eugène du Simitière.

Joachim Camerarius was a Bavarian physician who published four highly influential emblem books between 1593 and 1598. Collections of detailed drawings accompanied by moralistic mottoes, emblem books remained popular through the Revolutionary Era. They were largely responsible for introducing the subjects of art, symbolism, botany, zoology, and a philosophy of sorts to an illiterate public. The emblem of the eagle in the 1702 edition owned by Franklin showed it displayed (with wing tips up) over the olive branch on one side and a bundle of thunderbolts on the other. The accompanying description said he held the olive branch, the symbol of peace, in his right talon, the more favored position in heraldry. The Latin motto translated to "The left [talon] holds a thunderbolt, but the right an olive branch, That in peace and war I may be mindful of my duty."

Camerarius's eagle is not supporting a shield. As Patterson and Dougall point out in *The Eagle and the Shield,* Thomson may have been inspired to add the shield by a popular 1780 coin called the Maria Teresa *taler* (from whence we get our own word *dollar*). An eagle supporting a shield also appeared on several other earlier coins from Europe and in European heraldry. Shields alone were ubiquitous in heraldry, of course, and were included in all three of the previous committees' designs of the U.S. Great Seal. Usually a heraldic shield was supported by two figures on either side, and Thomson made an important change when he directed the eagle alone would support this shield. He emphasized that the eagle as the sole supporter of the shield demonstrated that America must stand alone on its own virtue.

The engraving of the die for the original obverse of the Great Seal, 1782 (note it is reversed so impressions made from it will be correct), based on Charles Thomson and William Barton's design. Compare this with Camerarius's eagle to see the likely source of inspiration. Notice also the long neck and the mistake of the tuft on the head. Illustration from Patterson and Dougall, *The Eagle and the Shield.*

Other Sources of Inspiration

As an expert in the classics, Thomson would have been familiar with the prominence of the eagle in myth, literature, art, and heraldry around the world. The eagle is seen on ancient Roman coins, and in Egyptian art and Greek poems. Because it is so often identified as the ruler of the sky, the eagle became associated with the sky gods and king gods of many religions, including Odin, Zeus, and Jupiter. From the Roman republic to the Holy Roman Empire, the eagle was a prominent symbol. As the Roman Empire split in two, a double-headed eagle was employed to show that Constantinople was looking over both the East and the West of the empire. The double-headed eagle is often used to imply a sense of dualism, and it remains a popular icon in this area to this day.

The eagle also appeared on a few pieces of Colonial money before Charles Thomson used it on the Great Seal. A 1715 South Carolina four-pound note depicted a double-headed eagle, and a 1779 South Carolina 70 dollar bill showed the dramatic scene of the eagle attacking Prometheus.[14] The strongest influence on Thomson's choice of the eagle, however, has to be its historical reputation in European heraldry as king of the birds. Many other countries were similarly influenced and also use the eagle in their national symbolism, though not the bald eagle, of course. Those using the eagle on their flags or in their national seals or coats of arms include Albania, Romania, Armenia, Mexico, and Poland. Others using eagles prominently in their national identity for hundreds of years include the Austrians, Germans, Greeks, and Spaniards.

The art or science of heraldry is a field rich in symbolism, perfected during the Crusades when designs for armor were developed to identify nation from nation and family from family. The rules are so strict that entire pages can be written deciphering the various symbols used in a crest or shield and the various meanings implied by the positions and placements of the items and colors. As with most animals in heraldry, the symbolic associations of the eagle predate heraldry and were adopted as is. Much attention is paid to whether the wings are up or down, and whether the bird is in flight or displayed, as each have distinct associations, but overall the eagle in heraldry is chosen as a symbol of strength and majesty.

> ### Illegal Eagles on Seals
>
> Popular authors and conspiracy buffs have made it an urban legend, but there is no truth to the suggestion that the head of the eagle on the Great Seal is turned during times of war to face the arrows instead of the olive branches. The design of the U.S. Great Seal has never been altered, nor can it be by law. The very similar Presidential Seal, however, can and has been altered several times at the discretion of various presidents. There is some evidence to indicate that even George Washington used a presidential seal that mirrored the Great Seal, but it is not until 1877 when Rutherford Hayes began using an official Presidential Seal that we have an undisputable artifact to examine. In Hayes's seal, the artist is unknown, as is the reason the head of the eagle was turned to its left to face the arrows instead of the olive branches. In heraldry, the head of the animal should always be facing its right side, which is what Harry Truman pointed out in 1945 when he finally corrected it with his own redesign.[15]
>
> From 1841 to 1885 the U.S. Great Seal depicted the eagle holding only six arrows instead of 13. This error most likely was the result of the engraver, John Peter Van Ness Throop, basing his design on a worn and faded version of the 1782 die. It's possible Throop was able to count only six arrows, and it's true that a bundle of arrows of indiscriminate number was an established heraldic device implying unification. Thomson's description did not suggest the number of arrows to be included in the bundle, but his sketch shows at least 10. It was heraldry student William Barton, when he revised Thomson's sketches and notes before presenting them to Congress, who called for 13 arrows to stand for the original Colonies. The Throop die with six arrows, known as the "illegal seal," was used for more than 40 years before being corrected with a new die cut in 1885. The unknown engraver of the original 1782 seal also apparently made the error of putting a tuft or crest on the head of the eagle, a detail often included on European heraldic eagles, but not appearing on bald eagles, which was clearly what Thomson intended.

America Adopts the Eagle

Have you heard the anecdote about Ben Franklin criticizing the choice of the eagle as our national bird, claiming he preferred the turkey instead? Similar to other American symbol legends, this story has been repeated out of context and with a disregard for Franklin's notorious penchant for satire. As we reviewed in Chapter 3, Franklin was fully aware that heraldic animals are chosen only for their qualities worthy of emulation, disregarding their lesser-attractive qualities. He also knew the bald eagle was chosen, in part, because, similar to the turkey, it was an indigenous American bird. As one of America's premiere adman sloganeers, however, he surely would have recognized the potential of the majestically beautiful bald eagle as a glamorous, magnificent national symbol and approved of it on its hype factor alone. More than almost anyone else among America's leaders, Franklin was intensely interested in the power of symbols in shaping public opinion. In 1775, when he designed the first federal paper money, he took the opportunity to proselytize once more for the causes of unity and independence. The simple admonitions and images he printed on the currency, the 13-linked chain and the 13-stringed harp, for example, became so popular that many were adopted for the flags and mottoes of militia regiments.

In addition, his remarks comparing the eagle to the turkey were not about the eagle on the Great Seal, but rather in response to the medallions of the newly created Society of the Cincinnati, designed by Peter Charles L'Enfant (who we will meet again in Chapter 7). In modeling this medallion after the new U.S. Great Seal, L'Enfant was the first in what was to become a long tradition of copying the device of the eagle and the shield for seals of state and government organizations. Franklin's criticism of L'Enfant's medallion was part of his larger critique of the society itself (though he would later accept an honorary membership in it). Many of the Revolutionary generation complained about the Society of the Cincinnati, calling it elitist for perpetuating hereditary rights. It was an exclusive club formed by General Henry Knox and other officers in the Continental Army who wished to stay in contact with each other after the war and work to establish pensions for veterans and their families. Because membership was open only to direct descendants of military officers, many Americans felt it was a step backward.

Also of significance, before Franklin wrote the letter to his daughter from which the turkey story is quoted, he was already using the eagle side of the new Great Seal with pride, printing it on the title page of a compilation of the 13 state constitutions, which he translated and printed from his press in France. So the next time Thanksgiving rolls around, and magazine writers make us feel nostalgic about turkeys by retelling that old chestnut of a partially exaggerated Ben Franklin story, don't let that sway you away from your respect for the bald eagle.

The Eagle Takes Flight

After the 1782 approval of the Great Seal, Americans immediately embraced the image of the bald eagle and it began appearing everywhere. Variations on the

Seal design were worked into needlepoints, tapestries, tavern signs, paintings, medallions, and sculptures. The bald eagle quickly became a shorthand way of pictorially saying America, and it was placed next to the Roman goddess Libertas, to more fully identify this goddess and ethic with the American cause. Thomson's final eagle and shield design has proven so popular that it has been adapted as a logo by a long string of federal government agencies, corporations, and clubs. Each one has made changes to the design, some slight and some major, as is the custom in heraldry, called "differencing." The changes are intended to show the distinctness of the government agency and yet retain the relationship to the national symbol. Elements from the eagle side of the Great Seal are used in many of our state seals, as well as in the seals of the Department of the Air Force, Department of Commerce, Department of Justice, Department of State, Department of Defense, CIA, FCC, Federal Reserve System, Supreme Court, and Library of Congress, to name just a few. The one with which we are most familiar is the Presidential Seal, seen on the podium every time we watch the president speak.

The United States Postal Service logo is one of the most familiar uses of the eagle that we see in our daily lives today. The eagle side of the Great Seal has been adopted with slight differences by dozens of government institutions. Used with permission of the USPS.

Esoteric and Mythological Symbolism of the Eagle

Rabbi Avraham Brandwein tells us that eagles are often seen as a symbol of compassion in the Jewish tradition, in part because of a legend about the eagle flying with her young sheltered on her back to shield them from any arrows shot from below. Rav Brandwein also reminds us that Ezekiel's chariot was surrounded by a lion, an ox, an eagle, and a man.[16] This is translated as the lion was king of the beasts, the ox king of the animals, the eagle king of the birds, and the man king of them all. Jewish people today also symbolize some of their great leaders as eagles, referring to both the medieval sage Maimonides and the Lubavitcher Rebbe, Rabbi Menachem M. Schneerson, as eagles. The Torah compares God Himself to an eagle. In Deuteronomy 32:11–12, Moses describes how the Lord protects his favored ones who obey his laws well, as Jacob did:

"Like an eagle that stirs up its nest, that hovers over its young, he spread His wings and caught them, He carried them on His pinions" (wings). In Exodus 19:4, God says, "You yourselves have seen what I did to Egypt, and how I carried you on eagles' wings and brought you to myself."

In the Christian tradition, the eagle is most commonly associated with St. John the Evangelist, which is why we see so many eagles carved into lecterns in Christian churches. The four gospel writers have been given the same animal symbolism as in the vision of Ezekial, with John being the eagle, Mark the lion, Luke the ox, and Matthew the man. Stained-glass windows sometimes show an eagle clutching a scroll with the first few words of his gospel: *In the beginning was the Word.* Because it soars straight upward, Christians have also linked the eagle symbol to Christ and His ascension. The author of the Revelation of St. John also had a vision very similar to that of Ezekiel, describing the throne of God surrounded by the same four creatures: "In the center, around the throne, were four living creatures, and they were covered with eyes, in front and in back. The first living creature was like a lion, the second was like an ox, the third had a face like a man, the fourth was like a flying eagle" (Revelation 4:7, New International Version).

In 17th-century alchemical symbolism numerous depictions of eagles represent the volatile principle or the element air. In astrological lore the eagle is associated with the sign of Scorpio. Some of the standard terms used to describe the nature of the sun sign Scorpio definitely describe an eagle: *intense, willful, proud,* and *purposeful.* Scorpio is a water sign, connecting water to eagles—a link verified by nature, after all, as the bald eagle is classified as a *sea eagle.*

Volumes could be written about the appearance of the eagle in world mythologies, and we will list here just a brief overview of some of the more famous mythological eagles. From the earliest historical records in Sumeria, the eagle played a prominent role. The eagle was a mode of transportation to and from the abode of the gods, and on missions to retrieve magical aid. This role of the eagle as a conveyance to heaven is repeated in many cultures. The constellation we know today as Aquila the eagle is named for the Greek and Roman god Zeus/Jupiter's eagle who was sent to Earth to pick up the favored Ganymede and bring him to Olympus. The Hindu mythology has a god named Garuda, which has the wings and beak of an eagle and the body of a giant man. Garuda is seen chiefly as the means of transportation for the god Vishnu. The Mabinogion, the ancient manuscript of Welsh mythology, tells of the hero Lleu Llaw Gyffes who is transformed into an eagle at the time of his death. Norse mythology features the giant Hraesvelg, who in the form of the eagle is said to create the wind with the beating of its wings. We've already discussed the Native American Thunderbird, who creates thunder with the beating of its wings. A Griffin is an eagle-headed lion from the Greco-Roman mythology, and Ningursu is a lion-headed eagle from Babylonian mythology. And we can't forget Gwaihir, the lord of the eagles in J.R.R. Tolkien's *Lord of the Rings,* who, with his fellow eagles, rescues both Gandalf and Frodo at their times of greatest need.

The Double-Headed Eagle

The double-headed eagle is often used to depict an organization formed by the joining together of two jurisdictions. It is also the most widely used emblem of the Scottish Rite Freemasons. "Deus meumque jus" translates to "God and my right." Photo credit: Supreme Council, 33°, S.J., U.S.A.

The popularity of the symbol of a two-headed eagle may be explained by its pleasing symmetry and implication of balance and strength. The double-headed eagle was popular among the ancient Hittites as early as the 18th-century BCE. This trend was picked up many centuries later with the foundation of the Seljuk empire in modern-day Turkey. The Greek Orthodox church to this day uses the double-headed eagle as an important symbol in their church designs, having inherited it from their predecessors, the Eastern part of the Holy Roman Empire. It is also found on flags, seals, and logos of sports teams all around this region. During the Middle Ages, the popularity of the double-headed eagle spread via the Crusades, and began appearing on crests and shields throughout Europe, Asia Minor, and Russia.[17] The double-headed eagle has been traced as far back as ancient Sumeria where it was found on cylinder seals in the city of Lagash.

The Scottish Rite Freemasons use a double-headed eagle in their symbolism to denote the 32nd and 33rd degrees. The earliest use of the double-headed eagle among Freemasons dates back to 1758 CE, when they may have adopted it (as many other organizations have done), to show the banding together of two powerful groups. In their case it was the formation of the Council of the East and West that led to the current system of 33 degrees in Masonry. Another way of interpreting the double-headed eagle along Masonic lines would be that Masons place a heavy emphasis on learning from the past (one head looking back) so as to experience a better future (one head looking forward). Masonic historian Arthur C. Parker summarized that the double-headed eagle "symbolizes a duality of power, a blending of two names, two functions and two dominions in one body. [In Sumeria] it stood for a union of solar and celestial forces; as a royal crest it has stood for power and dominion, and as a religious seal it stands for truth and justice."[18] Masonic esoteric author Manly Palmer Hall compares the double-headed eagle to the phoenix and says it foreshadows a male-female balance and the transmutation of ignorance into wisdom.[19]

The Phoenix

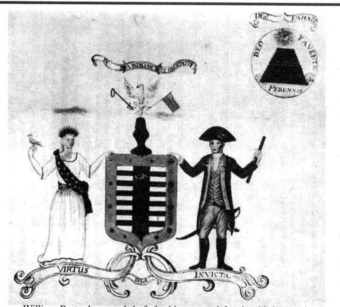

William Barton's second draft for his proposal for the third committee on the Great Seal, 1782, included a phoenix. Note the tiny phoenix on the shield is one of numerous other symbols, not the central image, as Thomson's eagle was to become. Barton considered the phoenix to be "emblematic of the expiring Liberty of Britain, revived by her Descendants, in America." Illustration from Patterson and Dougall, *The Eagle and the Shield*.

Because of its similarity to the eagle, the legendary phoenix bird would deserve mention in this chapter based on their symbolic connection alone. But in fact, the phoenix bird itself was also included in one of the rejected proposals for the design for the U.S. Great Seal. It is *not* true, as many fundamentalist-conspiratorialists will tell you, that the bald eagle supporting the shield was originally or secretly intended to be a phoenix. The phoenix appeared in William Barton's complicated design, which all together through various designs included a total of four birds: a dove of peace, a white eagle, a phoenix, and a rooster. A student of heraldry, Barton knew the mythological phoenix was a symbol of regeneration and renewal. Recording why he included it in his preliminary design for the U.S. Great Seal, he said it was, "emblematical of the expiring Liberty of Britain, revived by her Descendants, in America."[20] The concept of renewal from the ashes of tyranny depicted in the symbol of the phoenix apparently spoke to a number of the early Colonists as well, as the phoenix appeared on several designs of early Colonial money.

The phoenix is a legendary bird usually described as having features of both an eagle and a vulture. Because of its connection to the phoenix, David Ovason says we can view the eagle on the Great Seal as a reference to achievements in the past and contrast it with the need to finish the pyramid, or the achievements for the future.[21] Variations on this mythical bird that regenerates itself in fire are known by many cultures around the world. According to the Arabian tradition, the phoenix is a rare bird, only one of which lives at a time. After several hundred years, the phoenix returned to its place of origin and set itself up to receive the direct rays of the sun. It would burst into flames and turn into a pile of ashes, out of which would emerge a baby phoenix fully formed.

J.E. Cirlot says the phoenix is a symbol of periodic destruction and recreation.[22] Similar birds and legends are also found in the mythologies of Egypt (the Bennu Bird) and North America (the Thunderbird)[23], and in the Jewish tradition (the Milcham). Because of its miraculous resurrection, the phoenix was used as a symbol for Christ by the early Christian church, as referenced in the letter of St. Clement, Bishop of Rome, to the Corinthians. Early Christian allegories even added a three-day lag time in between the immolation and the rebirth of the phoenix to more closely match the tale of Christ rising from the dead.

The phoenix or firebird is a legendary creature known to several cultures around the world. At the end of its long life it was said to regenerate itself in a burst of flames. Though conspiracy theorists are incorrect to say the eagle on the Great Seal was originally intended to be a phoenix, the phoenix was included in one of the preliminary designs for the Seal to symbolize renewal. Courtesy of Toni L. Taylor, artist.

Why Fundamentalist-Conspiratorialists Fear the Eagle

Unfortunately for this discussion, the early renderings of the Great Seal were slightly crude, and they also included a mistaken tuft or crest on the head of the eagle. It was drawn with a long neck, allowing fundamentalist-conspiratorialists today to say it looks more like the long-necked phoenix. Manly Hall stated in his *Secret Teachings of All Ages* that the crest on the head of the eagle on the original Great Seal matched the crest on an Egyptian hieroglyph of a "phoenix-man." To him, this was evidence that the original Great Seal designers were trying to portray a phoenix instead of an eagle. David Ovason demonstrates how Hall was mistaken in his hieroglyphic interpretation of the "phoenix-man," but unfortunately this mistake has had wide repercussions in the fields of anti-Masonic and anti-American-symbolism critiques. Hall is also the source for the optimistic but factually unverifiable claim that "[o]f the fifty-six signers of the Declaration of Independence, nearly fifty were Masons."[24] This number is repeated regularly on television documentaries and anti-Masonic Websites trying to prove a Masonic conspiracy among America's founders. The historical records, however, document a much-less-dramatic total of nine verified Masons among the 56 signers of the Declaration of Independence.

Other than Manly Hall's discounted suggestion that the Great Seal designers intended their bald eagle to be a phoenix (and remember Hall was writing before the publication of the only authoritative book on the Great Seal, *The Eagle and the Shield*), there is not one hint or clue that can support this claim. But even if there were, it is clear the phoenix symbol meant something entirely different to the Revolutionary generation than it does to the fundamentalist-conspiratorialists. Despite its use by early Christians to symbolize Christ, the phoenix today is greatly feared by the fundamentalist-conspiratorialists who associate it with flames (Illuminati), pagan mythology (Satan), and reincarnation (rather than resurrection). Because of these conspiracy fear-mongers, millions of Americans today think the phoenix is a symbol for the Antichrist.

One group has attacked Hillary Clinton as an "Illuminist Witch" because she's been photographed wearing a lapel pin of an eagle holding a pearl.[25] I would think photos of American politicians wearing eagle lapel pins are probably as numerous as photos of them kissing babies, but these particular writers had already determined that Mrs. Clinton was a high-ranking member in the Satanic conspiracy, and this eagle lapel pin was just further "proof" in their eyes. Another group excitedly shows us how similar is the design of an eagle on a 2002 U.S. postage stamp to the Nazi eagle used by Hitler.[26] They may look alike, but that's because they are both eagles. It is not proof that the U.S. Postal Service is run by Nazis or Illuminati, but millions of people are believing this single level of interpretation thanks to the emotional "oh my gosh!" approach and a lack of historical background to dismiss it. Of course, the use of the double-headed eagle as a symbol by their currently designated bogey-men, the Scottish Rite Freemasons, is proof enough for some that the eagle is an evil symbol. Once again, I find myself repeating that that the double-headed eagle is a symbol used by the Freemasons *as well as countless other groups and countries around the world.* It is not a symbol that originated with or is exclusive to the Freemasons. It is the most elementary of mistakes to extrapolate that all instances of eagle symbols are influenced by the Freemasons.

Anti-Masonic author Texe Marrs has produced an entire video documentary to pick apart the symbolism used by NASA and connect it to his conclusion that the evil Masons are in control. He regales us with emotionally charged phrases claiming that both Buzz Aldrin and Neil Armstrong were Freemasons, and that they planted the Freemasonic double-headed eagle flag on the moon in a secret ceremony they held off camera, claiming the moon "for their Masonic God, Lucifer, the lord of darkness."[27] Marrs allegedly reveals a double meaning to "the Eagle has landed," when he describes how "Neil Armstrong carefully took out his Masonic apron and held it up for the cameras over his space suit as if to cover his genitals area-the power center, or dynamo, of Luciferian energy in Masonic ritual.

Today, a photograph of Armstrong holding his occultic apron hangs on a wall at the House of the Temple, the sanctuary of the Scottish Rite, in Washington, D.C."[28]

The American eagle has even landed on the moon with *Apollo 11*.

We checked his facts with Dr. S. Brent Morris, managing editor of the *Scottish Rite Journal*, who clarified, first of all, that Neil Armstrong was *not* a Freemason, though his father was. *There is no such photograph* of Neil Armstrong holding a Masonic apron on the moon. As Morris explained:

Each astronaut was allowed to take a small amount of personal items with him on a flight. The four astronauts who chose to take Masonic items that I'm aware of were John Glenn who wore a 33° ring when he orbited the earth, Walter Shirra, who took a small blue flag with a square and compasses with him on a *Gemini* flight, and Gordon Cooper and Buzz Aldrin, who each took small white flags with Scottish Rite eagles on them to the moon.[29]

Some of these astronauts' items are displayed proudly in various lodges, but there were no secret flag planting ceremonies, nor do Masons worship a "lord of darkness" named Lucifer (as we detail further in Chapter 8). The use of mythological symbolism by NASA can be explained simply as following good rules of heraldry and design. Unfortunately, however, as with anything symbolic, the fundamentalist-conspiratorialists try to find a way to link it to Satan or their concept of the evil "them."

The Price of Peace Is Eternal Vigilance: The Eagle Shall Have Your Power

The eagle should remind us that the people have the power and the responsibility to change their leaders when displeased. Our current administration may be acting like war-mongering imperialists with delusions of grandeur today, but that is definitely *not* the path envisioned for us by the Founding Fathers. Thomson deliberately placed the olive branch in the favored right talon of the eagle and turned his head to face peace. In his explanation of the symbol he wrote, "the olive branch...denote[s] the power of peace."[30] The first time the Great Seal was used was on a document beginning the peace negotiations with Great Britain after the war. The decade that followed was a very prickly and precarious time when decisions were made that would have enduring effects on U.S. policy. John Adams supported George Washington's belief that the United States should remain neutral in foreign entanglements, and peace negotiations must be pursued at all costs to avoid them. Adams lost his reputation by brokering peace with France during their own bloody revolution, and our country experienced its first ugly split into two diametrically opposed political parties.

When considering the eagle as a symbol, there are many distinct characteristics with which to identify. The Roman imperial eagle led the legions of soldiers into battle justifying the war as if on orders from Jupiter. Jupiter was often seen in artwork with his companion eagle, which leads to an interesting comparison. Because of the neoclassical influences on early American art, Washington and Franklin were sometimes depicted wearing togas, and very frequently next to the American bald eagle. Washington in a toga next to an eagle can look very similar to Jupiter in a toga next to his. But Washington's eagle was not Jupiter's eagle. The eagle of American symbolism stood for their new won independence and the need to stand on their own virtues. It was ever turned toward peace, while remaining vigilant and united against threats to this peace—from both within and without.

The eagle reminded our Founding Fathers to cherish their independence by pursuing peace. When our leaders misuse the "screaming eagles" of our military power (as evidenced by more than three-quarters of Americans opposing the War in Iraq, as the latest polls indicate), then it's time we remember that, as the Iroquois did, we have the power to impeach them. The eagle stands for vigilance, and vigilance is our power and the price we pay to maintain our liberties.

The American Eagle

Learning a little history is all it takes for a rational person to realize that the American eagle is not a dark or occult symbol. Rather, it is a beautiful, majestic, and inspiring symbol—or can be, if you allow more than one level of interpretation to guide you. Today, many companies and sports teams in America use the eagle as their emblem to give their group an instant national reputation by linking it with the national bird of the country. The eagle logo also associates them with the same majestic, strong, and far-seeing qualities that attracted early Americans to it in the first place. Popular eagle logos include Anheiser-Busch, Armani, the United States Automobile Association, Altair Airlines, the U.S. Postal Service, and the Philadelphia Eagles.

The eagle has forever dominated the sky in terms of man's symbolic rendering of this giant bird. Throughout its heraldic history, the eagle became associated with empires and imperialism, and even today it is seen as the symbol of the American empire instead of the far-seeing vigilant protector of the peace described by the League of the Iroquois. Charles Thomson did not write about what he intended for the meaning of the eagle, other than to say it was the lone supporter of the shield "to denote that the United States of America ought to rely on their own Virtue."[31] Although he was certainly aware of some of the other symbolic interpretations for the eagle that we have presented in this chapter, as would any great artist, he left us the liberty and freedom to interpret the symbols on our own.

CHAPTER 7

WASHINGTON, D.C.: HISTORY, MYSTERY, AND SYMBOLISM IN PLAIN SIGHT

As a city planned by the Revolutionary generation, *and* the result of the first great political compromise, *and* the first federal project on which a black man was invited to partici pate, the city of Washington, D.C. itself is an American sym- bol. A symbol full of symbols, if you will, and the abundance of classical art and architecture as well as the geometric shapes in the city map are brimming with possibilities for interpretation. We will spend most of our time in this chapter examining the city map itself, as so many of the symbol- hunters are speculating on the intentionality of the geometric patterns and sym- bols that can be found there. The style of the city can be revealing about our Founding Fathers' vision for the future of this unified nation, but it is even more revealing about the generations who followed in their footsteps and their chal- lenge to maintain that vision aesthetically while meeting the practical needs of the city. The continuing renovations and improvements that change the face of Wash- ington, D.C. from one decade to the next are also symbolic of this nation. New monuments, new streets, and new government institutions are added and modi- fied, as the American government of the people is constantly striving for improve- ment. The changes are not always for the best, but hopefully we will correct them with future changes requested by the ever-vigilant and vocal citizenry.

As with the other symbols in this book, the official history of Washington, D.C. does not correspond with the contemporary negative interpretations of its symbolism. Those finding Satanic symbolism in the street layout of D.C. are motivated by a mistrust of the current administration as well as by a fear of the

Freemasons. As was the case with the history of the Great Seal, however, there is no documentary evidence to verify that any of the contributors to the original city plans of Washington, D.C. were Freemasons—with the obvious exception of George Washington himself. George Washington's role in the development of the capital city was invaluable, but his input was more one of chief driver, cheerleader, and negotiator, rather than designer. By most accounts, his creative contributions were negligible, beyond his crucial support for the grand vision of the first engineer/architect, Peter (Pierre) Charles L'Enfant.

The Father of Our Nation Was Also the Father of Our Capital City

Unable to afford the classical or European education of many of his contemporaries, Washington taught himself the science of surveying. While still a young man, he perfected this skill by striking westward across the frontier land of Virginia, where he also contracted a serious case of what has been called "Potomac Fever." The father of our country had it bad. Those afflicted with Potomac Fever included all the large landowners and speculators in the Virginia territory who envisioned the Potomac River providing the means for expanding trade routes and settlement to the west. Some believed the future of the mighty river would even connect them to the unexplored western territories.[1]

After the death of his elder brother, Washington inherited his family estate, Mt. Vernon, located on a picturesque curve in the river overlooking what would eventually become the capital that would bear his name. Upon inheritance, he almost immediately expanded the 5,000 acres by 3,500 more. When he married the wealthy widow Martha Custis, Washington's financial situation was secured, and he began investing the way most thrifty Americans were doing: by buying more land. With the additional Custis money, he soon purchased another 60,000 acres, more than two-thirds of which was good land in the Potomac-Ohio river complex.[2] As soon as it became apparent to him that his place of honor in history was inextricably tied to the success of the American experiment, he probably started to ruminate on his beloved Potomac as a great location for the capital city of the new nation. It's quite likely that Washington picked the location for the capital long before it became an object of discussion for the Congress, as alleged by one of the dismissed designers of the city, Samuel Blodget, many years later.

By the time the debate over the location of the federal district became public, it was already common knowledge that Washington favored a site on the Potomac. Not only was it fairly equidistant from the northernmost and southernmost points of the 13 states, but he was also convinced that the Potomac would provide endless means of opportunity to grow the new nation westward. A capital on the Potomac would connect the north to the south, and also the east to the west.[3]

As soon as the war was over the Continental Congress resolved to find a home of its own. They began moving about from Philadelphia to Princeton to Annapolis before landing in New York. In 1787 they decided to create a 10-mile square federal district, and the debates began as to where to locate it. Marylanders were the first to propose sites including Baltimore and the area near Washington's home along the Potomac. Pennsylvanians thought Philadelphia had earned the right after so much of the important work of the revolution had happened there. New York City was putting on quite a show trying to keep the Congress right where it was by surging ahead with repairs and beautifications, cleaning up the considerable damage wrought by the British during the war. Returning to New York in 1789, the delegates to the first United States Congress were awed by the newly rebuilt Federal Hall designed by the French-American, Peter Charles L'Enfant. This was the building fondly remembered as the location where George Washington officially became the first president. It was strong and graceful in style, inspired by the neoclassical look of Greece and Rome, and yet uniquely American—what would soon be called "Federal style." It was just the kind of symbolism Americans were looking for as they set out to develop an entirely new system of government based on ancient Rome and yet uniquely American. Not shy of self-promotion, L'Enfant wrote to the new president in September 1789, with an attempt to parlay his success into the job for city planner of the future capital.

Competition for the permanent residence of the federal government was fierce, and it took the first constitutional crisis to pick a site. It was allegedly over a private dinner between Thomas Jefferson, James Madison, and Alexander Hamilton that the first great compromise was put into motion. Secretary of the Treasury Hamilton was being blocked from implementing his fiscal ideas, most notably the establishment of a national bank and the assumption of the war debt by the federal government. His opponents were a growing faction of anti-Federalists who feared the power of a centralized national government and preferred that the individual states retain more sovereign power. Southerners were opposed to a national resumption of the debt because most of their states had already paid their war debts. Nor did the agrarian South see the need for a national bank that would be of more use to the mercantile North. Many historians believe it was at this dinner party in June 1790 that the compromise was brokered. Madison would not openly oppose the national Bank of the United States in the Congress, and Hamilton would marshal support from New York to move the capital city to a location in the South as compensation. It was later worked out that in deference to Philadelphia's importance to the new republic, the Congress would reside there for the next 10 years while the new "Federal City," as it was called then, was built. Pennsylvania also got the consolation prize of having the most important avenue in the future capital named after it.

Once the Potomac location was determined with the Residency Act in July 1790, President George Washington was given nearly complete control over it from Congress, including choosing the specific location, the commissioners to manage the project, and the design. He was already working closely with his Secretary of State Jefferson to narrow in on the exact location, and Jefferson's role in the new city grew in importance each day. In January of 1791 Washington selected the first commission of overseers to consist of David Stuart of Alexandria, Thomas Johnson of Frederick, and Representative Daniel Carroll of Rock Creek. "Each held Potomac Company stock and, in the opinion of Jefferson, each stood ready to do Washington's bidding," says historian Kenneth Bowling.[4] Charged with managing the land sales and the construction process, they are the ones responsible for christening the city officially as "Washington" and the 10-mile square as the "Territory (or District) of Columbia," which was made official in September 1791.

In February 1791 Jefferson hired Andrew Ellicott, with Benjamin Banneker to assist him, to survey and lay the boundary stones around the border of the district. In March 1791 Washington's choice of designer, Peter L'Enfant, arrived ready to create the "capital of this vast empire."[5] Until his death in 1799, Washington spent an inordinate amount of time overseeing this frequently contentious project. He was involved in everything from the never-ceasing political attempts to move the capital elsewhere, down to small details such as street railings.[6] Because of missing records, there is some debate over who picked the sites for the two most important buildings on the city plan, the house of the Congress and the President's House. Washington and Jefferson certainly talked about it, and they may have made preliminary selections for these two sites before even announcing the square radius around the district, knowing as they did that land values surrounding these two buildings would skyrocket immediately thereafter. It was Washington's unwavering support for L'Enfant's creative control in these early months, however, that was the most crucial for the genesis of the city plan.

Before anyone claiming to see significant geometrical patterns in the street designs can make any conclusions about sacred geometry or symbolism, it's important to ascertain which plan and whose work is being considered. The five most often cited as responsible for inserting secret symbolism into the city plan are George Washington, Thomas Jefferson, Peter L'Enfant, Andrew Ellicott, and Benjamin Banneker. We will examine each of the latter three in turn, and review their backgrounds and the written explanations they left behind in order to consider the possible intentionality of symbolism in the city streets of Washington. We will return later to Washington and Jefferson.

The History of the Map: Ellicott, Banneker, and L'Enfant

Surveyor Andrew Ellicott (1754–1820) was born into a Quaker family, but nevertheless enlisted into the Maryland militia in 1775 to fight for America's independence and rose to the rank of major. In 1772 his father and uncles moved to Maryland from Bucks County, Pennsylvania, and formed the town of Ellicott's Mills, today called Ellicott City. Andrew's talents in mathematics and science drew him to the Philosophical Society, where he was befriended by Benjamin Franklin and David Rittenhouse. He worked with Rittenhouse and James Madison to complete the surveying work on the Mason-Dixon line separating Maryland from Pennsylvania. After the war he was elected to the Maryland legislature and then sent to the western frontier of Pennsylvania to determine what would become known as "the Ellicott Line," marking the boundaries for the Northwest Territories. Franklin recommended him to Washington, who hired him to mark the western boundaries of New York. During this trip he also made the first scientific survey of the Niagara Falls, accurately assessing its length and height and speed of descent. He also taught Merriweather Lewis survey-ing, a skill that served him well as he and William Clark explored the Louisiana Purchase territory. There is no documentation to indicate that Andrew Ellicott was a Freemason or interested in anything esoteric beyond his chosen fields of astronomy and surveying.

Benjamin Banneker (1731–1806) is one of the only well-known black Founding Fathers, and he's only well-known today due to the diligent efforts of contempo-rary African-American historians to publicize his remarkable story. He was a free man who so well educated himself and demonstrated such mental acuity that he attracted the attention of some of the leading minds of the day. His published almanacs are credited for helping prove to some of his contemporar-ies the fallacy of their arguments that black people were somehow mentally inferior to white people. He even took on Thomas Jefferson in the cover letter he included when presenting Jefferson with his first almanac in 1792. This letter is considered by many to be the first protest letter sent by an activist for black rights to an American official. Banneker scolded Jefferson, saying:

Andrew Ellicott and Benjamin Banneker surveying the 10-mile-square boundary of the new federal district. Detail of a mural called "Survey of the Federal Territory," painted by William A. Smith, located at the Maryland House in Aberdeen. Photo by Tony Browder.

...how pitiable is it to re-flect, that although you were so fully convinced of the benevo-lence of the Father of mankind, and of his equal and impartial distribution of those rights and privileges which he has con-ferred upon them, that you should at the same time coun-teract his mercies, in detaining by fraud and violence, so nu-merous a part of my brethren under groaning captivity and op-pression, that you should at the same time be found guilty of that most criminal act, which you professedly detested in others, with respect to yourselves."[7]

Jefferson responded immediately, not only with a letter saying how much he agreed that blacks and whites were equally talented but for "the degraded condition of their existence both in Africa & America,"[8] but he also forwarded copies of Banneker's almanac to the Academy of Sciences at Paris, which helped spread his fame as the United States' first black scientist.

Banneker is of most interest to me in our study of Washington, D.C. because of his knowledge of astronomy and astrology, and his stated fondness for the star Sirius. One of his biographers, Charles Cerami, says, "Banneker reportedly said Sirius was... a double star many years before professional scientists of the advanced world confirmed that fact."[9] Cerami couples Banneker's advanced knowledge about the star system Sirius, to his facility with weather forecasting and farming irrigation techniques, and suggests a conclusion that Banneker's ancestry was the Dogon tribe of Africa. (It should be noted here that Sylvio Bedini, another Banneker biographer, has concluded that Banneker's ancestry was from Senegal.) The Dogon are an isolated tribe in present day Mali whose mythology came to the attention of the Western world in the 1930s when French archeologists spent several decades living among them. The mystery is unsolved still as to how this remote African tribal people possessed astronomical knowledge about the star Sirius that was not confirmed visually until the invention of better telescopes in 1862. If Banneker was descended from the Dogon lineage, and if their sacred, advanced astronomical teaching was passed down to him through his grandmother, then it's possible that Banneker may have made a point to seek out the star system Sirius as he performed the surveying work for the district. His work for the Federal City was done at night, after all, by taking measurements from the stars. This is pure speculation, however, and there is no reason to believe that Banneker had any input into aligning any of the streets with the heliacal rising of Sirius as is claimed by some today. His job consisted exclusively of assisting Ellicott with the original boundary survey.

Banneker's ancestral stories are conflicting, but both Bedini and Cerami based their conclusions on the work of Martha Ellicott Tyson, daughter of George Ellicott, Banneker's closest friend. George Ellicott was the young cousin of Andrew Ellicott who befriended Banneker, though 30 years his senior, and maintained a lifelong friendship, mutually enjoying an appreciation of astronomy, math, surveying, and mechanics. Banneker never married and had no children, and most of his papers and books were destroyed in a fire soon after his death. In an attempt to record his remarkable life, in 1836 George's daughter, Martha, conducted interviews of surviving Banneker family members and neighbors. The neighbors all remembered hearing about Benjamin Banneker's grandfather, remembered as Banna Ka, and the seemingly remarkable knowledge that he had brought with him from his homeland. This inherited wisdom apparently included a knowledge of astronomy to make predictions for the weather, and the irrigation techniques that were so crucial to the success of their farm. These are also techniques in which the Dogon are known to have excelled.

Born in 1731, Benjamin lived and worked on the family farm in Oella, Maryland, next to the future Ellicott's Mills, all his life. Young Benjamin was mostly self-taught, and his photographic memory and mathematical and mechanical proficiency earned him a reputation as a child prodigy. Legend has it that he so admired one gentleman's watch that it was presented to him as a gift, and he immediately took it apart and put it back together again. Once he'd mastered how clocks were made, he proceeded to build a large wooden clock, which remained in use in for at least 30 years.[10]

It may have been this type of demonstration of his photographic memory that started the legend about him reproducing the D.C. map during a crisis in the production. Legend has it that after L'Enfant was dismissed or quit in a huff, he took all his plans with him back to France. (Note: He never went back to France.) It was then allegedly up to Banneker to reproduce L'Enfant's plans from memory, which he did, saving the day. Unfortunately, the dates of Banneker's known whereabouts contradict the possibility of this colorful story being true, as he was back home on his farm in March 1792, when L'Enfant left the job. From what we know about him, Banneker *could have performed* such a feat had it been asked of him, but we don't need to perpetuate an inaccurate legend about him to assure his greatness. He did contribute to the capital of our nation by assisting Ellicott's survey, and the fact that his self-taught surveying and astronomy skills were considered worthy enough to be chosen for such a monumental job is quite enough to earn him a place in history.

He does seem to have possessed a genius quality that went largely undocumented due to the societal barriers faced by all people of color in his time. By 1791, Banneker was already 59 years old, but many of his most famous accomplishments were yet to come. Later that same year he published the first of a series of almanacs that would bring him much acclaim. Cerami points out how far ahead of his time he was in his speculation about life on other planets, which was not to become a credibly discussed theory until two centuries later. Today there is a fine Benjamin Banneker Historical Park and Museum of Oella located on the original site of the Banneker family farm, and plans are in the works for a Banneker Memorial at L'Enfant Plaza in Washington, D.C.[11]

I have long been a great admirer of Benjamin Banneker, and in 1976 I included a portrait of him in a mural commissioned by the City of Baltimore that included a scene of Washington crossing the Delaware as seen in this detail. Much to the consternation of the historical sticklers who see it, however, I changed it so Washington is crossing Baltimore's Inner Harbor, and there is Benjamin Banneker riding along behind Washington in the boat. Of course, Banneker was not with Washington on this historic trip, but their paths did cross when designing the Federal City, and I took a little artistic license in order to pay homage to one of America's forgotten founders. This mural can still be seen at Baltimore's War Memorial Building.

And then there's L'Enfant (1754–1825). As with Banneker, his name is known to us today only after having lain in obscurity for about a hundred years. L'Enfant was rediscovered when the city was gearing up for its centennial and preparing for major renovations. Commissions were formed, and after some investigation two earlier maps were discovered validating that the Frenchman's design had pre-dated Ellicott's. It had long been assumed that Andrew Ellicott had designed the town, as his name was prominently displayed on the first published map. As we shall see, L'Enfant's name was on the map first, but it was deliberately erased from both the map and the official version of the story. Somebody wanted his memory erased so badly that they even ransacked his house immediately upon his dismissal and stole all his original papers, designs, and correspondence on the project, none of which were ever seen again.[12]

L'Enfant was a 22-year-old art and engineering student in Paris when he caught the spirit of liberty and independence, and decided to help the Americans take their stand. He came over with the Marquis de Lafayette to fight in the war as part of the Corps of Engineers and was eventually promoted to the rank of brevet major. After crossing paths with Washington in Valley Forge, he was wounded and taken prisoner in some of the heaviest fighting in South Carolina and later cited for bravery. His father had been a painter in the court of Louis the XV, and Pierre (who changed his name to Peter as soon as he arrived in America) had studied at the Royal Academy at the Louvre, where he would have had access to the plans of all the great European cities. After the war he went into business as an architect and engineer in New York, where he formed a special bond with Alexander Hamilton. On fundamentalist-conspiratorialist Websites, he is often identified as a Freemason, which is used as a key to their argument that there is a Freemasonic influence on the design of the streets of Washington, D.C. As of today, no historical evidence has surfaced to verify that L'Enfant was a Freemason. He was the obvious choice for the job, however, and Washington called him better qualified than anyone he knew in the country. Washington was to become the greatest defender of L'Enfant while the latter's ego and obstinacy grew more and more troublesome to the others on the committee.

The McMillan Commission of 1901–1902 that resurrected L'Enfant's memory assumed that his main influences on the Federal City had been Versailles and Paris, where he grew up. A superficial similarity does exist between their street plans, but J.L. Sibley Jennings, Jr., a supervisory architect with the Department of Justice, made his own study, published in the Library of Congress *Quarterly* in 1979, in which he makes a convincing case that L'Enfant was more interested in creating something unique and designing a city that blended well with its climate and topography. It's not as simple as noticing a pattern of radial streets in some northern European cities and concluding these were L'Enfant's inspirations.[13]

Thomas Jefferson left a record of the city plans he sent to L'Enfant for reference, and this has long been assumed to be a list of L'Enfant's inspirations—mostly northern European cities. Jennings discovered that

Jefferson's note indicates only the plans *that he had available to send,* not what L'Enfant was really looking for. L'Enfant had specifically requested city plans for mostly southern cities such as Madrid, Naples, Venice, Genoa, and Florence. This implies he wanted to consider how town planners in similar climates had capitalized on light and shade and cooling breezes. Jennings thinks Madrid, with its multitude of open air plazas and wide boulevards and fountains, is most like the city of L'Enfant's vision.

Also essential to L'Enfant's vision was his understanding that the human eye cannot appreciate the beauty of anything that is too far away, a consideration we also encountered in Bartholdi's ideas for the Statue of Liberty. The avenues of D.C. were not long and straight in L'Enfant's plan. On the contrary, travel along the avenues of L'Enfant's city would have been interrupted regularly with pleasing visual and airy surprises. Bends in the street and an abundance of public squares would have given the impression that around every corner was another architectural treat: a park opening here, a church appearing there, a fountain around the next bend. He spent weeks carefully studying the natural terrain in the federal district in order to naturally incorporate the landscape into the city structure.

The symbolic centerpiece of L'Enfant's plan for the capital was what he called the "People's House," where the elected members of Congress would meet (later to be called the Capitol, Jefferson's preferred term). He placed it on Jenkins Heights, a hill he described as "a pedestal waiting for a Superstructure."[14] He wanted a waterfall to cascade down from the Congress House and run into the canals that would be created out of the former Tiber Creek, connecting the area to the Potomac river trade. The corridor connecting the President's House to the People's House was to be a thriving commercial district. The passage connecting the People's House with the Washington Monument (which L'Enfant envisioned as a standard equestrian statue), today the National Mall, was meant to be his "grandest avenue in a city full of grand avenues."[15]

A right triangle was formed by three key points—the White House, the Capitol, and the Washington Monument—and above and beyond this triangle L'Enfant distributed 15 "round points" or public squares, each with a fountain or a statue to a future hero. He envisioned inhabitants from each of the 15 states moving into these neighborhoods, and the round points, with their refreshing features, were meant to be conducive meeting places for the neighbors. The monuments and important buildings in the city were connected by avenues named after the states radiating from these points, and a grid of north, south, east, and west streets was then placed over top. L'Enfant keenly considered that the populations of both the city and the nation were about to expand, and his grandly scaled city took this future growth into account.

It would have been a beautiful city, unique to the world. But it was not to be. In fact, the very boldness of L'Enfant's vision together with his blind determination to see it realized without deviation were the main reasons behind his clash with the commission that ultimately led to his removal from the job. Those appointed to be responsible for the actual construction and sales were understandably concerned about L'Enfant's insistence for delays to perfect his coordinated design, causing strife among the developers, contractors, and construction crews. They all felt pressured by the mandate to design and build, not just any city, but an incredible city, from scratch, in less than 10 years. Despite their panicky complaints, in hindsight, what L'Enfant was able to accomplish in just a few months is remarkable. He came on the job in March 1791, and showed the preliminary designs to Washington in June to get approval for the general direction. By August, Washington approved the revised plans. A copy of these plans is what is now believed to be in the Library of Congress, proving there were certainly copies around, and no one had to reproduce them from memory.

But by October, unfortunately, L'Enfant was still insisting the plan was not yet ready to be published, and the commissioners missed an important fundraiser. As the appointed overseer of the commission, Thomas Jefferson made it clear from the beginning that he preferred a very simple plan of a square gridded city similar to Philadelphia or Annapolis. An accomplished architect in his own right, Jefferson was not a fan of the grand scale of L'Enfant's vision, believing something more modest would better reflect the new American republic. The commissioners also complained of the immense sizes and distances in L'Enfant's plan, calling them better suited for monarchies than republics, but L'Enfant would not listen to anyone else's ideas.

At the height of this highly volatile situation L'Enfant tore down a house being built by Dan Carroll, nephew of the commissioner by the same name, who had begun construction amidst the confusion on the site that L'Enfant intended for his People's House. This error in judgment and his temper were the excuses cited to explain his eventual dismissal or resignation in the official version of events as recorded by the planning commission, certainly not an unbiased account. What actually happened remains unclear, but for some reason Washington suddenly ceased defending L'Enfant. In March 1792, following Washington's instructions, Thomas Jefferson sent L'Enfant a letter saying his services would no longer be needed. He was never again welcomed in Washington's presence. Jennings deduced that this snub resulted from L'Enfant somehow insulting Washington during their last-ditch efforts to negotiate the differences between L'Enfant and the commission.

As soon as L'Enfant discovered that his plan had been given over to Andrew Ellicott for finishing, he realized someone on the commission had betrayed him. Though everyone described the changes Ellicott made to the plan in terms of straightening, neatening, simplifying, practical, and welcome, L'Enfant vehemently disagreed. In a meeting with Washington's personal assistant, Tobias Lear, and in a subsequent letter to Washington, L'Enfant raged that his work had been "unmercifully spoiled and altered from the original plan to a degree indeed evidently tending to disgrace me and ridicule the very undertaking."[16] To understand why he became so upset over seemingly minor changes, a deeper appreciation of L'Enfant's intentions is required. The disregard for his deliberate integration of the terrain, the visual delight of the neighborhoods, and his allowances for the future growth make it understandable that he flew into a rage. In the interest of hurriedly completing a neatened plan for distribution to potential land buyers all these niceties fell by the wayside. Others have theorized that L'Enfant had embedded secret and sacred geometry into his design, and these measurements were altered significantly by Ellicott's straightenings. More obviously, L'Enfant had been looking forward to establishing his place in history with this magnum opus and was incensed to see Ellicott's name replacing his on the map.

Ellicott did not have L'Enfant's artistic and architectural background, and seems to have under-appreciated L'Enfant's visions of grandeur and his ideas about how the human perception is affected over vast distances. His long, straightened avenues may look tidy on paper, but they were ugly and monotonous in reality, as everything after a certain point turns fuzzy and gray to human perception. Ellicott also simplified L'Enfant's design by deleting more than half of the proposed public squares. L'Enfant never made any money from his plan and

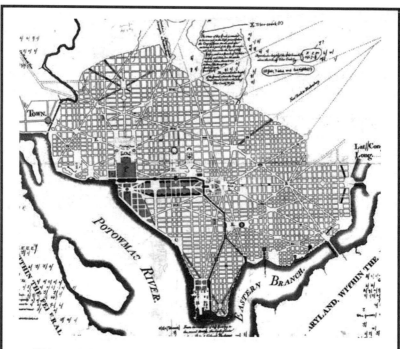

(This page) Peter Charles L'Enfant's 1791 "Plan of the city intended for the permanent seat of the government of the United States." Library of Congress. (Opposing page) Andrew Ellicott's 1792 "Plan of the city of Washington in the territory of Columbia." A careful comparison of Ellicott's map with L'Enfant's map reveals many changes that appear subtle on paper, but would create quite a different experience for the man on the street. Library of Congress.

spent the remainder of his years fading into obscure poverty, trying to win back the recognition he deserved. He lived on the farm of a friend in Maryland, where he was buried in 1825, virtually forgotten. The rediscovery of his input into the city plan by the renovation committees at the turn of the next century led to the re-interment of his remains with great pomp and ceremony at Arlington National Cemetery in 1909. On the outside of his tomb is an engraving of one of the earliest maps of the city—ironically one that Ellicott already altered.

The Speculation on the Symbolism

We are now leaving the historical and mostly documentable section and entering the more speculative regions about the design of the capital of our nation. Although some of the historical conclusions are also necessarily based on

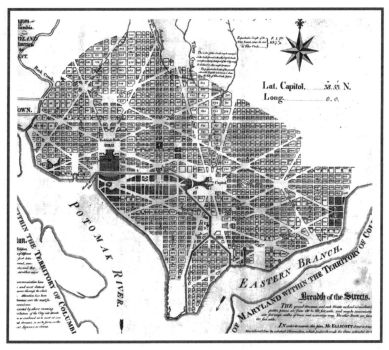

speculation due to missing data, they are pieced together reasonably by historical detectives who look for patterns, the backgrounds of the creators, and corroborating circumstantial evidence. Some of the conclusions we can make in this section about symbolism are just as strong in that regard, if not stronger, than those being made by the mainstream historians on who built the city. Others are less strong, especially in my assessment, lacking as I am in the years of specialization required to see the correlations. We will quote directly from some of the researchers who I think are on to something in their search for significant symbolism in the street plans of Washington, D.C. Even when they contradict one another we will leave each theory presented as is for the reader to pursue or dismiss. Geometers, land surveyors, alchemists, astrologers, and students of esoteric and ancient symbology will get the most out of the following section, but I hope it will also present interesting reading and launching points for more research by those less acquainted with these areas. Please remember: The theories of each of these researchers fill at least one and often several books each, and we are curtailed by space here to present to you only the most basic of thumbnail sketches.

David Ovason: Astrology and Virgo

David is a personal friend and has helped me considerably with my own research projects. I especially admire his exacting investigative technique and his facility with five or six languages, giving him the ability to read primary sources in their original. He has spent probably years' worth of time in the Library of Congress and other archives studying these records to supplement his conclusions. He is a trained and skilled astrologer and a longtime student of the hermetic mystery schools, and probably the best-qualified writer on the market to ascertain these symbols in Washington, D.C.

Ovason makes three central points in *The Secret Architecture of Our Nation's Capital* pertinent to our short discussion:

1. Both L'Enfant and Ellicott were probably Freemasons.
2. Someone with astrological knowledge helped select the dates for the official cornerstone laying ceremonies that marked the beginnings of all the important structures in D.C.
3. The right triangle that L'Enfant devised as the centerpiece of his city—the one connecting the White House, the Capitol, and the Washington Monument—was deliberately situated to mirror the stellar triangle that encompasses the constellation of Virgo.

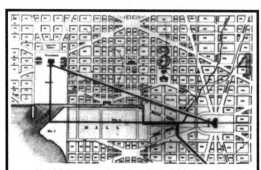

David Ovason says that L'Enfant placed on his earliest map of the city a right-angled triangle, with the 90-degree angle on the Washington Monument and the hypotenuse running down Pennsylvania Avenue, joining the White House with the Capitol. Reproduced with permission from *The Secret Architecture of Our Nation's Capital* by David Ovason.

First of all, the subtitle of Ovason's book: *The Masons and the Building of Washington, DC.* Though the abundance of Masons whose names pop up all over the history of the capital—from its inception right on through the 19th and 20th centuries—is undeniable, Ovason, for one, does not see any secret significance in that fact. Instead, he sees a group of the most highly skilled and qualified people for the many jobs of designing and constructing and surveying necessary to build a city. That many of them happened to be Freemasons does not to him imply that it was a Masonic undertaking:

> I am not for one moment suggesting that it was "the Masons who built Washington, D.C.," or that Masons' Lodges ever had a coordinated, formulated plan to influence the growth of the city in any way.... I am claiming merely that Washington, D.C. was designed and built on Christian hermetic principles derived from, or linked with, ancient cosmological ideas. In exploring this truth, I observe that some of the people involved in the building of the city, besides being architects, planners and artists, happened also to be Masons. I am reasonably sure that in just about every case these individuals were also committed Christians. It would be patently absurd (if only because it is so obvious) for me to labor the point that Washington, D.C. was built by Christians.[17]

I agree with brother David on this point, and therefore will not dwell on the list of names of important D.C. contributors who were also Masons. Lists of verifiable Masons can be found readily enough on the more reputable Masonic Websites,[18] where they are understandably proud of their members who were chosen for jobs of significance based on their accomplishments and merit. The implication that either L'Enfant or Ellicott were members of the Craft is slightly more important, however, because, if it could be proven, it would help strengthen the argument for intentionality in some of the significant angles interpreted in the street layout. But of course, *even if they were not Masons* they could have also intended these same deeper symbolic interpretations in their design. Sacred geometry is not exclusive to the Freemasons; it's just that Masons tend to be more familiar with and prone to use arcane symbolism than the average person.

Many Masonic historians argue that, because there is no record of a L'Enfant or Ellicott initiation, there is no proof that they were Masons. Ovason is fully convinced, however, that L'Enfant was a Mason, based on a careful assessment of his life and works. He also reminds us that L'Enfant served as an officer in the Revolutionary War, and many military lodge records were lost for fairly obvious reasons. His conviction that Ellicott was a Mason is based to some extent on the latter's presence at the Masonic ceremony when the first boundary stone was laid, though he admits no lodge records have as yet been found to prove Ellicott's membership, either.

The same situation of confusion applies to the maps. Barring any new discoveries, it seems likely there will always be contention over which one of these two, Ellicott or L'Enfant, contributed exactly what to the final design. Ovason tends to favor what is known as Ellicott's map. Ellicott himself apparently claimed to have set the precise angle of Pennsylvania Avenue,[19] but, of course, Washington was also said to have personally picked the site of the President's House, and the right angle triangle is already clearly indicated on L'Enfant's map. It was also L'Enfant's idea to create a city with diagonal streets radiating from "round points," making it possible to trace so many triangles and other geometric shapes all over the map. Ovason sees this as L'Enfant's tribute to the triangle and a reminder of "the tripart man: the thinking, feeling and willing within the human being."[20] Ovason's contention is that either Washington or Ellicott had, by setting the exact angle of Pennsylvania Avenue, worked into the map of Washington, D.C., a triangle that reflected a stellar triangle linked with the three first-magnitude stars that enclose most of the constellation Virgo, which we will return to in a moment.

Another of Ovason's key points is that someone with astrological knowledge picked the dates for many of the cornerstone laying ceremonies around the city. Back then astrology was still considered a sister science to astronomy and worthy of study by the best of educated men.[21] Having made a lifelong study of astrology myself, I appreciate the significance of the correlations Ovason found in the charts he cast for the various beginnings of Washington, D.C., but many Masonic historians today have a hard time with these ideas. Of course, few people today have the necessary intellectual training in astrology and related orientation theory to really appreciate what Ovason's theory claims. Although some Masonic historians state that astrology is not used officially in the Masonic ceremonies or rituals, that does not rule out that much of their symbolism is astrologically based or that astrology is used by individual members or lodges.

After making every effort to reestablish the precise moment of these rituals by reference to contemporary records, Ovason showed that the timing of the cornerstone ceremonies in the foundation rituals appears to have been determined astrologically. He argues that, because these foundations were laid by

Masons, then at least one or two Masons must have been involved in this use of horoscopy, if only to effect these historically important orientations. Realizing a number of key coincidences in the most important charts, Ovason concluded that these events were timed to coordinate a resonance with Virgo. The fact that original horoscopes for these events have not survived does not imply that the Masons are keeping such data secret, says Ovason. Many non-official documents relating to the founding of Washington, D.C. have been lost, but, in this case, little need would have been felt to preserve horoscopic records, of little interest to any but specialists.

Students of astrology may agree with Ovason that "the magical thing about the founding of the city, the White House, and the Capitol is that they're all tied together by this 23 degrees of Virgo."[22] The coincidence of these patterns in the sign Virgo seemed to Ovason to be beyond the confines of mere chance. Here are the similarities in several charts for important foundations in Washington, D.C.:

△ The first boundary stone for the district was laid at 3:30 p.m. on April 15, 1791. The planet Jupiter (the planet of beneficence) was in 23 degrees of Virgo.

△ The White House cornerstone was laid at noon on October 13, 1792. The moon and the Dragon's Head (the point where the orbit of the sun intersects the orbit of the moon, also thought to be a point of beneficence) were in 23 degrees Virgo.

△ The Capitol cornerstone was laid by George Washington sometime in mid-afternoon on September 18, 1793. The Sun was in 24 degrees Virgo, and Mercury and the Dragon's Head were also in Virgo.

△ The foundation stone for the Washington Monument was laid at noon on July 4, 1848. The Moon and the Dragon's Head were in Virgo.

△ The cornerstone for the Washington Monument—the ceremony for which took place when post-Civil War resumption of construction began—was laid on August 7, 1880, at 10:59 a.m. The Moon, Mars, and Uranus were all in Virgo. The one minute to 11 o'clock may have been a nod to the rising of Spica, the star that represents the sheaf of wheat in the constellation of Virgo.[23]

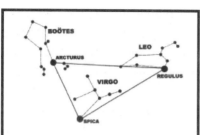

Ovason's theory extends L'Enfant's triangle to the skies, seeing almost the same right-angled triangle traced around the constellation Virgo. The stars of the Virgoan Triangle correspond with the L'Enfant triad as follows: Arcturus falls on the White House, Regulus on the Capitol, and Spica on the Washington Monument. Reproduced with permission from *The Secret Architecture of Our Nation's Capital* by David Ovason.

Freemasons have very publicly performed cornerstone-laying ceremonies to mark the start of construction on hundreds of buildings, bridges, monuments, and even churches throughout the country. On one level of interpretation the elements used in these ceremonies have symbolic meanings: Corn stands for nourishment, the oil stands for joy, and the wine for refreshment. On another level, however, the cornerstone-laying ceremonies are intended to create sympathetic harmony with the natural order. Ovason describes the spiritual background of the cornerstone ceremonials, tracing their origins as far back as temple-building in ancient Egypt. He concludes that these ceremonies are concerned with establishing a resonance between heaven and earth. Builders of cities, churches, and cathedrals would strive to establish orientation with a particular fixed star, in the belief that the cosmic powers invested in that star would empower and spiritually charge the building. In the ancient world, such rituals were designed to permit spiritual agencies to operate seminally on the material plane. As Ovason puts it, "A city which is laid out in such a way that it is in harmony with the heavens is a city in perpetual prayer. It is a city built on the recognition that every human activity is in need of the sanctification of the spiritual world, of which the symbol is the light of the living stars."[24]

The timing of the charts and the alignment of Pennsylvania Avenue with the stellar triangle are not the only links between Virgo and the capital. There are also countless artistic references to Virgo throughout the city in paintings, statues, and zodiacs. Calling D.C. a city of the stars, Ovason has catalogued more than 1,000 zodiacal and planetary symbols in Washington, D.C. There are at least 29 zodiacs in important buildings; one building alone has more than 21 individual zodiacs inside it. Other major American cities contain only a few zodiacs in public art, sometimes none.

Many of the references to Virgo were added during the City Beautiful movement at the beginning of the 20th century, when the tradition for Virgo symbolism was continued in several architectural details. Ovason doubts that anyone involved in the McMillan Plan realized that they were revealing the ancient mysteries inherent in the original building of Washington, D.C., but he believes at least someone must have been familiar with esoteric symbolism. He goes on to wonder whether either L'Enfant or Ellicott realized the connections to Virgo that their designs entailed: "[T]his program of arcane symbolism, which is perhaps the finest in the Western world, was not one visualized by L'Enfant or Ellicott. It was, however, made possible by the basic structures which these two great men provided at the heart of the city."[25]

Ovason describes a stellar moment that stargazers can appreciate as the annual solar mystery of Washington, D.C. It is best experienced between the 10th and the 12th of August and is best viewed from the top of the second tier of steps leading up to the West Front of the Capitol building. The best position is that to the north, from where you can gaze directly down Pennsylvania Avenue toward the White House. At that time of the year, the sun will set *directly* over the horizon, contiguously with the extended line of Pennsylvania Avenue. After sunset, and as the sky darkens, three stars begin to glow in the skies above the White House. Spica, Arcturus, and Regulus pick out in the darkening night sky a large right-angled triangle: The apex, marked by Regulus, hovers above the White House. The triangular pattern of this group of stars is reflected exactly in the shape of the Federal Triangle, with Pennsylvania Avenue as the hypotenuse. The Federal Triangle is a residue of the original map-making, whereby the plan of the three major public buildings, the White House, Capitol, and Washington Monument, was intended to reflect the plan in the skies. Neither the White House nor the Monument were built where the original designers intended, however, which is why Ovason now refers the stellar triangle to the Federal Triangle, rather than to the three major public buildings. Ovason, the first to reveal this solar-stellar orientation, claims that this magic of light links the design of Washington, D.C. with the ancient mysteries, wherein it was taught that every building on earth, from city to temple, should be designed to reflect meaningfully the hidden activities of the spiritual world.

Charles Westbrook: Creating Shapes From the Angles

Charles Westbrook deserves the largest share of credit for the explosion of theories using geometric shapes in Washington, D.C. to prove intentionality of its designers for some kind of secret plan. Baigent and Leigh in their 1989 *The Temple and the Lodge* pre-date his claims, but they merely suggested an octagon templar cross around the White House and the Capitol.[26] There was also material on the square and compass design around the Capitol published previously in Masonic literature. Westbrook's 1990 book, *The Talisman of the United States*, seems to be the first to go into great detail with claims that the streets of D.C. were an intricate web of intentionally placed geometric designs. Though not driven as much by an anti-Masonic agenda as many of those who have copied his research and diagrams, Westbrook does believe that the street designs of Washington, D.C. prove a conspiracy to deliberately embed occult symbols and astronomical calendrical sight lines on the ground.

Charles L. Westbrook, Jr., is a former professor of East Carolina University, a software programmer, and a mechanical and electrical engineer who has made a study of comparative religion, art, design, and American history. He proudly disclaims that he is not a Freemason, nor a member of any political group or religion. I was intrigued by the long subtitle of his 1990 self-published book, *America's Oldest Secret, The Mysterious Street Lines of Washington, DC, Signature of the Invisible Brotherhood,* and was the first radio show host in the country to invite him on the air to talk about it. Westbrook has since expanded his theories published in newsletters and on the Internet and is working on a fictionalized retelling of his work entitled *The Kabalyon Key*. His novel promises to further connect his research into the mystic intentionality of the design of Washington, D.C. to the city plans of Rome, Edinburgh, Jerusalem, and more.[27] Westbrook claims to own "unique family documents on the creation of the Washington Monument and other papers related to the history of Virginia and North Carolina," adding that he "grew up in a house where this stuff was discussed around the kitchen table."[28]

Central to Westbrook's thesis are the angles of certain streets, which he says are purposely designed to act as astronomical calendars. Westbrook also diminishes the input of L'Enfant on the design, but, unlike Ovason, Westbrook looks further back *behind* L'Enfant for the mysterious designers who must have preceded him. The most remarkable angles in Westbrook's theory are ones that enable an astronomer to predict eclipses, solstices, and equinoxes by watching the stars rise and set over certain natural landforms. Accurately predicting the equinoxes and solstices was a key to advancing civilization because it enabled early man to better plan and improve his agricultural skills. But with the long periods of time required to create such accurate landscape clocks, Westbrook figures someone in this vicinity must have been mapping out potential site lines as early as 1735—or 19 years before L'Enfant was born.

"There is a good possibility that there is another and older Founding Father involved with the development of the city plan for Washington, D.C.," said Westbrook in one of his newsletters.[29] Because the 56- to 57-year cycle of eclipses would have to be observed at least twice to determine its accuracy, he concludes that, "someone may have been working on the city plan for Washington, DC as early as 1679."[30] To support this idea, Westbrook points to some early plans of the towns that were later incorporated into the District of Columbia (Carrollsburg, Hamburg, Alexandria, and Georgetown surveyed between 1712 and 1755) and notes that "all include aspects of the basic angular street pattern for the future plan for Washington."[31]

Westbrook also points to Thomas Jefferson as the one who knew about these earlier attempts at sacred landscaping and who pushed them into the design for the nation's capital. He considers L'Enfant as "more or less a draftsman for Jefferson."[32] Both George Washington and Thomas Jefferson were interested in the origins and mystical beliefs of the First Peoples. The entryway to Monticello was known as "Indian Hall" for all the artifacts Jefferson had collected and displayed there. Being from the area, and active in surveying, it is quite likely that Washington had heard the legends that the Algonquin Indians used to hold tribal councils at the foot of Jenkins Heights, that grand hill that L'Enfant reserved for his Congress House, or his Superstructure. Other local legends about this district involve the Englishman Francis Pope who owned Jenkins Heights in the 1660s. Perhaps as a play on his own last name, Pope called the area "Rome," and the creek that ran nearby the "Tiber." Later retellings of Pope's ownership were embellished to include a vision Pope allegedly had for this hill, where in the future, a city more grand than ancient Rome would be built, enabling peaceful governance for all the nation.

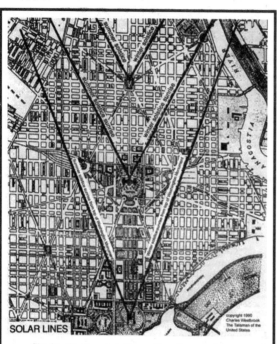

SOLAR LINES

Charles Westbrook believes the city map is a type of planisphere, allowing for solar and moon alignments of streets. This illustration shows the solar alignment pattern in the streets of Washington as measured from the center of the Earth. Permission granted, copyright 1990, Charles Westbrook, from *Talisman of the United States.*

Most important to Westbrook is the idea that the city map is a "type of planisphere," allowing for "solar and moon alignments of streets set as if measured from the center of the Earth, not from the ground level at Washington, DC."[33] This alignment is not merely wishful thinking, he says: "This sun/moon alignment is not a theory—as with the other 'Rorschach symbolism'—it is a measurable fact."[34] (See the illustration.) He also believes the alleged pentagram above the White House that we will discuss later has more to do with "the sigil for Jerusalem and the old pilgrimage routes for Rome, than any sort of devil worship."[35]

I asked Charles Westbrook to provide me with a summary indicating the observations that originated with him. By reprinting this summary here, I am not endorsing all these conclusions, and, in fact, must point out that other researchers have seriously questioned his measurements. I am not a mathematician, an architect, or a surveyor; I am a student of symbology. In symbology, we look for patterns, but are also wary of coincidences. My hope is to present all of these speculative researchers in their best light so that those more qualified than I can then dig into their theories and disprove what can be disproved, leaving us with the improvable mysteries to ponder.

Summary of Claims That Originated With Charles Westbrook

Most important to Westbrook's theory is his belief that the "L'Enfant Plan" is Jefferson's original design concept. Jefferson worked for George Washington in the supervision of the city plan before, during, and after L'Enfant was fired. According to Westbrook, Jefferson chose the site for the city, not Washington. Jefferson also supervised the design elements for the White House, the Capitol, and the Washington Monument, a supervision that extended into his presidency and continued afterward.

In *The Talisman of the United States,* Westbrook was the first to make the following claims:

1. The streets of Washington are laid in patterns of a Star of David east of the Capitol; a pentagram north of the White House; a pentagram east of the Capitol; and a pentagram encompassing the Capitol and the Mall.

2. The square and compass design west of the Capitol is related to the compass and level design of the Vatican Complex. (Westbrook was not the first to claim Maryland and Pennsylvania avenues west of the Capitol resemble the compass design of the Freemasons.)

3. A Kabbalistic Sephiroth Tree and Tarot card arrangement can be seen extending across the National Mall to Arlington Cemetery.

4. There is a measurable astronomical explanation for the design of the city, including solstice and moonrise information, and a 23.5-degree relationship to the tilt of the earth, an axis mundi, and the procession of the zodiac. The solstice and major and minor moon alignment of streets east of the Capitol lay out the city plan as a type of planisphere, stressing that these alignments are set as if measured from the center of the Earth, not from the ground level. (His new book, *The Kabalyon Key,* describes key locations in the city that use this alignment to invoke a shamanic spiritual awakening.)

5. The symbolism in the plan is associated with Edward Savage's "Washington Family Portrait" and the armillary sphere, compass, and map found in the portrait.

6. The sun and moon arrangement of the street east of the Capitol mirrors the astronomical alignment of the street plan for Rome.

7. The pentagram arrangement of Rome suggests a relationship between Rome and Washington. The Senate Park Commission of 1901 was aware of this relationship between the two cities and had as one of their redesign proposals one that followed the city plan for Rome.

8. The plan of Washington is associated with the Shield of the Trinity, a type of Kabbalistic sigil for the Christian god used during the Middle Ages in Europe.

9. There is a Society of Cincinnati connection to the design of Washington.

10. The plan for Washington, D.C. is related to the fabled Priory of Sion and the coded map of the Rennes region in France, as told in *Holy Blood, Holy Grail.*

11. The design of Washington, D.C. is connected to the astronomical alignments of the Temple Mount and the physical plan for Jerusalem.

12. The "legs of the compass" were aligned with the 1791 setting of the star Sirius. Since the publication of *Talisman,* however, Westbrook has disclaimed this idea: "It's not the reason the streets are laid out as they are in my opinion. It's not something I continued to investigate, although I saw a possible relationship in the alignment of the streets at one time."[36] Nevertheless this connection is repeated by numerous fundamentalist-conspiratorialists who enjoy any mention of the star Sirius for another opportunity to claim the founders were practicing Egyptian or Satanic magic.

Although I believe Charles Westbrook's inventory of coincidences indicates intentionality on the part of at least one city planner along the way, most of the work of the speculators in this section would be dismissed by mainstream academics without examination. I would like to see the discussion opened to other trained specialists who can verify the facts and figures so we can then weigh the conclusions extrapolated from their premises. But because "looks like" is "close enough" for most fundamentalist-conspiratorialists, the diagrams created by Westbrook have been seized upon and repeated all over the Web as proof that Washington, D.C. was designed by Satan-worshipping Illuminati Masons.

When "Close Enough" Is Not Good Enough

Unfortunately, this book will not be sufficient to convince many fundamentalist-conspiratorialists that the planners of Washington, D.C. were not intent on hiding evil symbols in the street map of our capital. When people already have their minds made up, they will often see similar symbols as "close enough" to serve as proof for their convictions. They are already convinced that the Masons are evil (for fallacious reasons discussed further in Chapter 8) and that Masons controlled the design of the city, an illogical assumption we addressed earlier in this chapter.

The angles of the streets of D.C. do indeed suggest some interesting symbols, all of which could be interpreted in positive ways, if any of them were intended to be interpreted at all. In a city replete with angles connecting highly significant buildings and monuments, anyone searching for clues to support a preconceived notion will find them. Although there is no official documentation to indicate that any of these patterns was placed there intentionally, I still find it thrilling to examine the geometrical beauty in some of these symbols—even more so if they were the result of coincidence. The researchers I chose to highlight in this section measured five- and six-pointed stars, the Masonic square and compasses, the vesica piscis, the pyramid and eye in the triangle, and the Kabbalistic Tree of Life, and I believe these quantifications are worthy of further study.

I'm not convinced that the unfinished and irregular pentagram in the streets north of the White House was placed there intentionally, but, if it was, it was certainly not put there because the designer was a Satan worshipper trying to put a hex on the White House. More than any other symbol, the one that the fundamentalist-conspiratorialists point to with fear is this incomplete, inverted, irregular pentagram. Because of superficial research they have concluded the inverted pentagram always means Satan, falling into that "one level of interpretation" trap. I tend to believe this incomplete and irregular pentagram is coincidental rather than intentional, mainly because when working with geometric symbols in magic, one should be careful to keep the angle measurements and the line connections complete and exact. Otherwise the magic is useless. But because this symbol is relatively easy to spot even on a contemporary map of D.C. (and because the star is upside down), there are countless Websites showing it filled in with a picture of the alleged Satanic goat head hovering over the President's House.

Even further far-fetched are some of these other symbols that fundamentalist-conspiratorialists have traced in the D.C. map in their attempt to prove that the city was planned by Satanists:

△ An owl can be spotted in the landscaping around the Capitol and Mall, which they claim is in honor of the mascot of the secretive Bohemian Grove attendees.

△ Bunny ears with a stick figure is created from the angles usually identified as the Mason's compasses (Maryland and Pennsylvania avenues radiating west of the Capitol), and fundamentalist-conspiratorialists say this is an ancient way of depicting the Devil.

△ The dreaded 666 is formed in the landscaping of the traffic circles north of the White House.

△ Those who are under the impression that 13 is somehow a Satanic number find great significance in the 13 blocks separating the White House and the headquarters for the Scottish Rite Freemasonry (depending on which streets you decide to include in the count).[37]

Fundamentalist-conspiratorialists have a frame around their vision that interprets most of what they see as Satanic. This frame explains why they conclude these suggested symbols were placed in the map by Illuminati Masons so that the leaders of our country could be manipulated by Satan. If Dan Brown's next book focuses on the secrecy of the Freemasons (as it is rumored to) and implies they hid occult symbols in Washington, D.C., it will only add to this confusion. It will surely unleash an avalanche of unsubstantiated speculation and connecting-the-dots research that is interpreted through fear. With our speculation in this book, we have instead attempted to remain grounded in the historical use and humanistic psychological interpretation of these symbols.

Chris Hardaker: A Funny Thing Happened on the Way to the Inauguration

Chris Hardaker is just the kind of person we need to step forward and give some thought to these mysteries of Washington, D.C. Trained as an archeologist specializing in the prehistoric southwest cultures of the Anasazi and Hohokam (see his "The Hexagon, The Solstice And The Kiva," posted online), Hardaker was looking for clues to indicate the applicability of classical geometry in prehistoric southwestern Pueblo cultures. He thought sacred geometry might be a potential tool for archaeological reconstructions of their town planning, architecture, and symbols. While he was working on his master's degree, his committee chairman suggested he test his theory on a more contemporary culture. Perhaps he could find evidence that the builders of a modern city had incorporated intentional geometrical symbolism. They chose Washington, D.C. for the subject of their test, not because they knew of any of this controversy, but for more practical reasons. They figured it was a planned city and would have a lot of historical documentation available about its plan that Hardaker could sift through to find his evidence. His chairman said it was all about methodology, regardless if anything was found. If he found proof that there was any sacred/classical geometry used in the planning of D.C., it would strengthen the value of his continuing to look for it among the ancient cultures of America.

I first heard from Chris Hardaker back in 1992, apparently when he was doing the research on this theory. He wrote to me after reading my 1989 book, *America's Secret Destiny,* and wanted to correspond about the reverse of the Great Seal. Unfortunately, my radio show schedule kept me fully occupied at that time, and our correspondence was very brief. To my great advantage, he re-contacted me in the summer of 2007 after seeing me in the documentary film called *Riddles in Stone,* and this time he sent me a copy of his by-now-completed, but still unpublished, paper, "The Seal and the City: Or a Funny Thing Happened on the Way to the Inauguration." In a most entertaining and informative style, Hardaker relates his journey of discovery and, in the process, describes how an academic would approach the question of intentionality in the symbols of the D.C. map.

Hardaker didn't enter into his investigation with any idea he would find anything at all. Almost immediately, however, he saw what appeared to be a pyramid in the Mall jumping out at him from the 1792 Ellicott plan. (See the illustration.)

As we will review in further detail later, when you turn the map on its side so that East is at the top, you can better appreciate the direction in which L'Enfant may have envisioned his city. We know he considered Congress House as the center of his city, and many of the major avenues were to originate there. He oriented this key symbolic element so that it pointed east to the light of the rising sun, and also facing the neighborhoods where he envisioned

The pyramid and the eye in the National Mall as seen by Chris Hardaker. Thirteen blocks long with an Eye of God associated with the Capitol Rotunda. On the modern map, the "Eye" is located at the Western Terrace, the present site of the presidential inauguration. Courtesy of Chris Hardaker, *EarthMeasure.com.*

many of the average people would live, thriving in the commercial and residential districts of the city. This eastward-facing symbolism was erased when Ellicott's revision turned the Capitol building around to face the west and the Washington Monument.

Hardaker discovered that when you turn the map of D.C. on its side this way, the triangles jump out at you. He recognized the way the streets align (with Pennsylvania and Maryland avenues radiating west from the Capitol, down either side of the Mall) could be interpreted as the reverse of the Great Seal, the unfinished pyramid with the eye in the triangle above it. The number of city blocks in this "pyramid" matched the 13 in the Great Seal pyramid. Hardaker says that at the top he noticed "the hint of the triangle containing the 'eye': three points expressed on the ground as the Peace memorial, Garfield's statue, and the Capitol's Rotunda."[38] After using his protractor to measure the angle of this pyramid on the map, he found it to be within 2 degrees of the base angle of the pyramid on the back of the one-dollar bill. This was enough to warrant further study.

He educated himself on the history of the planning of Washington, D.C., and interviewed Masons, architects, and others relevant to the field. None of them wanted to consider the hypothesis that the national seal was deliberately designed into the street plan of the national capital. Nowhere in the official documentation on the history of the city did he find anything more meaningful to indicate intentionality. More important in some ways to Hardaker was his conclusion that a designer with L'Enfant's professional background would not normally have been inclined to include symbols in his street plans. But then he discovered the means by which he could "cut the umbilical cord," as he called it, between L'Enfant and the city once and for all. Sibley Jennings's discoveries in the Library of Congress archives about L'Enfant's earliest designs led Hardaker to question the modern assumption that the city is *essentially* L'Enfant's design. In reality, the changes Ellicott made to L'Enfant's plan, which may have appeared minute, so radically altered L'Enfant's vision that it led to his de facto resignation in disgust. It also created a completely different city, especially in the three-dimensional experience.

With the only person with some formal training and experience in city planning eliminated from the project, Hardaker was better able to imagine the amateurs—George Washington or other members of the commission who were not tied into the precedence and history of city planning—suggesting the addition of symbols into the design. Maybe that's why the streets were straightened. Following this line of reasoning, it could explain why Washington was so insulted during the resignation/firing arguments that he refused to speak to L'Enfant ever again. Perhaps it was Washington himself who requested the changes that Ellicott made. When L'Enfant said the changes "unmercifully spoiled" his design, and tended to "ridicule the very undertaking,"[39] maybe he was insulting Washington rather than Ellicott. Because many of Washington's diaries from this time period are missing, we may never know.

Keeping in mind that it may have been *amateurs* who decided to slip in a deliberate symbol to the street map, Hardaker decided it was okay to use that "precious scientific device ignorantly referred to as 'connecting the dots'"[40] and test his sacred geometry theory. This specific pyramid shape is generated by the vesica piscis, a symbol used throughout history that is related to themes of fishes, Jesus Christ, and the goddess. It frequently appears as two intersecting circles, though more often the almond-shaped (or vaginal-shaped) opening that is created where they overlap is seen alone. The space formed by overlapping two perfect circles encloses a sacred object. Hardaker focused on the map of the modern Capitol grounds. As he explained:

> I found that the Peace Memorial and the statues for Marshall and Garfield were equidistant, forming a 60° triangle. Exploring further, I used the shared distance as a radius with the Marshall statue as a center and discovered that the other side of the circle fell at the base of the eastern steps. It also corresponded to a pair of corners comprising the base platform on which the Capitol was built. The next logical step was to construct another circle with the same radius, but this time using the eastern steps as the center; the construct is a device traditionally known as a vesica piscis. Here again, the circle skirts the corners of the foundation of the Capitol's platform just east of the western terrace, while the Capitol is fully enveloped within the intersecting zone. Finally, I located the middle of the vesica through intersecting lines; their intersection dramatically fell on the top of the Rotunda, the "Freedom" Statue.[41]

Unlike those spinning Westbrook images to suit their own anti-Masonic interpretations, Hardaker is as adamant as I am that none of these symbols can even remotely lead to a conclusion that our Founding Founders were Satanists. Instead, he makes reasoned assumptions that, if anyone deliberately placed that incomplete inverted five-pointed star over the White House, it was done as a symbol of protection. He goes on to show that by drawing a larger pentagon around that star, it is possible to then draw an even larger *upright* pentagram that is encasing the smaller one.

Looking for a simple planned city that might have evidence of the deliberate use of sacred geometry, Hardaker unwittingly selected one where the possibilities are practically endless. As he learned from his Masonic sources, "hints are okay," and "angles matter," concluding from this that incomplete symbols may still have been intentional: "[M]ajor nodes, monuments and statues would serve to investigate the idea of an underlying symbolic dimension to the city."[42] The founders never cut an official die for the pyramid side of our Great Seal, but Hardaker considers that they may have cut the pyramid into the very streets of the capital instead. He reminds us how mythologist Joseph Campbell described our Great Seal: "This is the pyramid of the world, and this is the pyramid of our society, and they are of the same order. This is God's creation, and this is our society."[43]

Rick Campbell: The Great Pyramid and the Keepers of the Plan

Another fortunate new addition to this field is Rick Campbell, who has been working as a surveyor for the past three years. While researching this chapter, I discovered his extensive Website based on his manuscript called "From Pentagram to Pyramids: Masonic and Kabbalistic Symbols in the Washington, D.C. Map."[44] Intrigued by his hypothesis, I invited him to be a guest on *21st Century Radio*. His work will soon be published in book form, making it available to a wider audience that will hopefully include people who can better evaluate it than I can. In the meantime, we invite you to visit his Website for much greater elaboration.

Campbell says he became interested in the idea of symbolism in Washington, D.C., by stumbling across the Internet debate over the pentagram above the White House. Figuring that, if there was one intentional symbol in the street plan, there would probably be others, he dove into the project. His work as a surveyor allowed him to step back in time and imagine how the project might have looked to L'Enfant, Ellicott, or Washington. As he says, the procedures of a construction project have not changed greatly since 1791, disregarding the obvious technical advances in the field. As the surveyors did 200 years ago, they start with the general survey, then make a map, over which is laid the plan, which is then staked out on the ground. Never in his years of operating in this procedure has he seen anyone trying to incorporate intentional symbols into a city plan.

Though not a Mason himself, Campbell spends a great deal of time on the history of the Freemasons, believing that if so many symbols used by Masons were incorporated into the design then it reveals a Masonic influence. From his studies of Masonic scholarship, he has concluded that Masonry "equals the study of philosophy plus the building arts of math, geometry and architecture."[45] He has found great value in an interesting book published in 1896, *Canon: An Exposition of the Pagan Mysteries Perpetuated in the Cabala as the Rule of All the Arts,* written by the mysterious William Stirling. As Campbell summarized: Stirling suggested "that the esoteric doctrine of the cathedral building clergy was synonymous with the ancient mysteries, and that the symbols of the church were disguised symbols of that mystery and the Kabbalah—the prime symbol of which is the Tree of Life."[46] These teachings were often concealed in mathematical formulae that could be decoded by anyone with the knowledge of sacred geometry. Without the right keys to uncover the teachings, they would remain hidden in plain sight. After finding what he believes to be some of these same geometrical indicators in the street plans for Washington, D.C., it became Campbell's contention that the city planners deliberately inserted architectural metaphors within their new town.

Although he is at a serious disadvantage by not being a Mason, I applaud his efforts to try to understand the Craft in order to better understand the symbols. Campbell acknowledges his degree is in philosophy, and that he is presenting his theories for those equally interested in philosophy and puzzles. Unlike most other Websites claiming a Masonic intentionality behind the symbols found in Washington, D.C., Campbell is not doing so from a position of attack.

Campbell asserts that the 1791–92 D.C. planning committee used three esoteric templates for their map: (1) the Kabbalistic Tree of Life; (2) Metatron's Cube (an intricate geometrical symbol thought to have magical properties containing a hexagram within a hexagram and the five Platonic Solids); and (3) the cross-section of the Great Pyramid. The Great Pyramid is symbolic in this sense in that it encodes knowledge that can be decoded. Both the Tree of Life and Metatron's Cube derive from a vesica based geometric exercise of doubling the circle, illustrating what he sees as the ideal template for the D.C. map.

Campbell is dismayed over how many of his contemporaries are misidentifying the maps they use in their symbolic analyses of Washington, D.C. According to Campbell, most people incorrectly see L'Enfant's own second draft map as Ellicott's revisions, meaning that L'Enfant himself made the "straightening" changes to the map before Ellicott's version. For his measurements, Campbell prefers to use the 1818 Robert King map as an early example of the current configuration of the D.C. map, because it is what he called a real features map that doesn't include the proposed landscaping around the Washington Monument as in the Ellicott plan.

Because some of the key points in the overlay of these symbols on the D.C. map remained as swampy marshland until just a few decades ago, Campbell's fourth assertion is the implication of a small group of what he calls the keepers of the plan and symbolism. In order for the future renovations and additions to the city to remain consistent with the grand scheme outlined by these templates, Campbell believes someone is designated to inherit the long-range plan and carry the symbolic intentions forward. One obvious candidate for this role in the early part of the 20th century was John Russell Pope (1874–1937), a non-Mason architect, who designed the monuments making up the last three points on his Tree of Life overlay: the National Archives Building, the House of the Temple, and the Jefferson Memorial.

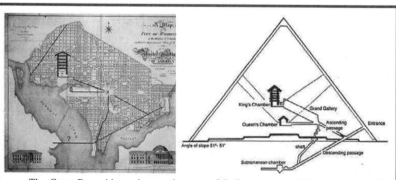

The Great Pyramid overlay on the map of D.C. as seen by Rick Campbell. The peak of the relieving stones is matched with Scott Circle north of the White House, and the junction of the ascending passage and the descending passages is matched with the junction of Pennsylvania and Potomac avenues. Courtesy of Rick Campbell.

Here's how Campbell summarized his theory for this book:

> Not all of what was planned fit on the land that was available then. The last element of the Tree of Life in the map, represented by the Jefferson Memorial, was completed in 1943 on land in the Tidal Basin that did not exist in Washington's day. The planners were forward looking. While the Jefferson Memorial location itself is not shown, the 1792 planning map has Maryland Avenue suggestively aimed at the bottom end of a projected 16th Street (the current location of the Jefferson Memorial), and Virginia Avenue points from the east branch of the Potomac to the yet-to-be-built Washington Monument location. That is, all 11 spheres of the Tree of Life are indicated in the 1792 plan, even the one that wasn't on dry land yet.[47]

Originally intrigued by the possibility of a pentagram north of the White House, Campbell started his investigation there. He noticed immediately that the pentagram is not a regular one, meaning the angles of its five points are not equal to one another, giving it that broad, squat look. He also noticed how New Hampshire Avenue runs down the left side of this pentagram, giving the impression of a triangle that could be traced around the entire "star." Though there is no street that does the same thing down the right side of the pentagram, Campbell decided to trace it in and see what would be revealed. What he found was a triangle of approximately 52 degrees, the same as the angle of the Great Pyramid of Giza. This opened up a whole new realm of possibilities to him:

> The map was intended as a representation of the pyramid cross-section. With the White House as the King's Chamber and the Washington Monument the Queen's Chamber, Potomac Avenue is the Descending Passage and Pennsylvania Avenue is the Ascending Passage and Grand Gallery. (See the illustration.) Note that this does not work well if the Washington Monument is not offset [the monument was officially moved out of alignment with the White House because the ground proved too soft where it was originally intended]. If we accept the notion that elements in the D.C. planning map correlate with features in the Great Pyramid cross-section, one has to ask, what is there under the river that represents the "subterranean

chamber," and what might the D.C. map tell us about features of the pyramid that we don't know about yet?[48]

Why would the planners of D.C. use the Great Pyramid of Giza as a template, you might be asking yourself? Campbell surmises it might have something to do with passing along the secrets of the Great Pyramid itself. He deduces this from the visual representation of the relieving stones of the Great Pyramid that were included in the street plan in 1792 (as seen by the lots between the White House and Scott Circle in the D.C. map). The actual relieving stones above the King's Chamber were not discovered in the real pyramid until 1837 by Howard Vyse, which would mean the creators of the 1792 D.C. plan knew something about the pyramid that no one else in the mainstream knew until 1837. This fits in with Campbell's theory that "Masons are keeping alive a tradition that is not only responsible for the sacred architecture of Gothic cathedrals, but also an inner doctrine of symbolic geometry that they say dates all the way back to the construction of Solomon's Temple."[49]

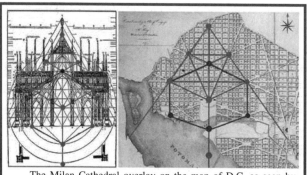

The Milan Cathedral overlay on the map of D.C. as seen by Rick Campbell. Courtesy of Rick Campbell.

Campbell also picked up on an idea from *The Canon* demonstrating how a template of the Tree of Life can be revealed in the Milan Cathedral and other examples of sacred geometry in architecture. He decided to compare the D.C. map to the plan of the Milan Cathedral, described as one of the most direct evidences of the old mystical rule of building. (See the illustration.) He found:

> The *quadratum* form is represented in the D.C. map by the oblique square that is the boundary of the District, and the orthogonal grid of east-west, north-south streets. The *quadratum* represents the floor plan in the cathedral. The same *ad triangulum* design elements show up not only in the D.C. map, but also the

U.S. Great Seal and the Washington National Cathedral, showing what appears to be an operative continuity of content.[50]

Asserting that the design for Washington, D.C. was created to correlate with these various templates, Campbell reminds us that "Masonic architecture is the pinnacle of the Craft it would seem, and since Masonry and the Kabbalah, like parables from the Bible, are symbolic and allegorical, we know that Masonic architecture is *symbolic architecture.*"[51]

Nicholas Mann: Sacred Geometry in L'Enfant's Plan

Nicholas Mann is a student of anthropology, classical philosophies, mythology, and sacred geometry. He has written a number of books on sacred sites in both the United Kingdom and the United States. Similar to David Ovason, who sees an astrologer behind the synchronicities in the astrological charts that can be cast for the various beginnings in the city, Nicholas Mann sees a sacred geometer behind the synchronicities that can be found in the layout of the street plan. He diagrams them in exquisite detail in his 2006 book, *The Sacred Geometry of Washington, D.C.*

Mann's research led him to conclude that L'Enfant's original and intended design can be found in the map held by the Library of Congress dated August 26, 1791, which they commemorated two centuries later, on August 26, 1992, with the publication of a full-color facsimile reproduction and a newly created digitized version of the plan. This map shows faint pencil corrections (including Thomas Jefferson's crossing out the "W" in Potowmac River) and is the one accepted by most mainstream academics as the last map produced by L'Enfant. Mann told us this map "reflects L'Enfant's original ideas however intuitively they were perceived. The later maps do not reveal intentions. They reveal the compromises reached by surveyors and engineers. We have to look at the original inspiration, and I think L'Enfant was as enthused and full of the ideals of the new democratic republic as anyone."[52]

Mann starts with the assumption that certain demonstrations of sacred geometry have been repeated in architecture and monuments around the world by many cultures. Unlike Campbell, however, Mann does not see a Masonic intention behind the symbolism in the city plan for Washington, D.C. He concludes that "any influence that Masonic symbolism and ideas could have had upon L'Enfant's design was indirect."[53]

Mann also admits that there is no documentation in any of L'Enfant's extant correspondence that indicates he had any intention of incorporating geometric patterns that were sacred to generations of mystics down through the ages. Nevertheless, there they seem to be, begging the question of how could they be accidental? I'm no geometry expert, but if Mann's calculations are right, then indeed there does seem to have been a geometer's hand behind L'Enfant's first draft. We know he was striving to achieve a symbolic rendering that was wholly unique and symbolic of the new balance of powers in the United States. While he worked on his draft for the new capital city, the Bill of Rights was being voted on by the States, after years of debate imperiling the passage of the Constitution. American citizens were gradually coming to grips with the concept of their dual-identity making them part of a federal system and at the same time citizens of their individual state. The battle of states rights versus federal rights was long from over, but at that moment in time, 1791, there was renewed optimism about the concept of "out of many, one." From the beginning, the federal capital was designed to reflect these unique ideals of American unity: from the individual to the state and from the state to the Union. Mann says this reflection can be found in the measurements of the city right down to the length between the important buildings and the patterns that can be drawn connecting them.

By focusing on the Capitol, L'Enfant followed a pattern for what Mann called the "architectural re-'Creation of the world'"[54]

> [He] first establish[ed] a new world center, an *axis mundi,* in the site for the US Capitol, the House of Congress. L'Enfant conceived of the Capitol as a primary point of origin in the center of the new country, with one vertical and two horizontal axes passing through it. He established an east-west axis across Washington with the Mall and East Capitol Street, and a north-south axis, that was to function additionally as a new, global, zero-degree meridian, running through North Capitol and South Capitol Streets. As is well known in Freemasonry, this creation of the symbolic definition of the world center and the six directions is the first step in all traditional sacred geometry. Marking the center and the cardinal directions were the first acts in the highly ritualized and geometrical laying out of any temple in classical, Egyptian, Hindu or any other early architectural tradition.[55]

By placing Congress at the center of the city he was making an important statement about America's government, that the law, the legislature—and not the presidency or the church—was the center of power. The elected representatives of the people were central to America's New Order of the Ages. According to Mann's theory, the changes to L'Enfant's plan from both the Ellicott revisions and the McMillan Plan in 1901 altered the city center, shifting it so that it now falls over the President's House, a move that is symbolically at odds with our founders' intentions.

Mann uses primarily the Golden Section and the pentagram to study L'Enfant's map. The Golden Section is one of the most geometrically beautiful natural phenomena in the known universe. To me, it is the perfect demonstration of the Pythagorean idea that "everything is number." The Golden Section or Golden Ratio can be expressed as a ratio of 1 to 1.6180339887 (phi), which has been found by artists and architects to be a most aesthetically pleasing ratio. Great artists capitalized on this knowledge and incorporated this ratio and the corresponding Golden Spiral into many of their greatest works, mirroring a cosmic harmony found in nature. The pentagram is one of the cleanest demonstrations of the Golden Section with several of its intersecting line segments being in Golden Ratio to one another.

In ancient traditions the number 5 and the pentacle represented life and humanity. Five stands between 4 (earth) and 6 (the heavens). The Egyptians identified the pentacle with the first architect, Thoth, the divine measurer of creation, and Christian mystics saw it as the human aspect of Jesus Christ. A five-pointed star is a harmonious, integrative, and balanced symbol, and the Neoplatonists and Pythagoreans were among those who said it reflected the idea of "as above, so below." In this regard, the five-pointed star is another way of symbolizing the "one from the many" in America's motto, *E Pluribus Unum.* (We further discussed the symbolism of the five-pointed star in Chapter 3.)

Mann encourages us to turn the map on its side, so that east is at the top, believing that this was the way that L'Enfant preferred to view his city. With Congress House serving as his center, Mann draws a circle with a radius of 0.618 of a mile around it and finds that the circle connects the intended locations for the Supreme Court, the District Courts, and City Hall. This is the same distance, 0.618 of a mile, "that each of the avenues radiating out around the Capitol runs

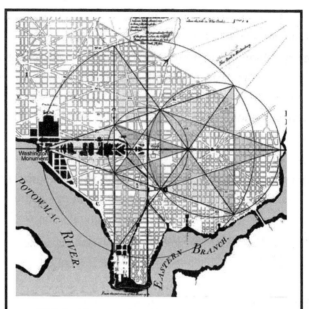

Nicholas Mann uses the Golden Section to draw three circles and pentagrams together in symbolically relating the Legislature to the People as they are related to the Executive. Reproduced with permission from *The Sacred Geometry of Washington, D.C.* by Nicholas Mann.

before arriving at its first square and principal buildings."[56] An eastern-facing pentagram can then be drawn inside this circle. Mann refers to this as the "Star of the Capitol." Directly above it, a second pentacle can be drawn, also pointing east and aligned to the main axis of the city. Mann calls this pentacle the Eastern Star, seeing it as a symbol of a free and independent people rising in the east and representing a government that supports their new found sovereignty, equality and economic freedom. He then draws a circle around the second pentagram, and uses the distance across the first circle to the center of the second circle to produce the radius of a third circle. This one also has the Capitol as its center, but its radius is 1.618 of a mile. According to Mann:

> This is the distance L'Enfant intended to separate the Capitol and the White House. 1.618 of a mile is in the same ratio to a mile as a mile is to 0.618. This ratio is that of the Golden Section, where the new is to the original as the original is to the whole.... The three circles are now related through a Golden Section ratio. The center,

the axes and the three Golden Section circles provide the key to the fundamental design of the city."[57]

In summary, Mann ties the three circles and pentagrams together in terms of the Golden Section: "The first pentacle, the star of the Capitol, is to the second, the star of the people, as both are to the third, the star of the President. The Legislature is to the People as they are to the Executive—from one, to two, to three to one."[58] (See the illustrationon previous page.)

Mann calls the Eastern Star pentacle both symbolic and sacred. Symbolic of the belief so popular at the time that civilization was on a march from the east to the west. This city was the new star with its beginnings in the east. Sacred in that it aligned the city with the heavens by throwing its rays over it:

> [The Eastern Star imprinted the city] and the continent that lay beyond, not only with the pattern of its many avenues but also with the new republican and revolutionary values that had originally come from Europe. Like a heliacal rising star, it is likely that the 108 degree angle of the pentacle aligned the primary avenues of the city to the rising in the east of such first-magnitude stars as Regulus and Sirius.[59]

Mann surmises that Benjamin Banneker might have been there during the initial surveying work to point out to L'Enfant the heliacal rising of Sirius so that it would correspond down the avenues of this Eastern Star.

Though most researchers talking about a pentagram in the streets of Washington, D.C. are referring to the incomplete, squat "star" traced in the streets north of the White House, Mann dismisses this one as incidental. He finds much more meaning in the equilateral triangle that can be drawn using the lower point of this same "star" and extending the legs upwards until the sides of the triangle are 2 x 1087 yards. This means "they are equal to the diameter of the first circle around the Capitol or $672 \times phi = 1087$."[60]

Mann's theory is all about L'Enfant's original intentions, however, and none of these patterns exists in the street plan today. It is unlikely those making the changes were aware they might be disrupting any cosmic or geometric harmony in the patterns, but, according to Mann, disrupt them they did. We will return to Mann's consideration that America would benefit by returning the focus of the city to the People's House and follow L'Enfant's idealistic vision of unity for this country.

Akram Elias: A Monumental Vision

As we have detailed, most of the people claiming there was a Masonic influence in the design of Washington, D.C. are not Masons themselves. At the same time, most contemporary Masonic historians will deny that there was any Masonic objective for our capital beyond the many cornerstone-laying ceremonies performed by them, and their overall wish to see the plan for America succeed. Most historians believe that the large number of Masons who are named as important players in the appearance of the city from 1791 through today is no more significant than the even larger number of Christians who have played important roles in creating the structures that are interpreted as Masonic. Most of the symbols that are called Masonic, in fact, are symbols used by a great many other groups and societies, and for very similar reasons that the Masons adopted them, so if they do appear anywhere in D.C. with intentionality, we cannot automatically assume it was for Masonic reasons.

One very articulate exception to this rule is Akram Elias, a 33° Freemason, who has authored numerous articles on Freemasonry and is a world speaker on the topic of "Freemasonry and the American Great Experiment." I discovered him through his 2005 film, *Unveiling the Masonic Symbolism of Washington, DC,* and invited him to be a guest on *21st Century Radio.* Elias is very active in the Grand Lodge of Free and Accepted Masons of the District of Columbia and the Scottish Rite Valley of Washington, D.C. He is the recipient of the Valentine Reintzel Medal for outstanding service to Freemasonry, awarded by the Grand Lodge of the District of Columbia. He is a member of the various York bodies of Freemasonry, the Ancient Arabic Order of the Noble Mystic Shrine, and the Royal Order of Scotland. Brother Elias is a naturalized citizen of the United States of Lebanese origin and the winner of three Telly awards for writing the treatment and co-producing the 2001 documentary entitled *Mr. Dreyfuss Goes to Washington* with Academy Award–winner Richard Dreyfuss.

Unlike David Ovason, Elias does not claim that either of the mapmakers, L'Enfant or Ellicott, were Masons. Instead, he stresses the importance of the Chief Executive overseeing the entire project from the beginning, the most important Freemason in the land: George Washington. According to Elias, from the very first directive Washington gave to the surveyors, his Masonic background came into play.[61] Washington instructed Ellicott and Banneker to survey the 10-mile federal district in the shape of a perfect square. The square is one of the main symbols of Freemasonry, and it still is one of the main building tools used by operative Masons to be sure their building blocks are at right angles. In speculative Masonry, they use the square as a symbol to remind them to keep all their activities "on the square" or "on the level," or, in other words, to be truthful and upfront. Symbolically the square shape of the federal district could be said to mean that the New Order of the Ages was a "square deal," as opposed to the old order of monarchy.

George Washington's influence on the city plan cannot be underestimated. Other gentlemen who had great impact on the design of the city and who Elias has identified as Freemasons include James Hoban, the architect who designed the White House; Benjamin Latrobe, who revised the original Capitol building design, served as Surveyor of the Public Buildings of the United States, and was responsible for several projects in D.C., including the construction of the canals; Charles Bulfinch, who further revised the Capitol building and built the original rotunda and dome; Thomas Walter, who designed the current dome and House and Senate wings on the Capitol building; Robert Mills, who designed the Washington Monument; and Thomas Crawford, who designed the sculpture of the goddess Freedom that is currently at the top of the Capitol dome.

The orientation to the east is Masonically significant according to Elias, as Masons are among the many societies who orient their temples and lodge rooms to face the direction of the rising sun. The east is symbolic of the source of light and wisdom. The statue of the goddess Freedom on the Capitol Dome is facing to the east, says Elias, because the east is the "source of light, with the sun rising in the east. The idea is that freedom is the result of enlightenment. Freemasonry teaches that a person can become truly free only when he or she is able to defeat the three enemies of the free mind: ignorance, fanaticism and tyranny. These can only be defeated by the person seeking more light and becoming enlightened through more knowledge."[62] The Capitol, the Lincoln Memorial, and the Supreme Court—all buildings that could be compared to temples—are all oriented east-west, as is the main axis of the city, as we have previously discussed.

In almost all of the fundamentalist-conspiratorialists' writings proclaiming there are "evil" Masonic symbols hidden in plain sight in the streets of Washington, D.C., you will find the traced outlines of the compass and the square, the most familiar symbol of the Freemasons. Elias demonstrates how this is drawn by connecting the White House to the Capitol down Pennsylvania Avenue, and then from the Capitol to the Jefferson Memorial down Maryland Avenue. This creates the symbolism for the compass, the measuring tool so important to operative Masons, and used today by the speculative Masons as a symbol to remind them to circumscribe their desires. Elias traces the square below the compass starting from the White House to the Lincoln Memorial, and then up to the Jefferson Memorial. It should be noted that these are imaginary lines; there are no streets that connect straight through in all these directions.

In Freemasonic symbolism, the compass and square are regularly seen laid out in this manner together with the letter "G" in the center, said to stand for "The Great Geometer," another way of referring to "God." When Elias traces this symbolic construction of the compass and square in the D.C. street plan, the center falls directly over the Washington Monument, where the letter "G" would complete the image. Most fundamentalist-conspiratorialist Websites trace the square up much higher on the compass, making it so out of proportion that it no longer resembles the Masonic emblem. They trace the square starting at Union Station and travelling down Louisiana Avenue to just below the Capitol, and then back up Washington Avenue/Canal Street for the other side.

Elias also makes some little-known connections between Masonry and the monuments, particularly the 555-foot Washington Monument. To the founders, obelisks, pyramids, and columned temples symbolized the great builders of ancient times. They were symbolic of the new Republic, which these men were struggling to create. L'Enfant's plan originally called for several obelisk monuments to be placed around his city,[63] though, of course, he thought the Washington Monument would be a simple equestrian statue.

The Washington Monument

As overboard as they have gone finding "Satanic/Illuminati" symbols in the street maps of Washington, D.C., fundamentalist-conspiratorialists are even more intolerant of the monuments. The Roman, Greek, and Egyptian influences on the architecture and monuments all over the capital are condemned as pagan or otherwise "anti-Christian." As we emphasized in Chapter 4, however, the prevailing tastes and styles of the times must be taken into account before we filter the messages of the symbolism through our current less-informed, and often less-accepting, framework. Today, due to a lack of this understanding, we have an Internet full of breathless claims that anything resembling the art of Egypt, Greece, or Rome is, by default, Satanic—apparently because it pre-dates Christ.

The most striking monument in the entire city is the 555-foot Washington Monument towering over everything else on the horizon. Anyone afraid of ancient Egypt as pre-Christian and therefore Satanic will obviously find this structure menacing. The rest of us might simply be curious to learn the connection in the designer's mind between George Washington and ancient Egypt. Discovering that the designer of the Washington Monument, Robert Mills, was a Freemason, Akram Elias decided that Freemasonry must be that connection. Although not accepted by contemporary Masonic historian sticklers, there is an old legend that the origins of Freemasonry date back to the builders of the monuments of ancient Egypt. Even the Masons who do not accept the idea that their rituals and teachings have survived from that long ago still hold a reverence for the building accomplishments of this ancient civilization. Of course, Freemasons are not the only ones who admire obelisks, but it is one way of explaining why Mason Mills designed an obelisk to honor Mason Washington.

Elias sees further corroboration to his proposal in the repetition of the number 5 in both the height and width of Robert Mills' obelisk-like design (555 feet high and 55 feet wide along each side of its base). Were these numbers significantly chosen? If so, the number 5 could have been another nod by Mills to the Freemasonic brotherhood he shared with George Washington. The number 5 is associated with the Fellowcraft, and in Masonry it is the number for the builder. George Washington was symbolically the chief builder of the nation, and this obelisk-like monument was designed to be the chief building in the capital of the nation. On a larger scale, the United States was designed to be the builder of the New Order of the Ages, where freedom is maintained through enlightened wisdom. An emphasis on five in this monument might be related to *building*.

An American Version of the Obelisk: Out of Many, One

Notice I am calling the Washington Monument "obelisk-like" rather than "an obelisk." That is because, fashioned out of many stones instead of one big stone, the Washington Monument is really only *symbolic of an obelisk* rather than the real thing. In many ways, the Washington Monument is symbolic of the American experiment, as well. It is an American version of the obelisk: out of many, one. Obelisks originated in ancient Egypt, where they are believed to have represented the rays of the sun, which, of course, was worshipped as the supreme creator god, Ra. Carved from one single stone, obelisks are found at temple entrances, where it was believed they would collect the rays of the sun god and distribute them into the earth as a form of protection. Tour guide and author Anthony Browder sees a great source for black pride in the Founding Fathers' penchant for Egyptian symbolism and uses it to educate his readers on our incredibly rich history. As he points out the several Egyptian references in Washington, D.C. (including the sphinxes at the House of the Temple, the lotus and papyrus garden at Meridian Hill Park, and of course the Washington Monument), he reminds his black listeners that their history did not begin with slavery. Rather, it dates much further back to the noble land of *Kemet,* a phonetic spelling for the name the Egyptians themselves called their own country. *Kemet* translates to "the country of the blacks."

The Washington Monument was completed in 1884. Unlike an Egyptian obelisk that is fashioned out of one single stone, this is a truly "American" obelisk, fashioned out of many stones: "Out of many, one." Photo credit: Jennifer C. Cortner.

Our current word *Egypt* derives from the Greek name for this country.

While touring the Washington Monument Browder tells the story of how in ancient *Kemet* the *tekhen* (obelisk in Greek) is seen as a symbol of the resurrection of the god *Heru* (Horus in Greek). He draws attention to the *bedhet* (sun disc) that is carved in the wall over the elevator inside the Washington Monument. The winged disc is symbolic of Horus's ascendancy to the heavens after triumphing over his evil uncle Set. In the center of the solar disc is a six-pointed star representing *Ausar* (Osiris) and *Aset* (Isis), according to Browder, or the union of the male and female, the balance of positive and negative. The Washington Monument obelisk is just one of the destinations on Browder's tour that shows present-day Americans the influence of ancient Egypt on the designers of D.C.[64] There are indeed multiple levels of interpretation in our national monuments.

L'Enfant's intended equestrian statue of Washington was delayed for many years by lack of consensus and funds. In 1833, during the celebration of Washington's 100th birthday, a committee was formed to get the project moving again. By 1836, when the call finally went out for submissions of designs, the mythology of the Father of our Country had grown exponentially, and it was no longer deemed fitting that he be memorialized in the same manner as other heroes. Baltimore architect Robert Mills won the contest with his plan to construct a monument very similar to the one he'd recently erected in his hometown, the first monument in any American city dedicated to George Washington. The Washington Monument in Baltimore is a 178-foot round column with a statue of Washington at the top. For the monument in the capital, Mills changed the round column to an obelisk, tripled it in size, and embellished it with an elaborate pillared colonnade at the bottom to include statues of 30 other Revolutionary War heroes.

There was concern over the proposed cost, and after much debate the monument committee decided to begin building the obelisk and leave the final decision about the colonnade for later. Determining that the ground was too soft to support the weight of the enormous monument, the city planners shifted it slightly to the east and south. Fundraising was slow and not without controversy, and the construction happened in stages. It stopped completely at the outbreak of the Civil War, and the Washington Monument stood frozen at 150 feet for more than 20 years. Finally growing embarrassed enough of their stump, Congress picked up the project again in 1876 and completed it in 1884. Even today you can see the two different tones in the marble marking the division line between the two construction projects. Robert Mills's plan for the colonnaded pedestal was never completed.

Without the colonnade, the stark simplicity of the Washington Monument became symbolic itself. We had built *one* large monument out of *many* stones, memorializing the American motto of *E Pluribus Unum* as much as it memorialized George Washington. The Washington Monument stands for the strength of our nation in the unity of our many stones. The Egyptians saw the obelisk as a shaft of white light. White is symbolic of all the colors uniting together into one color. Out of many, one. We see this concept repeated again and again in our monuments and architecture. Cirlot's *A Dictionary of Symbols* tells us that, because of its shape, an obelisk is a symbol of the ray of the sun, and, because of its substance, it is also related to the symbolism of stone. Its pyramidal point at the top is related to the myths of a penetrating spirit.[65]

Others see it as a gigantic phallic symbol, which, when considered that it sits in a circle, could symbolize the *linga* and *yoni* of the Hindu tradition, again another nod to balance through the union of male and female. Fundamentalist-conspiratorialists especially like this interpretation, tending to see phallic symbols in everything long and narrow. A symbol of resurrection as in the story of Horus, the Washington Monument can be interpreted as the mastery of one's lower nature, and identifying with one's immortal soul, becoming conscious of one's spiritual identity and purpose. Various secret societies of the ancients and of today are striving for a spiritual science to achieve this connection, which is why so many of them use Egyptian symbolism in their lodges, rites, and practices.

L'Enfant's grand vision had always included sites for future monuments to future heroes. He knew America and its capital would grow as the country grew, and made allowances for the celebration of nationwide accomplishments in this one city designed to symbolize the whole country. In its current configuration, the two monuments that seem to "complete" the area around L'Enfant's triangle are the Lincoln and Jefferson memorials, situated to appear as if they have been there all along. The Lincoln Memorial is directly across from the Capitol in the west, with the towering Washington Monument and Reflecting Pool between them. The Jefferson Memorial is directly south of the White House on land that was reclaimed from the Potomac River when the Tidal Basin was created. As Rick Campbell pointed out, L'Enfant left Maryland Avenue hanging suggestively unfinished, pointing toward the river, as if foreseeing the possibility for a future monument there someday, somehow. These two big monuments also enable us to trace an east-west rectangle connecting them, as Akram Elias demonstrates, creating the shape of an ancient temple or a Masonic lodge room.

The Lincoln Memorial

Abraham Lincoln was the one to whom it finally fell to stand up and solve the test this country faced over slavery. Avoided by so many generations of leaders before him, the abolition of slavery was deferred again and again by politicians with vested financial interests, until it finally came to a question of secession and war to maintain the union. Lincoln handled the tragedy of the Civil War with diplomacy and grace, reluctantly using those arrows from the talon of the eagle against its own citizens. When metaphorically the stars on the flag began fighting with each other, his goal was to keep them all on the same flag. Lincoln's words for peace, equality, and unity were so eloquent, and his demise so tragic, that he was acknowledged immediately as a permanent American hero. Official committees were formed to create a monument in his honor as early as 1867, but it wasn't until the McMillan Commission attempted to beautify Washington in 1901 that its location was selected. In one of its more symbolic aspects, the view from the Lincoln Memorial overlooks Arlington National Cemetery, once home of Robert E. Lee. The Lincoln Memorial is all about reconciliation.

The Lincoln Memorial, completed in 1922, is modeled after Greek Doric temple designs such as the Parthenon of Athens. Photo credit: Terry J. Adams, National Park Service.

Architect Henry Bacon designed it a decade later, with a model resembling the Greek Doric temple designs and the Parthenon of Athens. An inscription inside even refers to the structure as a temple, dedicated to both Lincoln and the ideal of unity. The original Parthenon in Greece was built in the fifth century BCE and was dedicated to Athena, the goddess of wisdom, who was especially known for wise counsel during times of war. It was built by the democratic ruler Pericles on the Acropolis, jutting forth over the horizon of the city of Athens, making it the striking center of attention even today. Researchers have shown how the Golden Section may have been used in the design of the

Parthenon, though sticklers point out that the mathematical properties of the Golden Section were not documented until 308 BCE by Euclid, so we can't be sure the architect of the Parthenon consciously incorporated this measurement.

A 19-foot-tall statue of a seated Lincoln sculpted by Daniel Chester French sits on an almost altar-like raised chair in the center of the monument. On the two arms of the chair are carved bundles of sticks called *fasces,* a Roman symbol to demonstrate, among other things, the same lesson on unity that was taught by the Iroquois League using arrows. Take one stick and you can break it easily, but put a bundle (of 13, for example) together, and you cannot break it. Fasces were frequently seen in Revolutionary art, especially on the propagandistic pieces of currency urging unity of the Colonies. Lincoln's awe-inspiring words from the Gettysburg Address and his second inaugural address fill the north and south chambers on either side of the statue, and people from all over the world leave there believing they can "do all which may achieve and cherish a just and lasting peace, among ourselves, and with all nations."

As soon as it was dedicated in 1922, the Lincoln Memorial became the perfect place for Americans to stand up and exercise their rights to freedom of assembly and free speech. It seems to draw people who have a protest to express. The spare beauty of the design spoke so well of Lincoln's sacrifice that Americans are compelled to lay their grievances down before him. This applied especially to the 20th-century fight for civil rights for blacks. Martin Luther King, Jr.'s famous "I Have a Dream" speech was delivered from the steps of the Lincoln Memorial, as was Marion Anderson's 1936 concert, arranged by Eleanor Roosevelt after Anderson had been barred by the "color barrier" from singing at Constitution Hall. When the mile-plus-long Mall is crammed full of people at a demonstration, the view from this location overlooking the Washington Monument with the Capitol Dome hovering in the distance has become iconic in itself of Americans' right to participate in their government.

Thomas Jefferson and Neoclassical Architecture

Even though they were built almost a century after he died, both the Lincoln and the Jefferson memorials were greatly influenced by the tastes of Thomas Jefferson. His own architectural elegance was demonstrated at his Monticello home and the University of Virginia, both in the neoclassical style. He selected the architects and oversaw the design of the public buildings in the capital city from its very beginning through its first decade and a half. He was the first president to live in the White House from the start of his term, the first to walk down Pennsylvania Avenue and back for the Inauguration Parade, and the one who suggested the neo-classical design of the Roman pantheon that inspires so many of the public buildings.

The Revolutionary generation, and especially Thomas Jefferson, saw themselves as carrying forward and relighting the torch of knowledge and wisdom that had been so effectively suppressed by the commingling of church and state powers. Our founders were excited about reviving the educational philosophies of the classical age, and the neoclassical movement in architecture was seen as another way of emulating what Pamela Scott calls the "correct principles of structure, form, and decoration, canons that had been slowly eroding since the Renaissance."[66] Washington and Jefferson were agreed that the neoclassical style should predominate over the more popular Georgian architecture of the time, as Scott continues, because of their "belief that America should erect public buildings that would transmit its political and social ideals both to the present generation and to all posterity."[67]

Jeffrey Meyer agrees, saying that:

> [Jefferson] perceived a congruence between this style of ar-
> chitecture, his personal ideals, and his conceptions of democracy....
> In favoring classical architecture Jefferson was selecting not just
> a style that appealed to him, but one that he believed was in har-
> mony with the fundamental principles of the universe, implanted
> by the Creator at the beginning, as compelling as the truths of
> physics discovered by Newton. In that sense, for him, classical
> architecture expressed eternal principles.[68]

The Roman Pantheon is considered the ultimate architectural inspiration piece, and Jefferson used it as his model for both Monticello and the University of Virginia. It was only logical for architect John Russell Pope to imitate it again in the memorial to Thomas Jefferson started in 1939. Pope, who was not a Freemason, also designed the exotic House of the Temple, the headquarters for the Scottish Rite Freemasonry, modeled after one of the seven wonders of the world, the Tomb of Halicarnassus. He also designed part of the National Gallery of Art, and is considered one of the leaders in the City Beautiful movement that strove to incorporate social reforms with architectural renovations. The Pantheon of Rome was built around 100–125 CE, and was comprised essentially of the "vaulted cylinder and the portico,"[69] the aspect that is repeated in the Capitol, and many other buildings in Washington, D.C. The Roman Pantheon is also believed to reflect the proportions of the Golden Section, though again there is no proof that it was intentional. Originally constructed as a temple to the seven deities of Rome, it still exists today, being used since the seventh century as a Christian church.

The Jefferson Memorial

Authorized in 1934 and pushed through by President Roosevelt, the Jefferson Memorial occupies land that was part of the Potomac River in L'Enfant's day. Because of Jefferson's prominence in the founding of the country, his memorial was given the last remaining space of prime real estate in relation to the Mall and the monuments to Washington and Lincoln. It is aligned directly south of the White House and located on the south side of the Tidal Basin, a man-made inlet and recreational space created during the city-beautification period of the late 19th century, adorned since 1912 with the famous Japanese cherry trees.

The Jefferson Memorial, completed in 1943, is modeled after the Roman Pantheon, Jefferson's own architectural inspiration for his University of Virginia and Monticello. Photo credit: Jennifer C. Cortner.

Thomas Jefferson was the visionary of the American Revolution. His definitive writings lifted us out of the status quo and allowed us to dream of a truly new way of life that centered more than almost anything else on the freedom of religion. These beliefs are expressed in his Virginia Statute for Religious Freedom, passed in 1786, that is excerpted on one of the walls of his memorial:

Whereas Almighty God hath created the mind free; that all attempts to influence it by temporal punishments or burdens...are a departure from the plan of the holy author of our religion...that

no man shall be compelled to frequent or support any religious
worship or ministry…or shall otherwise suffer on account of his
religious opinions or belief, but that all men shall be free to profess,
and by argument to maintain, their opinions in matters of religion….

Religious fundamentalism routinely reasserts itself into the political structures of man around the world, and the need for constant vigilance against its
attempt to control our freedom of choice is as pressing today as it ever was.

Jefferson's accomplishments were so various and his character so controversial, it seems fitting that his memorial would be so bare, allowing visitors to
project what they will on him. He was an inventor, a diplomat, a scientist, a
gardener, and a bibliophile in addition to being an accomplished architect and
political philosopher. His words covering the walls are enough to renew hope in
all Americans that our country and the freedoms he helped establish really are
unique and worth fighting to save. In the center he stands, a 19-foot-tall bronze
statue sculpted by Rudolph Evans, holding the Declaration of Independence
rolled in one hand and gazing into the future.

For Defending Freedom, Jefferson Was the 1st Target of the Conspiratorialists

I think it's worth noting the parallels of America's first Illuminati scare with
the conspiracy theories about them today. These are the same kind of people
who attacked Jefferson in 1800 when our fledgling nation was on the brink of
reverting back to a monarchy and/or despotism. Those who did not share
Jefferson's optimism for the ability of American citizens to govern themselves
wanted more than anything for Washington to become king. They wanted a
benevolent dictator. Fortunately for us, George Washington was more interested in the success of the American experiment than he was in achieving
dictatorial power, which he surely would have been granted had he not continu-
ally rebuffed such suggestions. All through the 1790s, while the capital city was
experiencing its many birth pangs and infighting, the leaders of the Revolution
were splitting into two definitive groups. The different factions that evolved into
the two political parties we know today were fighting for control: those who
favored a powerful federal government with fewer rights for the States and
thus for the individual, and those, like Jefferson, who favored restraining the
federal government and giving more power to the individuals and the States.

The attacks grew increasingly personal and dirty from both sides, and the contest was not resolved until Jefferson won the 1800 presidential election. After a decade of fighting with his pen, informing Americans of the dangers to their liberties, Jefferson's Inaugural Address of 1801 welcomed a new spirit of reconciliation: "Let us, then, fellow-citizens, unite with one heart and one mind. Let us restore to social intercourse that harmony and affection without which liberty and even life itself are but dreary things.... We have called by different names brethren of the same principle. We are all Republicans, we are all Federalists."

Jefferson's victory put the nation firmly in the hands of those willing to give power to the people in the form of a democratic republic. When his two terms in office were followed by several decades of leadership modeled on his ethics, America began leading by example, showing other countries that *freedom* was the best hope for the world.

Few Americans today are aware of how close we came to returning to a monarchy just a decade after the War for Independence was won. Fewer still are aware that it was this political controversy that first introduced the specious scare tactic of calling your political rivals "the Illuminati." All the fear-mongers tossing around the label "Illuminati" today are urged to read Vernon Stauffer's excellent historical examination of this first great conspiracy scare in the new American republic. They need to understand how these claims came to America in the first place. Stauffer describes the atmosphere of confusion after the Revolution, especially in New England where the church had always had greater control over the state than in the south. The uncertainty for the future was parlayed into hysteria by Jefferson's political enemies who used the inflammatory writings about "the Illuminati" to throw doubt and suspicion on Jefferson.

The legend of the Bavarian Illuminati infiltrating America was agitated by clerics preaching sermons based on the writings of Abbé Barruel and John Robison. As Stauffer explains it:

> The grave fault of the clerical 'friends of order' was that they had not preached the Gospel. Instead, they had insulted the intelligence of the people by revamping the fables of a Scotch monarchist and a Catholic abbé. They imputed infidelity to the Democrats, while they themselves caused infidelity to abound. They directed

all their darts of 'democratic infidels' and 'infidel philosophy' against one man, Thomas Jefferson....[70]

Stauffer also shows that the Federalists were well aware that Robison and Barruel were "miserable mixtures of falsehood and folly" when they launched their charge of infidel philosophy against Thomas Jefferson and his party. He explains:

> The Federalists were simply desperate. They were determined to go to any lengths to keep Jefferson out of the presidency. All their works were saturated with sacrilege and impiety. Their public fasts were kept for political purposes. Their cry, "The church is in danger!" was hollow and insincere. Their praise of the federal administration had no other object than to effect the abasement of the Democrats. Their "Church and State Union" freely sacrificed the highest interests of religion and government to the cause of party.[71]

Those attacking Jefferson and the future of American independence were mostly from the aristocratic mercantile classes. The ones who preferred the monarchical system were the select few who managed to parlay royal favor. They fomented fear about a fabricated Illuminati scare to justify the imposition of more order. They even objected to the goals of the American Revolution, calling them impossible to attain. Stauffer concludes: "Nothing could be clearer than that the word 'Illuminati' had lost all serious and exact significance and had become a term for politicians to conjure with."[72] Ultimately, however, it was revealed that Barruel and Robison were founded on lies and exaggeration, and Jefferson won the election.

Sound familiar? These same kinds of lies and exaggerations about the Illuminati are again debasing America's credibility at home and abroad, dragging down many of our symbols as a result. The ultra-right-wing fundamentalists are tossing out the label "Illuminati" and distracting us with fabricated conspiracies about our symbols. This tactic not only delays us from our duty of keeping vigilant over our leaders, but also prevents us from gaining a deeper appreciation of the mystical power of our symbols by attaching to them rumors of a fabricated Satanic conspiracy. The worst casualty is the noble concept of America's destiny. America was designed to show the rest of the world how the individual man can honorably rule himself. The New Order has to be a consciously willed choice, and will not work at the point of a gun. Our destiny is not to force democracy on anyone, just to do it right at home and lead by example. If by defending freedom in the footsteps of Jefferson means you will be accused by the ultra-right as being a member of the Illuminati, then at least you are in good company.

The White House

That Jefferson epitomized the opposition party to those who preferred a monarchical rule is evident in the architectural styles in the capital city he helped to design. For example, he penciled over "Presidential Palace" on L'Enfant's map and inserted "Presidential House." L'Enfant was raised in the school of royal patronage, and his father worked for the king of France. As enthusiastic as anyone about the new republic, L'Enfant's courtly background influenced his belief that the leader of this great new country should live in a grand style worthy of the honor. This idea was overturned early on, though it took some time to settle on what they *did* want in its place. All they knew for certain was that it would *not* resemble a palace for a king in Europe. More enthusiasm went into the design for the Capitol, considered by all as the symbolic center of the city. The Capitol housed their novel concept of leadership by the people, and was where they poured their best innovative energy and ideas for symbolic architecture. The White House did not get the neo-classical treatment, and is usually described as belonging to the Georgian or Federal style. It has been added to and modified by almost every resident, redefining it thoroughly through the years. It changes with America, yet we always identify it with the seat of power (an identification that may be symbolically misdirected, as previously discussed).

The location of the President's House was also regarded in a highly symbolic way in relation to its distance and angular placement respective to Congress House. In L'Enfant's vision the distance separating them and the clear, enormously wide avenue connecting them were meant to symbolize simultaneously that these two were separate and equal powers and they were to keep an eye on each other.

The Power of the White House

Freemason Akram Elias compares the route traveled at the beginning of the Inauguration Parade from the White House to the Capitol, to the route taken by an initiate traveling to the east for initiation. Traveling from the White House in the north to the swearing-in ceremony at Capitol Hill in the east, Elias says, should serve to remind the newly elected president that his residence is not the source of the power. He should consider himself a candidate taking the oath to administer his term according to the law of the Constitution.

Chris Hardaker compares the swearing-in ceremony to an ancient ritual on a mountain, taking place at the top of what he sees as the pyramid and eye in the triangle symbol in the street plan. The mountain is Capitol Hill, where the chosen leader (the president-elect) places his hand on the holy word of God and, says Hardaker, "utters the sacred words at the behest of the High Priest (Chief Justice)."[73] After this the leader walks metaphorically "down the mountain," proceeding down Pennsylvania Avenue back to the White House, or metaphorically down one side of the pyramid.[74]

Rick Campbell's Great Pyramid cross-section overlay on the street map matches up the White House with the King's Chamber, taught in the ageless wisdom teachings to have been the place where initiates went to experience a sort of vision quest to determine their life purpose.

All three of these symbolic interpretations of the White House see the resident as an initiate, a student, or one who is learning. He is not the boss. He is not the king, or "the decider,"[75] as our current resident calls himself. Contrary to the image of a student, President Bush routinely applies the theory of "unitary executive," which basically assumes unitary power to the president to interpret the law. By issuing more controversial signing statements than any other president,[76] he has appointed himself the decider.

According to Nicholas Mann, during the various revisions to Washington, D.C., the axis of power shifted in the design away from Capitol Hill and toward the White House. This architectural shift has resulted in a new mindset regarding who is really in charge. In the last century, as more power was ceded to the executive branch, the change in focus has even rippled out to a more selfish mindset across the country in general:

> [I]n structural terms, they have lost a relationship of mutual reciprocity with the sovereign powers of the States and the people... This over-developed Executive symbolism in the city plan is not only indicative of an increasing predominance of Executive and federal authority over the State authority and individual rights. It also points to another, equally valid reading, of materialistic and self-centered ambitions running unchecked and beyond the law on the continent.[77]

Washington and Jefferson put out the call for design submissions for the President's House in 1792, and from them Washington chose James Hoban's design of a country house. He asked the Irish-American to make it a bit bigger and add a large receiving room similar to the one he had in Mount Vernon. Jefferson had also submitted a design for the house anonymously, probably along the lines of his earlier expressed vision for a more modest design for the city. Hoban's house was originally much simpler-looking than the one with which we are familiar, described as a fine Georgian home in the Dublin style. Today we recognize the façades with the semi-neoclassical square north portico, and the more Federal-style rounded south portico, created in 1824 and 1829 respectively. Both were fashioned after designs by Benjamin Henry Latrobe, another architect with lasting impact on the look of Washington, D.C.

Built largely by slaves and immigrants, the original building was finished enough in November 1800 for John and Abigail Adams to move in. She was appalled watching slaves bought and sold across the street, a painful dichotomy that would remain in the capital city of the "land of the free" for six more decades before slavery was outlawed in D.C. in 1862. Abigail Adams also complained about having to hang her laundry in the grand reception room (very few other rooms had been completed), and she was happy to return to Massachusetts a few months later after Adams lost the election to Jefferson. Jefferson's architectural itch immediately went to work after he moved in, and he added an east and west wing to better separate the living quarters from the office spaces. Hoban was to work on this building for the next 40 years, making additions and adjustments along with Latrobe and several other architects.

The south portico of the White House was created in 1829, fashioned after designs by Benjamin Henry Latrobe. ©iStockphoto.com/ mrbfaust.

The British occupation and torching of the brand new Federal City in 1814 was hugely demoralizing to the young country. The inconvenience of losing their meeting places and residences inspired a whole new round of debate with contingents trying to move the location of the capital back north all over again. Not only did President James Madison, a Jefferson protégé, resist all these efforts and insist on rebuilding on the same ground, but his charming wife, Dolley, exercised her formidable social skills to breathe life back into the entertainment and cultural scene making the city attractive again as a place to live. She also became a national heroine by rescuing the famous Gilbert Stuart portrait of George Washington from the flames. James Hoban went back to work and rebuilt the White House, taking the opportunity to enlarge it yet again. Incidentally, it is commonly believed that the name the "White House" originated after the fire-blackened walls received a coat of whitewash, but this is probably not true. Not only were the walls of the President's House almost entirely knocked down and rebuilt after the War of 1812, but there is evidence to show that it was being called the White House as early as 1811. The first structure was also made of sandstone in the distinctive white color and this white house always stood out among the numerous red brick buildings surrounding it.

The White House is often included in lists of famous haunted places. People who study ghostly phenomena report that locations of great emotional intensity are places that are more likely to become home to ghosts. The White House is a perfect example, where daily concern and emotion are experienced over great decisions that have American lives hanging in the balance. Ghost story compiler Jeff Belanger quotes former First Lady Rosalynn Carter speaking on the History Channel saying of the Lincoln bedroom: "They were so overwhelmed by being in that place.... Most of our friends who spent the night in the Lincoln Bedroom didn't sleep."[78] Abraham Lincoln is probably the most frequently spotted ghost in the White House (seen by Winston Churchill, Queen Wilhemina, Mrs. Calvin Coolidge, Mrs. Roosevelt's secretary, and many others), but he is far from the only one. Others have reported seeing a small boy thought to be Lincoln's son William, who died in the White House in 1862. Another famously retold story is how the Rose Garden was saved from Mrs. Woodrow Wilson's decision to tear it out when the ghost of an angry Dolley Madison scared off the gardeners.

Belanger quotes White House Chief Usher Gary Walters from a Halloween online chat, saying, "The presidents who I have worked for have all indicated a feeling of the previous occupants of the White House and have all talked about drawing strength from the fact that the previous presidents have lived here."[79]

The U.S. Capitol

The Capitol is also haunted, according to many eyewitness accounts. The September 4, 2006, issue of *The Irish Times* included the report of Bill Clinton's remark to Bertie Ahern, prime minister of Ireland, during a visit to the Capitol in 2000, when Clinton said he sometimes felt haunted by the ghost of the Irish-American architect James Hoban.[80] In addition to designing the White House, Hoban served as America's first superintendent of public buildings and was also closely involved with the U.S. Capitol building as architect, surveyor, and project manager, so he is as likely a candidate as any for still hanging around. The ghost of Peter L'Enfant has also been seen scurrying through the hallways of the Capitol, possibly still on his endless mission to receive appropriate recognition for his city plan. The ghost of John Quincy Adams has not only been seen in the Capitol, but also heard. Both President James Garfield and his assassin, Charles Julius Gusteau, have been seen lurking about. Grant's vice president, Henry Wilson, who died of pneumonia in the Capitol, has been heard coughing and sneezing in the Senate wing. Kentucky Congressman William Preston Taulbee was shot by a reporter in 1890 on the stairs leading to the pressroom and died a few days later. His bloodstains are still visible on the stairway, and it is thought his ghost is responsible for tripping visitors, and especially reporters, in this location. There are also reports of the ghost of a custodian who helps people do their work. As is the White House, the Capitol is a prime location for ghostly activity with its intense rivalries and heated debates over portentous issues.

The Capitol is also similar to the White House in that it continues to be a work in progress. As America added states and therefore the number of representatives and senators increased, the Capitol was expanded. Soon after L'Enfant was fired or resigned, in March 1792, Washington and Jefferson launched a public competition to design the Capitol. They wanted a design that would convey America's nascent political structure and its social order, but in the first round of submissions, none pleased them. Additional designs were sought, and, in April 1793, the design of Dr. William Thornton, again based partly on the Roman pantheon, was chosen. Washington also made Thornton one of the district Commissioners so he would eventually oversee the construction of this and many other buildings. His Capitol design would be significantly altered by James Hoban, Benjamin Latrobe, Stephen Hallet, and several other architects involved through the years. The most notable addition came from Charles Bulfinch, who designed the first dome.

The original building was completed enough by November 1800, for Congress to move in, but was badly burned by the British in August 1814. The reconstruction and expansion were overseen by Latrobe and Bulfinch, who finally completed the construction in 1829, more than 30 years after George Washington laid the corner stone. In 1856 Bulfinch's low wooden dome was replaced by a larger cast iron dome to better match the proportions of the still-expanding building. Overseen by the fourth architect of the Capitol, Thomas Walter, the current dome measures 288 feet high on the outside and is said to be modeled after the domes of St. Paul's Cathedral in London and St. Peter's Basilica in Rome.

The Capitol Dome is one of the most recognizable features of Washington, D.C. Symbolically, the dome is an image of the spiritual world above the city. From the first plan, this building was intended to be the axis from which the city would radiate its spiritual influence. Photo credit: Architect of the Capitol.

It's difficult to imagine the Capitol building without its trademark dome, and in fact it appears the founders of the city would have agreed. L'Enfant's drawings for the "People's House" suggest a domed structure, and Jefferson certainly favored a central dome as well. David Ovason says the center of the Capitol dome can be considered the center of a compass, and that originally "a whole sunburst of avenues and roads"[81] were to radiate from it. The whole city was designed to "accommodate the arc of sunset to the west of the Capitol building in a very distinctive way.... This consideration of the cosmic importance of the sunset to the Capitol building shows that the dome—itself an image of the spiritual world above the city—was to be the spiritual fulcrum of Washington, DC.... It was the center from which the city was to radiate its spiritual influence."[82] Nicholas Mann agrees: "By placing the Capitol on primary axes in the center of the plan, and relating all the other key buildings to this site in a ratio that is fundamental to the structures of the natural world, L'Enfant gave formal, visible expression to the all-powerful, central and representative qualities of the Legislature and its generative position in the New World order."[83]

Charles Westbrook's suggestion of a Masonic compass and square in the map center on the Capitol. He believes the landscaping and streets arranged to the east of the building provide the fine details, including the "handles, moving joints, and even a compass spring that can be seen in the layout based around the Capitol building."[84] The symbolism of the square and compass centered on the Capitol could be interpreted to mean that our congressional representatives should monitor their actions by the "square of virtue," and "exercise self restraint and self control" to better lead our nation.

Crowning the impressive Capitol dome is the 19.5-foot-tall bronze statue officially known as "Freedom Triumphant in War and Peace," which we mentioned briefly in Chapter 4. This American goddess resembles the Statue of Liberty, though she is much smaller and predates her by several decades. Thomas Walter, the designer of the current dome, originally called for it to be capped by a statue of "Liberty," but sculptor Thomas Crawford's proposal for an allegorical "Freedom" was just as suitable. This "Freedom" is very similar to the American goddess Columbia (also discussed in Chapter 4). In her right hand she holds a sheathed sword, and in her left hand she holds the shield of the United States with 13 stripes and 13 stars. Over the shield she is also holding a laurel wreath of victory. Her helmet is adorned with nine visible stars, which Crawford explained indicate her heavenly origin. Topping the helmet is the head of an eagle with great plumage flowing behind, hearkening to the days of allegorizing America as the Indian Princess.

Freedom is crowned by the eagle, just like the Great Tree of Peace. The eagle is standing vigilant at the very summit of Congress, ever watchful and far-seeing for threats to our liberty. The Statue of Freedom is facing east instead of toward the Mall perhaps to reinforce the idea that freedom is dependent on enlightenment, which symbolically comes from the east, the direction of the rising sun. This goddess is more than a reminder that freedom is the guardian of our republic. As our enlightener, she is also an image of the spiritual world overseeing its progeny.

Many American cities have copied this dome for their state Capitols and topped them with female goddesses. On Georgia's dome she is called Miss Freedom holding a torch in her raised right hand and a sword in the other. Montana's dome is topped by Lady Liberty holding a torch in her right hand and the laurel wreath and shield in her left. Texas's dome bears the Goddess of Liberty holding a five-pointed star in her raised left hand and a sword in the other. Americans have always considered the goddess a protector of our freedoms.

Beyond its role as the temple of liberty, the Capitol is also a vast artistic treasure house. Inside are the works of such famous artists as Gilbert Stuart, Rembrandt Peale, and John Trumbull, not to mention the more than 200 statues in the Rotunda. Most striking is the ceiling of the dome, where there is a 4,000-square-foot mural painted by Italian American artist Constantino Brumidi. It took him just 11 months to complete this enormous mural, which he finished right at the end of the Civil War in 1865. A master of the fresco painting technique, Brumidi spent a good part of 25 years working in the Capitol. His work can also be seen in the decorated hallways now known as the "Brumidi corridors."

The ceiling of the Capitol Dome features a 4,000-square-foot mural by Constantino Brumidi called *The Apotheosis of Washington*, a triumph of allegorical symbolism depicting most of the major Revolutionary heroes supported by Roman and Greek gods and goddesses. Photo courtesy of the U.S. Capitol Historical Society.

On the curved inside surface of the Capitol Dome 180 feet above the floor of the Rotunda is the gigantic mural, *The Apotheosis of Washington.* Apotheosis means the glorification of a person as an ideal or a god, and the apotheosis of Revolutionary figures, most notably Washington and Franklin, was a regular sight in the celebratory years following the victory of the War of Independence. Brumidi's version is a triumph of allegorical symbolism, depicting most of the major Revolutionary heroes supported by Roman and Greek gods and goddesses, all with their accompanying symbolic elements and colors. The central group in the Apotheosis finds Washington being raised up to heaven and supported by the goddesses of Liberty and Victory or Fame. Completing the inner circle are 13 maidens with a star above each head symbolizing the 13 colonies. The perimeter of the dome is composed of six scenes representing areas of important focus to the United States: agriculture, science, commerce, mechanics, navigation, and war. Making an appearance in this tapestry of American history are the goddesses Columbia, Minerva, Venus, Ceres, and America; the gods Mercury, Vulcan, and Neptune; and heroes from Ben Franklin to Samuel Morse. Most of the figures are more than 15 feet tall in order to be seen from the ground.

Outside the dome we have "Freedom" on guard, and inside the dome we have the father of our country ascending into the spiritual worlds assisted by "Liberty." *The Apotheosis of Washington* depicts an event that all humans will eventually experience as they become conscious of the higher planes of existence. As we render compassionate service to the material earth, nature, and its inhabitants, we will find the key of balance and attain the higher worlds of spirit. There is an energy in the Capitol that is conducive to opening these doors.

The City of Washington: May Time Render It Worthy of the Name It Bears

In fact, we might say that there is an energy in the entire city that is conducive to opening the doors to the world of the spirit, but most of its current inhabitants are not interested in learning the procedures necessary to experience this level of consciousness. A meditation experiment was held in Washington, D.C. in 1993, when a group of 4,000 experienced meditators gathered with the intention of praying peace. The skeptical chief of police agreed to share crime statistics with them and was stunned to see the rate of violent crime significantly drop during the eight weeks of the experiment. This same experiment has been performed successfully in other cities as well, but I do believe they might have more success in Washington due to the sympathetic geometries in the streets and the vibrations of hope and inspiration emanating from the memorials. Even the high expectations laid down for us by our founders in their very blueprints for this city inspire us to peace. Activities that are in harmony with unity, republicanism, and wisdom will resonate best with the patterns and structure of the deliberate layout of this city.

If a fundamentalist-conpiratorialist has his mind made up that our founders were evil and placed Satanic symbols in the design of our capital, then his frames will keep him from seeing other levels of interpretation. For example, why do they never point out that the five prominent monuments on the Mall can be connected in the shape of a cross? Do their preconceived ideas prevent them from considering the inclusion of a Christian symbol into the city plan? Whereas it can be viewed as Christian, this is America's cross, and it has multiple meanings, as all symbols do. Many other civilizations used the cross as a symbol before Jesus was crucified. In basic symbology, the two components of the cross are a vertical line symbolizing spirit and a horizontal line symbolizing the material world or matter. It is a union of spirit and matter, or a duality of masculine/vertical and feminine/horizontal, or a joining of heaven and earth. This union is also an accurate description of the human

The McMillan Plan for the National Mall in 1901 shows how the placement of the five main monuments creates the shape of a cross. Photo courtesy of the National Capital Planning Commission.

being as each of us possesses both masculine and feminine genetic traits, and a mortal body and an immortal soul. This American cross symbolizes the foundation that makes America the New Order of the Ages—a foundation based upon enlightenment.

Prayer, intention, and visualization have always played powerful roles in shaping this country. Many of our founders described the guiding hand of Providence behind the auspicious events in our early success. Consciously or not our founders created a capital city that enjoys a resonance with the natural law of harmony. To assist the completion of our destiny, we could visualize Washington, D.C. and all its structures, sculptures, art, and architecture fitting together and connecting our elected leaders within the macrocosm of American symbology. The destiny of America is to demonstrate representational liberty, and each of us has an individual responsibility to assist this manifestation. The resonance patterns found in Washington, D.C. assist these kinds of prayers for our current leaders, motivating them to make better decisions for the highest good. The design of Washington, D.C. gives the inhabitants of this city every advantage to continue that beneficent relationship with Providence started by our founders.

CHAPTER 8

OUR FOUNDING FATHERS WERE NOT SATANISTS

As ludicrous as the chapter title is going to sound to the average reader, it is a growing sentiment among a large body of people thanks to the cut-and-paste methods of research on the Internet. In order to interpret our American symbols as evil, the fundamentalist-conspiratorialists are forced into the conclusion that our founders were morally corrupt and controlled by Satan. For "proof" they point to all the pagan symbols around us. Without a background of classical references, it is dangerously easy to make these unfounded conclusions, and to identify some of America's strongest patriots and idealistic visionaries as part of the mysterious "them." Racist conspiratorialists have played this same "game" against the Jews for a long, long time, diagramming complex theories to show that behind all atrocities is a Jewish secret society planning to enslave the world and destroy Christianity. The Freemasons, liberal intelligentsia, and artists ("commies") have all suffered the same types of attacks from fundamentalist-conspiratorialists identifying them as the root of all evil. These days the conspiracy buffs have turned on American history and symbolism and begun to pick them apart for clues.

When faced with conflicting interpretations of anything, the best thing to do is to quiet your mind through regular prayerful meditation. When your intuition is strong, the unknown no longer has the power of fear. On fear, Rollo May said, in *Man's Search for Himself,* "When people feel threatened and anxious they become more rigid, and when in doubt they tend to become dogmatic; and then they lose their own vitality. They use the remnants of traditional values to build a protective encasement and then shrink behind it; or they make an outright panicky retreat into the past."[1]

A quick check at the reference sources behind the claims that American symbolism was designed by Illuminati Masons in league with the Devil reveals many of the same sources. Most of the descriptions and diagrams on the Web are lifted straight from one of the more prolific sources. These include Texe Marrs, David Icke, David Bay, and Jack Chick, who, in turn, are quoting self-described "insider sources." Their sources claim to be "ex-Illuminati," "former Masons," or "converted Satanists" revealing "for the first time" the secret truths behind the historical mirage the rest of us live in. These are the references cited for quotations such as "this symbol was designed by Freemasons," or "that symbol was designed by the Illuminati." Those who go to the trouble of providing more authoritative sources for their claims refer back to the works of Barruel and Robison, the inflammatory 18th-century books we described in Chapter 2. Barruel and Robison were both anti-Masons and, in their fervor to condemn them, they created many falsehoods about the Illuminati and their supposed infiltration of the Masons.

Speculation is fine as long as it is identified as such, but speculation is not valid unless all the historical facts are considered first. For example, those claiming Masonic input on the Great Seal simply have their facts wrong, as revealed in the authoritative book on the subject, *The Eagle and the Shield*. Although it was published by the State Department in 1976, it was not released until 1978, and before that time the State Department did not have anything publicly available on the reverse of the Great Seal. I know, because I tried in vain to get it, and corresponded with the authors of *The Eagle and the Shield* as they were assembling their book. This means that anything written before 1978, including my own work and that of Manly Palmer Hall, who is quoted as a Masonic historian on countless fundamentalist-conspiratorialist Websites,[2] was based on incomplete facts, and could be subject to question in the area of speculation. Many critics of the Great Seal today are basing their facts on just such information published before 1978.

Although I have a high regard for Manly Palmer Hall and corresponded with him frequently in the 1960s and '70s, he was not a Masonic historian.

He also got a number of his facts wrong about the Great Seal, writing as he did before Patterson and Dougall published. The reason Hall is cited so regularly as a historical reference on Masonry is because the fundamentalist-conspiratorialists are trying to prove that Masons are interested in the occult. Arturo de Hoyos and Brent Morris explain why this connection is invalid:

> Manly Hall did not become a Mason until 1954, so his *Lost Keys of Freemasonry* (1923) and *The Secret Teachings of All Ages* (1928) actually represent the personal theories of a non-Mason. Further, Mr. Hall (who passed away in August 1990) was a self-avowed mystic, not a "leading authority" of Freemasonry. He was a promulgator of mysticism and theosophy, topics of interest to some Freemasons; but his writings have not received official sanction by any Masonic bodies. The fact that he held the Thirty-third Degree and was respected by many Masons and honored by the Supreme Council 33 degree is no more significant than the fact that various Baptist, Anglican, or Methodist authors have also been so honored.[3]

The Léo Taxil Hoax

Though Hall's writings contained inaccuracies caused mainly by missing data or honest mistakes, the writings of Léo Taxil were far more destructive (and intentionally so) to the reputation of the Masons. Léo Taxil was the pen name of con man Gabriel Antoine Jogand-Pagès (1854–1907), who single-handedly fabricated the grand hoax that Freemasons worship a devil named Lucifer. Taxil's self-confessed hoaxed writings are the original source for those today accusing the Freemasons (and through them the Founding Fathers) of devil worship. De Hoyos and Morris describe Taxil as "notorious for his irreligious and pornographic writings."[4] After joining the Freemasons in 1881, he was expelled after less than a year when his character was revealed. In revenge, he constructed a complicated scheme intended to embarrass both the Freemasons and the Catholic Church.

In 1890 he began publishing a series of books alleging to expose the Masons, but, because he never advanced beyond the first degree, his descriptions of the initiations and rituals grew more fictionalized as the series progressed. The tales also grew more lascivious, something that attracted more readers. His climax described a secret sect of Freemasonry, something he invented entirely and called Palladism or Luciferian High-Masonry. He claimed this inner secret society was led by the recently deceased Albert Pike, the Sovereign Grand Commander of the Supreme Council, 33°, Southern Jurisdiction in the United States. De Hoyos and Morris summarized Taxil's romance tale as culminating in secret instructions from Albert Pike to the other Masonic leaders of the world that allegedly said:

> [T]hey could now reveal to their high-degree members that the 'Masonic religion' is the worship of Lucifer. Readers loved the increasingly lurid details, but as the fabrication grew more complicated, it threatened to collapse under the weight of unsubstantiated details. Finally, on April 19, 1897, in the hall of the Geographic Society in Paris, Lèo Taxil confessed all to a stunned audience, after which a riot nearly broke out.[5]

The biggest lie about Freemasonry is based on a hundred-year-old deliberate hoax by a confessed liar. Though some anti-Masonic writers acknowledge Taxil is the source of the lies about Freemasonic devil worship (even the *New Catholic Encyclopedia,* the Masons' old nemesis admits these accusations are based on the Taxil Hoax), unfortunately most anti-Masonic writers prefer to titillate fear and emotions by continuing to repeat and elaborate on it. Those today quoting Taxil as an authority "proving" that Masons worship the devil include: Jack Chick, J. Edward Decker, Des Griffin, Jack Harris, Texe Marrs, Eustace Mullins, Pat Robertson, Williams Schnoebelen, and Martin Short.[6]

Not all critics of Freemasonry fail to check into their sources, however. In his critique of Freemasonry, called *The Truth About Masons,* Robert Moray concluded, "Of all the attacks against the Craft, none is so vicious as the charge that Masons are a secret cult of Devil worshipers or Satanists and that at some point in the higher degrees they must pass through a Luciferian initiation."[7]

Moray also lamented, as I have been lamenting throughout this book, the low standards of research most other anti-Masons use. As he points out, most anti-Masons, "[i]n their zeal to attack Freemasonry, have been willing to use fantasy, fraud, and deceit. They have even created bogus documents when needed. Their writings must not be taken at face value."[8]

In his foreword to De Hoyos and Morris's book, James Tresner called them out on this lie: "They are not innocently mistaken; they are not led into error; they are not merely confused. They lie. Bear that in mind as you read the examples of what anti-Masons do when 'quoting' Masonic writers."[9] Tresner goes on to make this simple request: "It is not that Freemasonry considers itself above criticism. It is a human institution and, like all such institutions, imperfect and open to improvement. Criticize us if you wish—most Masons do. Examine us in depth, we have nothing to hide. But do not lie about us. And, especially, do not lie about us and then dare to claim you are doing the work of God."[10]

A defense of Freemasonry is not within the scope of this book, but I felt it was necessary to include some of it here because it was a prime motivator for me to write this book in the first place. Almost all of the contemporary attacks on American symbolism are linked in some way to the critics' condemnation of Freemasonry. A few of the critics of our national symbols, however, are not motivated by a fear of the Freemasons, but rather by a fear of the Roman Catholic Church. There are many writers and *Youtube.com* film makers who see pagan idolatry and the Antichrist in the means by which Catholics choose to worship. These critics also take the low road by fabricating evidence and making inaccurate historical links, but they use a lot of the same language to accuse our founders of Satanism. They simply insert the word *Vatican* for *Freemason* when pointing the finger of accusation for all this so-called Roman influence on American symbolism. Neither group takes into account the artistic tastes of the time period.

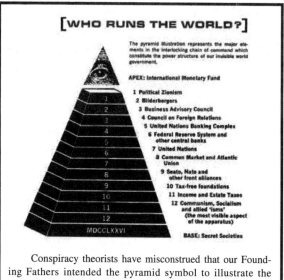

Conspiracy theorists have misconstrued that our Founding Fathers intended the pyramid symbol to illustrate the power structure of our invisible world government. This fallacy completely disregards the influence of the neoclassical movement and the Enlightenment on America's founders, who chose the pyramid for our Great Seal as a symbol of strength and duration. Illustration from June Grem's *Karl Marx Capitalist.*

The Enlightenment and American Symbols

Any examination of American symbols is invalid without considering the time period in which they were formed. The Age of Enlightenment was a tremendous factor of influence on both our founders and their symbols. But when the fundamentalist-conspiratorialists acknowledge it at all, they tend to spin it as another negative factor, saying Satan must have cleverly orchestrated the movement to lead man into the sin of personal freedom. The Age of Enlightenment is so called because it was responsible, in effect, for the throwing off of the feudal monarchical system of government, the eventual complete change in paradigm about the practice of slavery that had existed worldwide since the beginning of time, and the disconnection between the state and religion. It led to freedom for the individual to follow any religious beliefs preferred, at least in this country and most Westernized ones. Reason was advocated as the primary basis of authority reflected in the liberalism of our Bill of Rights.

The Age of Enlightenment also coincided with the organization of the brotherhood of Freemasonry. A great need for secrecy accompanied the spread of these new ideas, as it was dangerous in those times to make statements about the individual's rights to freedom. People espousing such ideas contrary to the establishment were hung or tortured as traitors and heretics. The lodges of Freemasonry became safe havens for the discussion of such radical shifts in consciousness, as some researchers believe they had done earlier by protecting the escaped Knights Templar. Through the years, they have maintained their high value on secrecy, even though the climate today is far more open to their teachings. The practiced skill of keeping secrets among the many Masons who were generals in Washington's Continental Army may have helped them win the war, as keeping secrets is of utmost importance among any group trying to throw off the control of a tyrannical power. To those who say the secrecy of the Masons is outmoded today, I would point to how many of our civil liberties have been revoked by our current administration, which believes in giving a president dictatorial powers. George W. Bush has made us remember there may yet be a time in the future when secrecy will be the only way of sharing ideas the government decides are bad for you, or at least bad for their control of you.

Education or enlightenment was key to freedom, says Jeffrey Meyer:

> That freedom requires knowledge became a central tenet of the American creed. An educated citizenry preserves democracy, a democracy protects individual freedom. Despite all the political wrangling in the last twenty-five years of the eighteenth century, all participants agreed on these essential points. The enemies were authoritarian monarchs who controlled bodies and ecclesiastical hierarchs who controlled minds. Authoritarian power had to be resisted, vigilance maintained, lest freedom be diminished. The best weapons were education and knowledge.[11]

Lying About the Freemasons

Freemasonry defined its rituals and chose its symbols in the same climate that inspired the Americans in their revolution. Both the Masons and the leaders of the American Revolution tended to choose symbols to honor the spread of knowledge and information as the keys to freedom. It's not that the Founding Fathers chose Freemasonic symbols; it's more that the Freemasons and the Founding Fathers were choosing their symbols from the same well. To slander the Founding Fathers by saying they conspired to place "Masonic" or "Satanic" symbols all around us with the future goal of brainwashing us into accepting the New World Order or the Antichrist is a 180-degree reversal of their intentions. The founders' goals for America were in large measure about granting freedom of worship to all inhabitants. Regardless of their personal religious beliefs, they went out of their way to protect your ability to chose whatever religion or social club to which you want to belong.

Attacking the Freemasons as evil is also completely contradictory to the Masons' goals of personal moral development, and their focus on charitable works and community service activities, especially in medical care for children, nursing homes, and educational grants. They have a greater appreciation for symbols than the average person, having used them as a "private language" for centuries. As Brent Morris explains, "Masonic lodges use symbols to teach moral lessons and ethical behavior," and "[i]t requires a deeper appreciation of the symbols for the significance to come out."[12]

Because those who attack Freemasonry are often the same ones attacking American symbols, it's important to examine their credibility. Others have already done an excellent job of refuting the attacks on Freemasonry; I especially recommend a well-referenced and organized Website run by Trevor McKeown[13] for quick rebuttals to the common rumors and accusations about them. Here is one final example from De Hoyos and Morris's book to show how much fraud and deceit surround the arguments of the anti-Masons. Chapter 8 of *Is It True What They Say About Freemasonry* reviews the work of Rev. James Dayton Shaw, a minister of the Gospel of Jesus Christ and author of *The Deadly Deception*. De Hoyos and Morris walk us through the six claims made on the cover of the book to show that four of them are outright lies. A fifth was determined to be an exaggeration added by the publisher, and therefore De Hoyos and Morris did not count this claim as a lie by the author. Only one claim on the cover is actually true. The best face that can be put on the veracity of all the statements on this anti-Masonic book is that only 33 percent of them are semi-true. And that's just the cover! Lie after lie are also revealed inside the pages as well.

Lying About American Symbols

Without considering documented history, it is easy for the fundamentalist-conspiratorialists to claim that if something looks Masonic, then it must be Masonic. Attacking American symbols is just their latest way of shocking their audiences into leaping to the conclusion that clues of an Illuminati or Satanic conspiracy are all around us. One of the most outspoken critics of American symbolism is David Bay, a prolific author of books and films that appeal to the emotions of fear and prejudice. His writings are cut and pasted all over the Internet. Here's just one example:

> "Washington D.C., Planned By Masonic Founding Fathers As
> The Most Powerful Occult Capitol [sic] In World History! Subtitle:
> Satanists believe that a city must be built by the Serpents of Wisdom
> and continually receive Serpent spiritual power if that city is ever to
> be great. Masonic American Forefathers built Washington, D.C., to
> be THE capitol [sic] in world history, unparalleled in occult power
> and influence. Serpent symbols in our Federal Mall tell the story!"[14]

This article has been reposted elsewhere identifying its author as Texe Marrs, but Bay assured us it is his original writing. The article details which symbols he sees as serpent-like, declaring with no citations that the "serpent is a symbol of the devil." Maybe sometimes, but the serpent is also used in the Bible as a symbol for wise defense, as in Matthew 10:16, when Jesus said, "Behold, I send you out as sheep in the midst of wolves; so be shrewd as serpents and innocent as doves." And in John 3:14 Jesus is quoted as comparing himself to the brass serpent on the staff of Moses that God instructed him to hold up before the children of Israel in order to heal them. Serpents in classical times were often symbolic of wisdom or of healing, as in the staff of Asclepius, the Greek healer whose serpent-entwined rod was adopted as a logo for the American Medical Association. Around the world, we find snakes often symbolize energy, which can be used for good or evil. The regular shedding of its skin has also given the snake a symbolic association with resurrection. If the Founding Fathers did incorporate any symbolism of the serpent in Washington, D.C., it was chosen because in early American art snakes were symbolic of wisdom.

David Bay also gives us a completely fabricated interpretation of the Washington Monument, crediting his information about the symbolic meaning of the obelisk to one of the standard sources, a self-proclaimed former insider. Bays says that "former Black Magick Satanist, Cisco Wheeler, now a Born Again Christian,"[15] informed him that, "An obelisk is taught to Masons as a symbol of the phallus, but the deepest level meaning is that it is really a 'frozen snake.' Obelisks support the Serpent Life Force as it spirals between Heaven and Earth. The shape of the Obelisk was inspired by huge generator crystals, Atlantean 'fire stone,' the life force accumulators and amplifiers."[16] Bay concludes from this unsubstantiated bit of creative writing that the Masons erected the phallic Washington Monument in the center of the capital in order to "arc the Serpent Life Force between Heaven and Earth, powerfully driving the government of the United States to be the most influential mover and shaker of the coming Kingdom of Antichrist, the New World Order."[17]

Bay's next claim in his subtitle is that "Masonic American forefathers built Washington, D.C." As we showed in Chapter 7, among the designers of this city, the only verified Freemason was George Washington, who had no creative input into the street designs. Though it seems that some examples of sacred geometry can be suggested in the street plans of D.C., none of these symbols is exclusive to the Freemasons. Just because they look Masonic does not prove that Masons placed them there. They may even be coincidental and have no meaning at all. The one source that Bay does cite for asserting that a Masonic fraternity was responsible for the plan of the city explicitly denies making any such assertion.

Bay frequently misconstrues the work of David Ovason (as he also does my own), bending statements to suit his own purposes until they are diametrically opposed to the original intent. Ovason foresaw that he would be quoted out of context and thus stated categorically that he was *not* saying that Masons coordinated a formulated plan to influence the city in any way.[18] Bay further fabricates a reference to Ovason as his source for stating that "when the

Mall was being conceived, and individual buildings were being built, Washington, DC was dedicated, and oriented, to the Dog Star Sirius, which in the Egyptian Mysteries, is Satan."[19] Just to be sure, I contacted David Ovason and asked if he claimed D.C. was dedicated or oriented to Sirius. He replied, "*No,* I did not claim that anywhere. That would, indeed, be a very foolish claim, for it is not true."[20]

Bay also errs in claiming that in the Egyptian mysteries the star Sirius was equated with Satan. Most Egyptian mythologists equate our concept of Satan with the Egyptian figure known as Set, who murdered and dismembered his brother Osiris. The dog star Sirius is usually linked to the goddess Isis and was welcomed as a harbinger of their agricultural season, universally considered a positive event. Unless Bay is referring to Isis as Satanic on the basis that all things in classical mythology of the ancients were pagan and therefore Satanic, the statement that Sirius in the Egyptian mysteries is Satan is another factual error.

Usually, however, conspiracy authors do not rely on works of historical documentation. Most of the time they are quoting from each other in an endless cycle of non-documentable and easily refutable, but always inflammatory, claims. For example, Bay quotes from Bill Cooper's book *Behold a Pale Horse,* where in turn Cooper[21] is quoting from Stan Deyo's book *The Cosmic Conspiracy.* Bay says that Cooper says in *Behold a Pale Horse*[22]:

> In the Great Seal of the United States, we see the ancient symbol of the Brotherhood of the Snake...which as you already know is the all-seeing eye in the pyramid representing Lucifer in the form of wisdom.... There are: 13 leaves on the branches, 13 bars and stripes, 13 arrows, 13 letters in 'E Pluribus Unum', 13 stars in the green crest, above, 13 stones, or layers, in the pyramid, 13 letters in 'Annuit Coeptis'. Thirteen is the mystical number assigned to Satan, according to Stan Deyo in his excellent book entitled *Cosmic Conspiracy.*[23]

So, it appears that the *Brotherhood of the Snake* and the *Brotherhood of the Bell* are interchangeable terms for the Illuminati in the writings of the fundamentalist-conspiratorialists who are intent on finding a secret society of devil worshippers to blame for all that is wrong with the world. Not surprisingly, many of the assertions in this quote are factually in error. For example, snakes are not a symbol associated with Freemasons. The all-seeing eye of the Great Seal is not situated *in* the pyramid, but rather above it. The designers of the Great Seal are on record stating the all-seeing eye represents the eye of Providence or God, not Lucifer. And finally: 13 is the mystical number assigned to Satan? Says who?

No reference is provided for assigning 13 to Satan in Bay's quote from Cooper's book, or Cooper's quote from Deyo's book. So I looked it up in Deyo's book and found he is referencing a small book from Australia called *Seal of God* by F.C. Payne, which appears to apply a numeric code to words in the Bible. I found a copy of this book posted online and verified that Mr. Payne assigns the number 13 to sin, linking it to Satan with a gematria chart for the various titles assigned to Satan showing how each is divisible by 13. His only reference for these conclusions is "students of the Scriptures."[24] As we discussed in Chapter 3, many ancient societies associated the number 13 with rebirth and regeneration and considered it lucky. It is a number of evolution and progress, and is sacred to many traditions. The reason our founders used this number repeatedly was to symbolize their union of 13 states, which they hoped would begin a rebirth of the enlightened policies of the ancient world.

Stan Deyo's *Cosmic Conspiracy* is also full of factual errors and unreferenced statements. Just before Deyo announces that "the Great Seal of the United States of America is not what it appears to be," he gives us the historical background: "[T]he Constitutional Congress officially adopted two major constructions on the 15th of September 1789; the U.S. Constitution and the Great Seal of the United States of America."[25] Well, as far as I can tell, the Constitution was officially adopted on the 17th of September 1787, and the Great Seal was officially adopted on the 20th of June 1782. He then proceeds to tell us that *Annuit Coeptis* the motto on the Seal, means "announcing the birth creation or arrival," and *Novus Ordo Seclorum* means the "New Secular Order."[26] As established in Chapter 2, the proper translation by the Latin scholar Charles Thomson, who selected these mottoes, is "He [meaning God] prospers our undertaking" and "The New Order of the Ages" (standing for the new form of democratic republicanism).

It appears that Deyo is copying his facts from William Guy Carr's notorious *Pawns in the Game,* the McCarthy-era update of Nesta Webster's Illuminati-Jew conspiracy theory. Carr's comments linking the Illuminati to the reverse of the Great Seal do appear to be literally cut and pasted into his book from an earlier source, and we will continue to search for a source that pre-dates Carr. Whoever first claimed (speciously) that the Bavarian Illuminati used a symbol similar to the eye in the triangle over the pyramid is probably the same one who originated these false translations of the Latin mottoes.

Deyo follows right along with Carr in claiming that the "Great Seal of the U.S. was designed...by the Illuminati. This is certain."[27] He gives not one reference to back up this assertion. So I ask, for the umpteenth time: Which one of the designers of the Great Seal was a member of the Illuminati? None of the true designers of the Great Seal was a member of ANY secret Society— THAT is what is certain. All writers should make a careful study of *The Eagle and the Shield* before they publish any further claims regarding the history of the Great Seal.

Another prolific and highly quoted source defaming American symbolism with lies and half-truths is David Icke. His 1999 book, *The Biggest Secret,* also lists the incorrect Latin translations for the Great Seal mottoes as "announcing the birth of a new secular order."[28] He declares authoritatively with no references cited that the obelisk and the dome were Egyptian symbols for the star Sirius, and that the all-seeing eye on the Great Seal is the eye of "Horus, Lucifer, Satan, whatever name you want to use, and... also symbolizes the reptilians looking into this world from the lower fourth dimension and if you look at a magnification of the eye you will see that the skin texture even looks reptilian."[29] The reverse of America's Great Seal is a symbol embraced by the reptilians, says Icke, because it represents the New World Order of a global fascist state.[30]

Whereas most fundamentalist-conspiratorialists use fear of Satan as their weapon, David Icke has found another way to spread fear. His conspiracy of "them" originates with extraterrestrial (or inner terrestrial) beings called the reptilians who manipulate our planet through various bloodlines of the ruling elite humans. Icke's theory describes reptilians as interdimensional beings that do not have a natural energy source such as a physical dimension, and therefore need to use humans as their energy source.

According to Icke the reptilians control humanity by breeding with the families of planetary rulers who have managed to stay in control more or less from one generation to the next since the beginning of recorded history. Though outwardly in opposition to one another, these ruling families and nations are secretly working together. The wars the rest of us see as shaping human history are actually organized conflicts designed to lead to global fascism.

Although his "them" is quite a bit different, and his teachings are sprinkled with so-called New Age ideas, Icke and his followers spread irrational fear the same way the fundamentalist-conspiratorialists do—that is, by creating an un-provable source that they in turn accuse of fear mongering. Unlike his other critics, however, I will not dismiss Icke simply because he brings extraterrestrials into the equation. During the past 20 years I have interviewed hundreds of aca-demics and professionals examining the UFO mystery, and from them I have this perspective to add to the question of David Icke: Very few of them support Icke's view on reptilians and what he claims to know about their purpose in visiting our physical dimension.

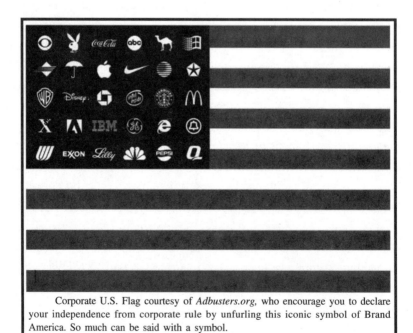

Corporate U.S. Flag courtesy of *Adbusters.org*, who encourage you to declare your independence from corporate rule by unfurling this iconic symbol of Brand America. So much can be said with a symbol.

The Constitution as a Symbol

Our current president, George W. Bush, was elected and supported in large measure by appealing to the Evangelical Christians, many of whom—though not all, by any means!—share the same mindset as the fundamentalist-conspiratorialists we write about in this book. My opinions of Mr. Bush are probably clear from several other comments I've made, but I would like to discuss briefly one event that demonstrates how little regard he has for one of America's most important symbols: the U.S. Constitution. (He has also shown disdain for the Geneva Conventions and the U.N. Charter, but we won't detail here all the abuses his administration has perpetrated on the American public in the guise of "protecting us from terror.")

Most Americans probably still believe we are protected by the Constitution from any one arm of the government assuming dictatorial powers. To make that assumption, however, we must have faith that our chief executive honors and upholds the Constitution and is not working against it to operate under "unitary executive" privilege. A November 2005 incident, unfortunately, revealed Bush's true feelings about the Constitution. He called it "just a goddamned piece of paper"[31] in a room full of congressional representatives and a few journalists.

They were there to review the controversial renewal of the Patriot Act, which had passed easily in the aftermath of September 11, 2001, but had since given many Americans, including prominent Republicans, second thoughts about its sweeping powers. Bush said he couldn't understand why anyone was upset about what he considered necessary measures, and, when one aide spoke up to say the Patriot Act contradicted a number of rights granted by the Constitution, he reportedly barked out, "Stop throwing the Constitution in my face! It's just a goddamned piece of paper!"[32]

In an appropriately titled book, *George W. Bush versus the U.S. Constitution*, Rep. John Conyers published the report by the House Judiciary Committee on the lies and hoaxes used by the Bush administration to increase the public fear level and lead us into the war in Iraq. The mindset that approved unauthorized domestic spying and torture has also rolled over other Constitutional rights in the past six years. Exclusive power has been granted to the president to determine any American citizen an "enemy combatant" and imprison him without trial indeterminately. Complete surveillance over every aspect of our daily lives is in place. In defense of these actions, the president claims he has the power to override any law during wartime. The problem with this picture is that a poorly defined "war on terror" may go on forever. By allowing George W. Bush so much unitary privilege, we may have inadvertently changed the course of America's destiny forever. I find it interesting that his approach with the "war on terror" has been very similar to the fear-mongering used by the fundamentalist-conspiratorialists about our symbols. By successfully manipulating fear, the Bush administration has infringed upon our civil liberties in ways Americans of earlier days never would have accepted.

The Procter & Gamble Logo Scare

I want to point to one final example of a corporate logo to demonstrate why I get so upset when people publish lies about our American symbols. It has to do with how "great is the power of steady misrepresentation," as Charles Darwin once said. One of America's oldest and best-loved consumer products companies was pressured to change their logo after many years of complaints from a fundamentalist-conspiratorialist campaign. It doesn't really matter that the campaign was based on lies and fueled by fear and emotional outrage as far as the fate of the discontinued Procter & Gamble (P&G) logo is concerned. The lie was picked up by hundreds of thousands of people who didn't check their facts. This same kind of attack is currently underway against our beautiful and powerful American symbols, which is why I hope you will stand up with me to defend them.

Procter & Gamble was founded in 1837 by William Procter and James Gamble as a soap and candle factory. The original Procter was known to be a devout Episcopalian who lived by the rule of tithing even before he started his soap company. His grandson and heir continued this tradition. Their original logo was developed as a trademark in 1851 to identify crates of their products in the shipping yards by workers who could not read. They described their logo as based on the man in the moon, a very popular motif in the mid-1800s, enclosed in a circle with 13 five-pointed stars. (See the illustrationon the opposire page.) The 13 stars were from America's first flag and in honor of the 13 original colonies.[33] They used this same logo with slight artistic modifications, without incident, for more than a hundred years. P&G continued to prosper throughout the next century, inventing such mainstay brands as Ivory Soap, Tide laundry detergent, Crest toothpaste, and Pampers diapers. Their early support for the medium of radio even spawned an entertainment industry called the soap opera.

The controversy started as early as the 1960s when someone generated a fake letter linking P&G to Satanism, using a misinterpretation of their logo as part of their proof. The main point of the hoax was to urge a boycott of P&G products. As the decades passed, the hoax lived on with interesting modifications to match the times. The earliest versions of the letter described the president of P&G swearing his allegiance to Satan on the *Merv Griffin* or *Phil Donahue* television show. Later versions have him appearing on *Sally Jesse Raphael, Jenny Jones,* or *Oprah.* Future talk show names will probably be inserted in future versions of the letter, for it is still out there, and still being believed and acted upon.

The fundamentalist-conspiratorialists decided that the P&G logo was a Satanic mockery of the Bible verse Revelations 12:1, where a woman appears with the moon under her feet and 12 stars in her crown. Because the P&G logo had a man in the moon instead of a woman on the moon, and 13 stars instead of 12, it was called Satanic. If you hold the logo up to a mirror and turn it upside down, you can see 666 in the curlicues of the man's beard. The two curlicues at the tips of the man's beard were called horns of the devil.

The Moon and Stars Logo used by Procter & Gamble from 1930 to 1991. A much-publicized letter-writing campaign by fundamentalist-conspiratorialists speciously claimed this logo to be Satanic. Used by permission.

After receiving more than 150,000 phone calls and letters from people incited under false pretenses to protest a misunderstood logo, the board members decided in 1985 to change their logo. Their company rep says this decision was "based partially on this discontent, as well as the need to have a logo that resonated globally with consumers."[34] They also do not give the letter-writing campaign the full credit for changing the logo: "While consumer complaints about Satanism contributed to an update on the logo, P&G made the final decision based on the fact that the moon and stars didn't translate well in the regions where the company was expanding its global operations."[35] Even after they changed their logo, however, they still continue to receive questions about this rumor.

P&G sued more than a dozen Amway products distributors as sources of the rumors, and was awarded more than 30 million dollars in damages. They also received public letters from the talk show hosts disclaiming that the P&G president ever appeared on their show. National Christian leaders including Billy Graham, Jerry Falwell, and Pat Robertson urged their followers to realize they had "been had" and to apologize. In the end, however, the man in the moon logo had been so effectively misrepresented and misunderstood that it was discontinued.

Don't Let This Happen to American Beauties

When fundamentalist-conspiratorialists set out to prove a preconceived opinion, they are not hindered by historical facts or the truth. Their minds are made up. If lies and deception are necessary to prove their point, it matters not. They are looking for examples to support their belief that Satan is everywhere, leaving clues in symbols to tempt you into sin. Spreading a little knowledge is all that is necessary to keep this rumor mill at bay about the alleged Satanic intentions of our Founding Fathers. If you share with others the true histories of our symbols and the context of the times in which they were created, we can forestall an ill-informed e-mail or letter-writing campaign that could do to the Great Seal what they did to the P&G logo.

When we don't do our homework, we can waste a lot of energy over specious connections leading to the loss of a symbol. Rather than attacking anyone's logo, your time would be better spent protesting the pollution record, controversial chemicals, or unfair labor practices of any particular corporation or government agency. Letter-writing campaigns of 150,000 strong protesting against some of these practices might make some truly significant changes, rather than merely cosmetic ones.

Despite my obvious disagreement with the conclusions of the fundamentalist-conspiratorialists, however, I still believe it is important to read their books and to do so with an open mind. Many of their conclusions are ludicrous, as I hope we have shown with the preceding chapters, but they are on the right track as far as there being an organized force in the world that is determined to distract us from our spiritual lives and entrap us in the material. As already noted, there are definitely groups of powerful elites who organize together to try to control the masses to their advantage. To find them, you only have to look into the connected boards of the major media, lobbying groups, big corporations, and professional politics. I believe it is a waste of time to get caught up in a hyper-analysis of their logos in an attempt to link them to the eye in the triangle or the torch or the pentagram. These symbols do not prove our Founding Fathers were Satanists. They prove they were children of the Enlightenment.

CONCLUSION

American symbols "worked" for the first 150 years or so after the Revolution, but they gradually grew outmoded and some of them became passé. Already in the 1960s I was writing in defense of America's symbols, but in those years I was objecting more to the young people's thoughtless dismissal of these symbols as icons of the older and non-hip generations. Blind patriotism was seriously called into question at that time, and some of our symbols were being pulled from their pedestals as a result. As I learned from humanistic psychologists, without meaningful symbols a society will be unstable and anxious. I set out to defend America's symbols as the very formative agents of our community. Symbols supply both the psychological and organizational foundations of social life, and, rather than pull them down, we need to more deeply appreciate them.

Today, America's symbols are suffering from a new series of attacks by a very different and very vocal element of our society. The pendulum has swung the other way, and now instead of the "hippie liberals" criticizing our symbols as too authoritarian, the fundamentalist-conspiratorialists are criticizing our symbols as too liberal. Just a casual Internet search for "hidden meanings of American symbols" will reveal the stranglehold on this topic that is held by those spewing negative interpretations. I hope that this book has presented a balance between these two schools of interpretation, both of which tend to result in misdirected boycotts, bans, and poorly advised logo changes.

Valid symbolic meanings that were not consciously intended by the designer of the symbol can sometimes be attributed to a work after the fact. Unless the intent was strongly held throughout the creative process, however, any magical effects this symbol might have are not going to be truly effective. The interpretations I have suggested for these American symbols can be used to explain why they struck a chord with our collective unconscious, but they can't be used to conclude that the creators *intended* any of the meanings. Speculative interpretations can be used effectively to gather more positive or negative attention to a symbol, but speculation should never disregard the historic record. Most of the time, the historic documentation does not validate any symbolic interpretations at all, either positive or negative. It is likely that in most cases, in fact, the creators of our American symbols did not even consider deeper symbolic interpretations beyond superficial allegory.

And yet, a deeper interpretation of these symbols can provide a deeper positive appreciation for the potential of the nation behind them. Our symbols should inspire hope. Hope that a *united* America can remain ever vigilant to protect our peace and our liberty. Only by *uniting* can we be strong. We need to embrace these symbols that inspire us to be as one. With the coming earth changes the best action any American can take right now is service to the community. Get to know your neighbors; volunteer your time to a worthy cause or for those less fortunate; plant trees; plan ahead.

We are not just the people from any city or state in the union.

We are not just Americans, or North or South Americans,

or people from the East or West Hemisphere.

We are people from the planet Earth.

We are Earth people, becoming enlightened beings.

Our form of representational government can only succeed with the active participation of its members remaining ever vigilant against threats to our peace. That includes threats from corrupted leaders within. It is my hope that a deeper appreciation for the symbols designed by our founders will add the necessary meaning to our lives and inspire contemporary Americans to activate our inherited role as defenders of an enlightened liberty. That is why I am so defensive about America's symbols. Because they really do have that much power.

Notes

Chapter 1

1. Clark, *The Sacred,* pp. 134 and 160.

2. Hieronimus, J.Z. *Kabbalistic.*

3. Cirlot, *A Dictionary,* p. xiii.

4. *The World Christian Encyclopedia* lists a mid-2000 estimate of Evangelical Christians at 40,640,000 (p. 772), but, of course, not all Evangelical Christians are proponents of the fundamentalist-conspiratorialist mindset.

5. As quoted in Cirlot, *A Dictionary,* p. xxix.

6. Cirlot, *A Dictionary,* p. xxix.

7. As quoted in Campbell, J., *Myths,* pp. 89–90.

8. Singer, *Boundaries,* p. 385.

9. May, *The Courage,* p. 153.

10. Tillich, *Dynamics,* p. 43.

11. Campbell, J., *The Hero,* p. 382.

12. Ibid., pp. 11–12.

13. Clift, "Symbols," p. 52.

14. Campbell, R., *Our Flag*; Heline, T., *America's.*

15. Heline, T., *America's,* pp. 7–8.

16. Jung, *Two Essays,* p. 91.

17. Singer, *Androgyny,* p. 266.

18. Campbell, J., *Myths,* p. 255.

19. Actual quote from President George H.W. Bush when being peppered with questions at the 1992 annual convention of the National League of POW/MIA Families.

20. Purged voter rolls, the prevention of more than 350,000 voters in Ohio from casting ballots or having their votes counted, and the use of touch-screen electronic voting machines (which leave no paper trail) are some of the ways our past two elections have been hijacked. The Government Accountability Office confirmed the Diebold system is "eminently hackable." With a touch-screen system even one corrupt staffer can throw an election. Convicted lobbyist Jack Abramoff was paid $275,000 to secure the installation of Diebold machines in Ohio. As of April 2007, four election board members of the most populous county in Ohio have been forced to resign because of the recount rigging charges and voter machine problems. Rep. John Conyers's Judiciary Committee report, *What Went Wrong in Ohio,* is now available in trade paperback.

21. Singer, *Androgyny,* p. 247.

22. Ray and Anderson, *The Cultural.*

Chapter 2

1. Schoch and McNally, *Pyramid.*

2. Patterson and Dougall, *The Eagle,* pp. 22–24.

3. Ibid., p. 531.

4. Ibid., p. 85.

5. Thomson, I.L. *The Great Seal*, p. 5.

6. Ovason, *The Secret Symbols,* pp. 121–22.

7. According to Denslow, *10,000 Famous.*

8. Weiss, "Masters." See also Domhoff, "Social."

9. Domhoff, "Social."

10. Weiss, "Masters."

11. From Steve Jackson, personal correspondence with the author, 6/16/07: "We are cynics, silly people and parodists, rather than either historians or conspiracy loonies. We assigned the pyramid symbol to the Bavarian Illuminati in the game, because somebody had to get it, and because lederhosen aren't very scary." The Steve Jackson Games Website (*www.sjgames.com*; accessed 6/2/07) further explains their game: "The phone company is controlled by creatures from outer space. The Congressional Wives have taken over the Pentagon. And the Boy Sprouts are cashing in their secret Swiss bank account to smash the IRS! Two to six players compete to grab powerful groups and increase their wealth and power."

12. McKeown, "Anti-Masonry Frequently."

13. Birch, *Secret.*

14. Sparks, *The Writings,* p. 377.

15. Jefferson was slandered as being an atheist during his political campaign, though his true religious beliefs were Christian in the broadest and truest sense of the word. For 16 years he worked on compiling *The Life and Morals of Jesus of Nazareth,* now known as the *Jefferson Bible.* He confided in few people about his studies, but in 1816 Jefferson wrote to Charles Thomson: "I too, have made a wee little book...which I call the philosophy of Jesus; it is a paradigm of his doctrines.... A more beautiful or precious morsel of ethics I have never seen; it is a document in proof that I am a real Christian, that is to say, a disciple of the doctrines of Jesus" (Jefferson, *Life,* p. x).

16. *The Writings of Thomas Jefferson,* vol. vii, p. 419, as quoted in Stauffer, *The Bavarian,* p. 312.

17. Ibid.

18. Heckethorn, *The Secret,* p. 306.

19. In his *Guide to Freemasonry* (p. 188), Dr. S. Brent Morris notes that the first time the all-seeing eye was officially described in any Freemasonic literature was in 1819, 37 years after the design of the Great Seal.

20. *The Protocols of the Elders of Zion* has been exposed as a hoax by several independent investigations, beginning with *Times* in London in 1921. The famous Berne Trial in 1934–35 declared *The Protocols to be plagiarized forgeries.*

21. Blanton, "The CIA's."

22. Alexandra Robbins, interview by Dr. Bob Hieronimus, *21st Century Radio,* 2/22/04.

23. Ibid.

24. "CBS."

25. Elizabeth Ellers and Danielle Marcey, interview with the author, 4/19/07.

26. Ibid.

27. Ibid.

28. Ibid.

29. Hanchett, "Nice."

30. "DARPA."

31. "Statement."

Chapter 3

1. As quoted in Corcoran, *For Which,* p. 86.

2. Basler et al., *The Collected,* pp. 240–41.

3. Furlong and McCandless, *So Proudly,* p. 118.

4. "The Rattle-Snake as a Symbol of America," by An American Guesser (BF), *Pa. Journal,* Dec. 27, 1775. As quoted in Isaacson, *Benjamin,* p. 305. For the full text of the letter, see MacArthur's article, "Ben Franklin on the Rattlesnake as a Symbol of America," in the Bibliography.

5. Furlong and McCandless, *So Proudly,* p. 101.

6. Patterson and Dougall, *The Eagle,* p. 61.

7. Ibid.

8. Dave Martucci, personal correspondence with the author, 2/18/07.

9. Furlong and McCandless, *So Proudly,* p. 117.

10. Dave Martucci, personal correspondence with the author, 2/18/07.

11. "Betsy Ross Homepage."

12. As quoted in Corcoran, *For Which,* pp. 37–38.

13. Cirlot, *A Dictionary,* p. 332.

14. *The Great Seal,* p. 5.

15. Ibid.

16. Ibid.

17. Wilhelm, *The I Ching,* p. 56.

18. *The Great Seal,* pp. 8–9.

19. For the rather convoluted explanation for how easy it is to cut a five-pointed star in one snip, see "Cut a 5-Pointed" in the Bibliography.

20. Case, *The Great,* p. 19.

21. Case, *The Tarot,* p. 10.

22. Wilhelm, *The I Ching,* p. 641.

Chapter 4

1. Bartholdi, *The Statue,* p. 36.

2. Paige, *The Liberty,* p. 28.

3. Weisberger, *The Statue,* p. 36.

4. As quoted in Weisberger, *The Statue,* p. 90.

5. "Our Society"; "The Unified"; and Duke, *Jewish.*

6. Cockran, *Cherokee Frontier,* p. 4. As quoted in Grinde and Johansen, *Exemplar,* p. 221.

7. Fleming, "From Indian," p. 46.

8. Patterson and Dougall, *The Eagle,* p. 65.

9. Joseph, *The Atlantis,* p. 22.

10. Fleming, "From Indian," p. 39.

11. Ibid.

12. Bartholdi, *The Statue,* p. 37; Weisberger, *The Statue,*p. 184.

13. Moreno, *The Statue,* p. 33.

14. Hancock and Bauval, *Talisman,* p. 442.

15. According to Ligou, *Dictionnaire.*

16. Jung, C.G. *Symbols of Transformation,* (Collected Works, 5). London, 1956. As quoted in Cirlot, *A Dictionary,* p. 70.

17. Hieronimus, J.Z., *Kabbalistic.*

18. As quoted in Gaskell, *Dictionary,* p. 590.

19. Cirlot, *A Dictionary,* p. 223.

20. Hieronimus, J.Z., *Kabbalistic.*

21. Barry Moreno, personal correspondence with the author, 8/29/07.

22. Weisberger, *The Statue,* p. 44.

23. Cirlot, *A Dictionary,* p. 29.

24. Weisberger, *The Statue,* p. 47.

25. Maxwell, *Matrix,* p. 17.

26. "Our Society."

27. Personal correspondence with the author and Caroline Lam, 7/20/07.

Chapter 5

1. Kimball, *The Story,* pp. 19–20; Paige, *The Liberty,* p. 5.

2. Kimball, *The Story,* pp. 32–33; Paige, *The Liberty,* p. 24.

3. Edmund C. Burnett, ed. *Letters of Members of the Continental Congress* (8 vols.; Washington, D.C.: Carnegie Institution of Washington, 1923), II, 8. As quoted in Paige, *The Liberty,* p. 24.

4. Kimball, *The Story,* pp. 19–39; Paige, *The Liberty,* pp. 3–16.

5. As quoted in Kimball, *The Story,* p. 45.

6. Ibid.

7. "Not Your."

8. *Philadelphia Inquirer* article, March 7, 1873. As quoted in Paige, *The Liberty,* p. 47.

9. Hart, "The Other."

10. As quoted in Giannini, "Factual Flier."

11. As quoted in Paige, *The Liberty,* pp. 49–50.

12. Ibid.

13. Ibid.

14. Ibid.

15. See the "Chapter 1 Addendum" to Westcott, *Bells,* on the following Web page: *www.msu.edu/~carillon/batmbook/chapter1.htm* (accessed 9/5/07).

16. Westcott, *Bells,* pp. 86–90.

17. Fox-Davies, *A Complete,* p. 287.

18. "Guided."

19. "The Story."

20. "The World."

21. "Schwedagon."

22. Maxwell, *Matrix,* p. 18.

23. "Bell."

24. Icke, *The Biggest,* p. 186.

25. "Illuminati." Post by "Truth Advocator" on 1/24/05.

26. Westcott, *Bells,* p. 15.

27. *The Zohar.*

28. Bergquist, "Doorways."

29. Cirlot, *A Dictionary,* p. 23.

30. See Wolf, *The Dreaming* and Goswami, *Physics.*

31. Nakkach, "The Secret."

32. Ibid.

33. Thompson, "Methods."

34. Bergquist, "Doorways."

Chapter 6

1. Adams, *Works from Adams* 4:296. Quoted in Grinde and Johansen, *Exemplar,* p. 200.

2. Paine, "Agrarian Justice" (1797), in Foner, ed., *The Complete Writings of Thomas Paine* (New York: Citadel Press, 1945), 1:610. Quoted in Grinde and Johansen, "Sauce," p. 630.

3. Columbian Magazine, II, 3, p. 136. As quoted in Grinde and Johansen, *Exemplar,* pp. 246–48.

4. The famous poem, "The Song of Hiawatha," by Longfellow is referring to a different person with a similar name or title.

5. As quoted in Grinde and Johansen, *Exemplar,* p. 160. For Thomson's role in creating the Northwest Ordinance, see his most recent biographer, J. Edwin Hendricks, *Charles Thomson and the Making of a New Nation, 1729–1824* (Rutherford, N.J.: Fairleigh Dickinson University Press, 1979).

6. This is a common saying attributed to many original sources, including Thomas Jefferson and Wendell Phillips. Wikipedia gives the honors to a 19th-century British politician named Leonard Courtney. It seems, however, that this quotation had existed in various renditions for many years before these various men used it.

7. Grinde, *The Iroquois,* pp. 8–9.

8. Grinde, *The Iroquois,* p. 31.

9. Johansen, *Forgotten,* pp. 65–66.

10. *The Bagatelles from Possy* (New York: Eakins Press, 1967), p. 34. Quoted in Grinde and Johnson, *Exemplar,* p. 199.

11. U.S. Fish and Wildlife Service Data from "Bald Eagle."

12. Patterson and Dougall, *The Eagle,* pp. 93–102.

13. Ibid., p. 61.

14. Newman, *The Early,* pp. 401 and 420.

15. Patterson and Dougall, *The Eagle,* pp. 409–50.

16. Rav Brandwein, personal correspondence with the author, 7/9/06.

17. Fox-Davies, *A Complete,* pp. 17, 231–38.

18. Parker, "The Double-Headed."

19. Hall, *The Secret Teachings,* p. 91.

20. Patterson and Dougall, *The Eagle,* p. 68.

21. Ovason, *The Secret Symbols,* p. 140.

22. Cirlot, *A Dictionary,* p. 242.

23. The Thunderbird is considered a legendary bird in many different Native American traditions, though cryptozoologists Mark Hall and Loren Coleman have collected numerous eyewitness accounts of the physical reality of such a monstrous bird, reported as recently as 1977 in Illinois. See their book, *Thunderbirds: America's Living Legends of Giant Birds* (Paraview Press, 2004).

24. Hall, *America's,* p. 96.

25. "Hillary."

26. Quayle, "The Fourth."

27. Marrs, "Magic."

28. Ibid.

29. S. Brent Morris, personal correspondence with the author, 8/29/07.

30. *The Great Seal,* p. 5.

31. Ibid.

Chapter 7

1. Berg, *Grand,* pp. 98–99; Bowling, *Creating,* pp. 39–44.

2. Bowling, *Creating,* p. 44.

3. Arnebeck, *Through,* p. 3; Bowling, *Creating,* p. 109.

4. Bowling, *Creating,* p. 88.

5. Berg, *Grand,* p. 68.

6. Bowling, *Creating,* p. 79.

7. Banneker's letter to Jefferson, dated August 19, 1791, is reproduced in Bedini, *The Life,* pp. 159–60.

8. Jefferson's letter to Banneker, dated August 30, 1791, is reproduced in Bedini, *The Life,* p. 165.

9. Cerami, *Benjamin,* p. 218.

10. Banneker's was not the first striking clock made in America, as is claimed in some overly zealous biographies of him.

11. "Benjamin Banneker Memorial" and "Benjamin Banneker Historical."

12. Jennings, "Artistry," p. 262.

13. We are grateful to author Chris Hardaker for introducing us to Jennings's work.

14. Berg, *Grand,* p. 13.

15. Ibid., p. 105. Berg contrasts L'Enfant's "grand avenue" with the greensward of Versailles with which is it so often erroneously connected. He points out how conceptually they were complete opposites. At Versailles, the king's bedroom was the focal point, and none of the citizens was ever allowed on the beautiful greens without the king's permission. In L'Enfant's city, the house of the people (Congress) was the focal point, and the citizenry were invited to congregate in any of the beautiful green spaces between the important buildings at any time.

16. Ibid., p. 184.

17. Ovason, *The Secret Architecture,* p. 355.

18. "Famous" and "A Few."

19. Ovason, *The Secret Architecture,* p. 60.

20. David Ovason, interview by Dr. Bob Hieronimus, *21st Century Radio,* 2/11/01.

21. The libraries of both Ben Franklin and Thomas Jefferson included serious books on astrology, as did those of the majority of cultured men and women. Benjamin Banneker was also familiar with astrology, as seen in his almanacs.

22. David Ovason, interview by Dr. Bob Hieronimus, *21st Century Radio,* 2/11/01.

23. Ovason, *The Secret Architecture,* pp. 255–56.

24. Ibid., p. 350.

25. Ibid., p. 324.

26. Baigent and Leigh, *The Temple,* p. 262. Also of note, the international best-seller written in 1982 by Baigent and Leigh with Henry Lincoln, *Holy Blood, Holy Grail,* was the launching point for a whole new way of looking for clues in history, art, architecture, and the landscape.

27. "The Kabalyon."

28. Charles Westbrook, Jr., personal correspondence with the author, 9/23/07.

29. Westbrook, *The Talisman Newsletter.*

30. Ibid.

31. Charles Westbrook, Jr., personal correspondence with the author, 9/23/07.

32. Ibid.

33. Ibid.

34. Ibid.

35. Ibid.

36. Charles Westbrook, Jr., personal correspondence with the author, 10/13/07.

37. The following Web pages provided the information for the Satanic interpretation of Washington, D.C. (all accessed 10/10/07): "Freemasonry and Washington D.C.'s Street Layout," (*freemasonrywatch.org/washington.html*); "Satanic Occult Symbols in Washington D.C." (*www.jesus-is-savior.com/False%20Religions/Illuminati/dc.htm*); and "Masonic Symbols of Power in their Seat of Power-Washington, D.C." (*www.cuttingedge.org/n1040.html*).

38. Hardaker, "The Seal," p. 2.

39. Berg, *Grand,* p. 184.

40. Hardaker, "The Seal," p. 2.

41. Hardaker, "The Seal," p. 8.

42. Ibid., p. 3.

43. Campbell, J., with Moyers. *The Power.*

44. "From Pentagram."

45. Rick Campbell, personal correspondence with the author, 9/14/07.

46. "From Pentagram."

47. Rick Campbell, personal correspondence with the author, 9/2/07.

48. Ibid.

49. Ibid., 9/14/07.

50. Ibid.

51. Ibid.

52. Nicholas Mann, personal correspondence with the author, 10/28/07.

53. Mann, *The Sacred,* p. 168.

54. Ibid., p. 2.

55. Ibid.

56. Ibid., p. 4.

57. Ibid., p. 8.

58. Ibid., p. 178.

59. Ibid.

60. Ibid., p. 119.

61. As stated in the film *Unveiling the Masonic Symbolism of Washington, DC.*

62. Ibid.

63. Berg, *Grand,* p. 109.

64. Browder, *Egypt* and "IKG."

65. Cirlot, *A Dictionary,* p. 227.

66. Scott, *Temple,* p. 48.

67. Ibid., p. 26.

68. Meyer, *Myths,* pp. 170–71.

69. Meeks, "Pantheon," p. 1.

70. Stauffer, *The Bavarian,* p. 357.

71. Ibid., p. 359.

72. Ibid., p. 360.

73. Hardaker, "The Seal," p. 1.

74. Ibid.

75. April 18, 2006, press conference defending Donald Rumsfeld as Secretary of Defense.

76. "Presidential."

77. Mann, *The Sacred,* pp. 179–80.

78. Belanger, *The World's,* p. 100.

79. Ibid., p. 95

80. O'Connell, "An Irishman's."

81. Ovason, *The Secret Architecture,* p. 84.

82. Ibid., pp. 83–84.

83. Mann, *The Sacred,* p. 171.

84. Westbrook, *Talisman,* p. 31.

Chapter 8

1. May, *Man's.*

2. Sites that call M.P. Hall a Masonic historian include the Illuminati Conspiracy Archive (*www.conspiracyarchive.com/NOW/Freemasonry.htm*); Religion-Spirituality.org (*www.religion-spirituality.org/freemasonry/ties-occult.php*); and The Cutting Edge (*www.thecuttingedge.org/FREE001a.html*).

3. De Hoyos and Morris, *Is It,* p. 24.

4. Ibid., p. 28.

5. Ibid., p. 29.

6. Ibid., pp. 44–45.

7. Moray, *The Truth About Masons,* p. 23, as quoted in de Hoyos and Morris, *Is It,* p. 30.

8. Ibid., p. 17.

9. De Hoyos and Morris, *Is It,,* p. 14.

10. Ibid.

11. Meyer, *Myths,* pp. 103–4.

12. Morris, *The Complete,* pp. 217–18.

13. McKeown, "Anti-Masonic Claims."

14. "Washington, D.C."

15. Ibid.

16. Ibid.

17. Ibid.

18. Ovason, *The Secret Architecture,* p. 355.

19. "Washington, D.C."

20. David Ovason, personal correspondence with the author, 9/25/07.

21. How credible was Bill Cooper as a source? Here's how James Moseley, a one-time friend and supporter of him, described him in his obituary printed in *Saucer Smear* (12/1/01): "William Milton ('Bill') Cooper, 58, died on October 6th in a hail of bullets while shooting it out with sheriff's deputies outside his home. Cooper was an important figure in the extreme right-wing Militia movement in this country.... Cooper had spent the past few years holed up in his house, avoiding a warrant regarding unpaid taxes for the years 1992 to 1994. He was a hard-core tax evader, and made no secret of it, for he believed the federal government had no right to collect income taxes at all. We knew Bill Cooper quite well, mainly from having spent long periods of time with him at the bar, at various conventions. Cooper was quite a drinker, and one excuse for this was pain from having to walk on an artificial leg.... One good thing we will say about Cooper—he was one of the best public speakers we have ever heard, in regard to technical performance. (The content was something else again!) Cooper never used notes, and yet he never faltered or repeated himself. In the heyday of Beckley's western conventions, Cooper would draw several hundred people and earn perhaps a couple of thousand dollars!"

22. From pages 93–94 of Cooper's book.

23. "Washington, D.C."

24. Finck, "The Seal."

25. Deyo, *Cosmic,* p. 70.

26. Ibid.

27. Ibid.

28. Icke, *The Biggest,* p. 359.

29. Ibid.

30. Ibid., p. xiii.

31. Thomson, Doug, "Bush."

32. Ibid.

33. "Proctor."

34. Statement from Robyn Schroeder, Corporate Media Relations, 11/16/07.

35. Ibid.

BIBLIOGRAPHY

Abrams, Richard, and James Bell. *In Search of Liberty: The Story of the Statue of Liberty and Ellis Island*. Garden City, N.Y.: Doubleday, 1984.

"A Few Famous Freemasons." Grand Lodge of British Columbia and Yukon Website. *www.freemasonry.bcy.ca/textfiles/famous.html*. Accessed October 3, 2007.

"Anti-Masonic Claims Refuted." Grand Lodge of British Columbia and Yukon Website. *freemasonry.bcy.ca/anti-masonry/index.html*. Accessed November 1, 2007.

Arnebeck, Bob. *Through a Fiery Trial: Building Washington, 1790–1800*. Lanham, Md.: Madison Books, 1991.

Appleman, Roy, Milo Quaife, and Melvin Weig. *The History of the United States Flag: From the Revolution to the Present, Including a Guide to its Use and Display*. New York: Harper & Row, 1961.

Ashton, E.B., and Hertha Pauli. *I Lift My Lamp: The Way of the Symbol*. Port Washington, N.Y.: Ira J. Friedman, 1969.

Assagioli, Roberto. *The Act of Will*. New York: Viking Press, 1973.

Baigent, Michael, and Richard Leigh. *The Temple and the Lodge*. New York: Little, Brown Company, 1989.

Baigent, Michael, Richard Leigh, and Henry Lincoln. *Holy Blood, Holy Grail*. New York: Dell, 1983.

"Bald Eagle Population Size: Chart and Table of Bald Eagle Breeding Pairs in Lower 48 States." U.S. Fish and Wildlife Service. *www.fws.gov/ midwest/eagle/population/chtofprs.html*. Accessed August 27, 2007.

Barreiro, José, ed. *Indian Roots of American Democracy*. Ithaca, N.Y.: Cornell University's Northeast Indian Quarterly, 1988.

Barrett, David, and George Kurian and Todd Johnson, eds. *The World Christian Encyclopedia: A Comparative Survey of Churches and Religions in the Modern World*. New York: Oxford University Press, 2001.

Barruel, Augustin. *Memoirs Illustrating the History of Jacobinism*. Translated by Robert Clifford. Whitefish, Mont.: Kessinger Publishing's Rare Reprints, 2007.

Bartholdi, Frederic Auguste. *The Statue of Liberty Enlightening the World Described by the Sculptor*. New York: North American Review, 1885.

Basler, Roy P. et al., eds. *The Collected Works of Abraham Lincoln*, 9 vols. New Brunswick, N.J.: Rutgers University Press, 1953–55.

Beauchamp, William. *A History of the New York Iroquois, Now Commonly Called the Six Nations*. Port Washington, N.Y.: I.J. Friedman, 1962.

Bedini, Silvio. *The Life of Benjamin Banneker: The First African-American Man of Science*. Baltimore, Md.: Maryland Historical Society, 1999.

Belanger, Jeff. *The World's Most Haunted Places*. Franklin Lakes, N.J.: New Page Books, 2004.

"Bell." *Online Etymology Dictionary*. *www.etymonline.com*. Accessed August 31, 2007.

"Benjamin Banneker Memorial Website." *www.bannekermemorial.org*. Accessed October 30, 2007.

Berg, Scott. *Grand Avenues: The Story of the French Visionary Who Designed Washington, D.C.* New York: Pantheon, 2007.

Bergquist, Carlisle. "Doorways in Consciousness: An Exploration of Resonant Being." *Future Harmonix*, Spring (1998).

"Betsy Ross Homepage Resources: Affidavits." *USHistory.org*. *www.ushistory.org/betsy/flagaffs.html*. Accessed August 15, 2007.

Birch, Una. *Secret Societies: Illuminati, Freemasons and the French Revolution*. Edited by James Wasserman. Lake Worth, Fla.: Ibis Press, 2007.

Blanton, Thomas, Ed. "The CIA's Family Jewels: Agency Violated Charter for 25 Years, Wiretapped Journalists and Dissidents." The National Security Archive, George Washington University Website. *www.gwu.edu/~nsarchiv/NSAEBB/NSAEBB222/index.htm.* Accessed September 17, 2007.

Bowling, Kenneth. *Creating the Federal City, 1774–1800: Potomac Fever.* Washington, D.C.: The American Institute of Architects Press, 1988.

Brands, H.W. *The First American: The Life and Times of Benjamin Franklin.* New York: Anchor Books, 2002.

Browder, Anthony. *Egypt on the Potomac: A Guide to Decoding Egyptian Architecture and Symbolism in Washington, D.C.* Washington, D.C.: IKG, 2006.

Brown, Dan. *The Da Vinci Code.* New York: Doubleday, 2003.

Bunker, Robert. *Nonlethal Weapons Terms and References.* Colorado Springs, Colo.: USAF Institute for National Security Studies. 1997.

Burland, Cottie. *North American Indian Mythology.* Seltham, England: The Hamlyn Publishing Group, 1970.

Burnett, E.C. "Charles Thomson." In *Dictionary of American Biography* Vol. 12. New York: Charles Scribner's Sons, (1933): 481–82.

Camerarius, Joachim. *Joachimi Camerarii symbolorum ac emblematum ethico-politicorum centuria quatuor.* Mainz, Germany 1697, 1702.

Campbell, Don. *The Mozart Effect: Tapping the Power of Music to Heal the Body, Strengthen the Mind, and Unlock the Creative Spirit.* New York: Harper Paperbacks, 2001.

Campbell, Joseph. *The Hero with a Thousand Faces.* Bollingen Series 17. Princeton, N.J.: Princeton University Press, 1972.

Campbell, Joseph, with Bill Moyers. *The Power of Myth.* New York: Doubleday, 1988.

———. *Myths to Live By.* New York: Bantam Books, 1973.

Campbell, Robert. *Our Flag or the Evolution of the Stars and Stripes.* Chicago: H.E. Lawrence, 1890.

Capitman, Barbara. *American Trademark Designs: A Survey with 732 Marks, Logos and Corporate-Identity Symbols.* New York: Dover, 1976.

Carr, Lucien. *The Social and Political Position of Women among the Huron-Iroquois Tribes.* Salem, Mass.: Salem Press, 1884.

Carr, William. *Pawns in the Game.* Glendale, Calif.: St. George Press, 1970.

Carter, David. *American Corporate Identity 2001.* New York: HarperCollins, 2000.

Case, Paul Foster. *The Great Seal of the United States: Its History, Symbolism and Message for the New Age.* Santa Barbara, Calif.: J.F. Rowny Press, 1935.

———. *The Tarot: A Key to Wisdom of the Ages.* Richmond, Va.: Macoy Publishing, 1947.

"CBS at 75: The Eye." CBS Website. *www.cbs.com/specials/cbs_75/eye.shtml.* Accessed April 15, 2007.

Cerami, Charles. *Benjamin Banneker: Surveyor, Astronomer, Publisher, Patriot.* New York: John Wiley & Sons, 2002.

Champlin, John D., Jr. "The Great Seal of the United States: Concerning Some Irregularities in It." *The Galaxy* 23 (1877): 691–94.

Cirlot, J. *A Dictionary of Symbols.* Translated by Jack Sage. New York: Philosophical Library, 1962.

Clark, Rosemary. *The Sacred Tradition of Ancient Egypt.* St. Paul, Minn.: Llewellyn, 2000.

Clift, Wallace. "Symbols of Wholeness in Tillich and Jung." *International Journal of Symbology* 7 no. 2 (1976): 45–52.

Colden, Cadwallader. *The History of the Five Indian Nations Depending on the Province of New York in America.* Ithaca, N.Y.: Cornell University Press, 1958.

Corcoran, Michael. *For Which It Stands.* New York: Simon & Schuster, 2002.

"Cut a 5-Pointed Star in One Snip." *USHistory.org. www.ushistory.org/betsy/flagstar.html.* Accessed August 15, 2007.

"DARPA Over the Years." DARPA Website. *www.darpa.gov/body/overtheyears.html.*

Day, Sara. "With Peace and Freedom Blest! Woman as Symbol in America, 1590–1800." *American Women: A Library of Congress Guide for the Study of Women's History and Culture in the United States.* Library of Congress, 2001.

De Chardin, Pierre Teilhard. *Future of Man.* Translated by N. Denny. New York: Harper & Row, 1964.

De Hoyos, Arturo, and S. Brent Morris. *Is It True What They Say About Freemasonry?* New York: M. Evans and Company, 2004.

Denslow, William. *10,000 Famous Freemasons.* Columbia, Mo.: Missouri Lodge of Research, 1961.

Deyo, Stan. *Cosmic Conspiracy.* Kalamunda, Western Australia: West Australian Texas Trading, 1978.

Domhoff, G. William. "Social Cohesion and the Bohemian Grove: The Power Elite at Summer Camp." Who Rules America Website. *sociology.ucsc.edu/whorulesamerica/power/bohemian_grove.html.* Accessed September 15, 2007.

Duke, David. *Jewish Supremacism: "My Awakening to the Jewish Question."* Covington, La.: Free Speech Press, 2002.

Edinger, Edward. *Ego and Archetype.* Baltimore, Md.: Penguin, 1973.

Eliade, Mircea. *Cosmos and History.* Translated by W.R. Trask. New York: Harper & Row, 1959.

Ellis, Joseph. *Founding Brothers: The Revolutionary Generation.* Minneapolis, Minn.: Turtleback Books, 2004.

Epperson, A. Ralph. *The New World Order.* Tucson, Ariz.: Publius Press, 1990.

"Famous Freemasons, A through I." Anti-Masonry Points of View Website. *www.masonicinfo.com/famous1.htm.* Accessed October 3, 2007.

Ferling, John. *Adams vs. Jefferson: The Tumultuous Election of 1800.* New York: Oxford University Press, 2005.

Finck, E.R. "The Seal of God in Creation and the Word: An Unanswerable Challenge of an Unbelieving World." Memorial University, Department of Religious Studies Website. *www.mun.ca/rels/restmov/texts/efinck/ GODSEAL.HTM.* Originally written by F.C. Payne. Accessed October 18, 2007.

Fleming, E. McClung. "From Indian Princess to Greek Goddess: The American Image, 1783–1815." *Winterthur Portfolio* 3 (1967): 37–66.

Ferguson, Marilyn. *The Aquarian Conspiracy.* Los Angeles: Jeremy Tarcher, 1980.

Fox-Davies, Charles. *A Complete Guide to Heraldry* New York: Skyhorse Publishing, 2007.

Frankfort, Henri, and H. Frankfort. "Myth and Reality." In *Before Philosophy.* Baltimore, Md.: Penguin, 1963.

Frankl, Victor. *Man's Search for Meaning: An Introduction to Logotherapy.* New York: Washington Square Press, 1965.

———. *The Will to Meaning.* New York: New American Library, 1969.

"From Pentagram to Pyramids." *www.geocities.com/jussaymoe/dc_symbolism/index.htm.* Accessed September 14, 2007 and October 6, 2007.

Fromm, Erich. *The Revolution of Hope.* New York: Harper & Row, 1974.

Fuller, R. Buckminster. *Operating Manual for Spaceship Earth.* New York: Pocket Books, 1970.

Furlong, William, and Byron McCandless. *So Proudly We Hail: The History of the United States Flag.* Washington, D.C.: Smithsonian Institution, 1981.

Gaskell, G. *Dictionary of All Scriptures and Myths.* New York: Julian Press, 1960.

Gerber, Richard. *Vibrational Medicine.* Rochester, Vt.: Bear & Company, 2001.

Giannini, Robert L., "Factual Flier #178," February 25, 1997. Independence National Historic Park. Philadelphia, Penn.

Goswami, Amit. *Physics of the Soul.* Charlottesville, Va.: Hampton Roads, 2001.

The Great Seal of the United States. Washington, D.C.: Department of State, Bureau of Public Affairs, 2003.

Greaves, John. *Pyramidographia: The First Book on the Pyramids.* Baltimore, Md.: The Maryland Institute Press, 1992.

Grinde, Donald, Jr. *The Iroquois and the Founding of the American Nation.* San Francisco: The Indian Historian Press, 1977.

Grinde, Donald, Jr., and Bruce Johansen. *Exemplar of Liberty: Native America and the Evolution of Democracy.* Los Angeles: American Indian Studies Center, 1991.

————. "Sauce for the Goose: Demand and Definitions for 'Proof' Regarding the Iroquois and Democracy." *The William and Mary Quarterly* 53, no. 3 (July 1996).

Guinness, Desmond, and Julius Trousdale Sadler, Jr. *Mr. Jefferson, Architect.* New York: Viking Press, 1973.

Hall, Manly. *The Adepts in the Western Esoteric Tradition: Masonic Orders of Fraternity. Part 4.* Los Angeles: Philosophical Research Society, 1950.

————. *America's Assignment with Destiny: The Adepts in the Western Esoteric Tradition. Part 5.* Los Angeles: Philosophical Research Society, 1951.

————.Abrams, Richard, and James Bell. *In Search of Liberty: The Story of the Statue of Liberty and Ellis Island.* Garden City, N.Y.: Doubleday, 1984. *The Secret Destiny of America.* Los Angeles: Philosophical Research Society, 1972.

————. *The Secret Teachings of All Ages: The Encyclopedic Outline of Masonic, Hermetic, Qabbalistic and Rosicrucian Symbolic Philosophy.* Los Angeles: Philosophical Research Society, 1967.

Hanchett, R. Stephen. "Nice Guy? Or the Devil's Spawn?" *www. bushisantichrist.com.* Accessed September 17, 2007.

Hancock, Graham, and Robert Bauval. *Talisman: Gnostics, Freemasons, Revolutionaries, and the 2000-year-old Conspiracy at Work in the World Today.* Hammersmith, London: Element Books, 2004.

Handlin, Oscar. *Statue of Liberty.* New York: Newsweek Book Division, 1971.

Hardaker, Chris. *The First American: The Suppressed Story of the People Who Discovered the New World.* Franklin Lakes, N.J.: New Page, 2007.

————. "The Seal and the City: Or, a Funny Thing Happened on the Way to the Inauguration." Unpublished paper delivered to the Society for American Archaeology, April 1990.

Harman, Willis. *Global Mind Change.* Indianapolis, Ind.: Knowledge Systems, 1988.

Harris, Alex. "William Barton." In *Biographical History of Lancaster County.* Lancaster, Pa.: Elias Barr & Co., 1872.

Harwood, Jeremy. *The Secret History of Freemasonry.* London: Lorenz Books, 2006.

Heath, Richard. *Sacred Number and the Origins of Civilization.* Rochester, Vt.: Inner Traditions, 2007.

Heaton, Ronald. *The Masonic Membership of our Founding Fathers.* Silver Spring, Md.: Masonic Service Association, 1965.

Heckethorn, Charles. *The Secret Societies of All Ages and Countries. Vol. 1.* New York: University Books, 1965.

Heline, Corrine. *America's Invisible Guidance.* Los Angeles: New Age Press, 1949.

Heline, Theodore. *America's Destiny: A New Order of Ages.* Oceanside, Calif.: New Age Press, 1941.

Henriques, Peter. *Realistic Visionary: A Portrait of George Washington.* Charlottesville, Va.: University of Virginia Press, 2006.

Hewitt, J.N.B. "A Constitutional League of Peace in the Stone Age of America: The League of the Iroquois and Its Constitution." Washington, D.C.: National Anthropological Archives, Smithsonian Institution, 1918.

Hieronimus, Robert. *America's Secret Destiny.* Rochester, Vt.: Destiny Books, 1989.

———. *E Pluribus Unum.* Baltimore, Md.: AUM Center, 1985.

———. *Founding Fathers, Secret Societies.* Rochester, Vt.: Destiny Books, 2006.

———. *The Growth Experience Depicted in the American Seal's Reverse.* Baltimore, Md.: AUM Center, 1982.

———. "An Historical Analysis of the Reverse of America's Great Seal and Its Relationship to the Ideology of Humanistic Psychology." Unpublished doctoral thesis. San Francisco: Saybrook Institute, 1981.

———. *Mythologies Expressed in the American Seal's Reverse.* Baltimore, Md.: AUM Center, 1982.

———. *Psychology of the Talisman.* Baltimore, Md.: AUM Center, 1982.

———. "Symbols: Agents through Which Consciousness Is Expressed in Art." *Saybrook Review* 5 no. 2 (1985): 47–54.

———. *The Two Great Seals of America.* Baltimore, Md.: Savitriaum, 1976.

———. *The 200th Anniversary of America's Great Seal*. Baltimore, Md.: AUM Center, 1982.

———. "Were Our Founding Fathers Occultists?" Parts 1 and 2. *Gnostica News* 4 no. 9 (1975); no. 11 (1975).

Hieronimus, J. Zohara Meyerhoff. *Kabbalistic Teachings of the Female Prophets: The Seven Holy Women of Ancient Israel*. Rochester, Vt.: Inner Traditions, (Forthcoming)2008.

"Hillary Clinton Wears New Lapel Pin That Absolutely Proves She is an Illuminist—Clinton's Fatal Leadership Series—Part 6H." The Cutting Edge Website. *www.cuttingedge.org/news/n1259.cfm*. Accessed June 27, 2007.

Hinrichs, Kit, and Delphine Hirasuna. *Long May She Wave: A Graphic History of the American Flag*. Berkeley, Calif.: Ten Speed Press, 2001.

"Hiroshima Peace Memorial Museum." Hiroshima Peace Site Website. *www.pcf.city.hiroshima.jp/top_e.html*. Accessed September 1, 2007.

Hunt, Gaillard. *The History of the Seal of the United States*. Washington, D.C.: Department of State, 1909.

Icke, David. *The Biggest Secret: The Book That Will Change the World*. Wildwood, Mo.: Bridge of Love Publications, 2000.

"Illuminati Symbols and Their Meanings." Black Chat Website. *www.blackchat.co.uk/theblackforum*. Accessed June 23, 2007.

Inner Wealth: Eight Ways to Discover Your Hidden Dimensions With the Symbols on the Dollar Bill. Fairfield, Iowa: Harmony International, 2002.

"IKG Cultural Resource Center Website." *www.ikg-info.com*. Accessed October 15, 2007.

Isaacson, Walter. *Benjamin Franklin: An American Life*. New York: Simon and Schuster, 2003.

Jacobi, Jolande. *Complex Archetype: Symbol in the Psychology of C.G. Jung*. Princeton, N.J.: Princeton University Press, 1974.

Jefferson, Thomas. *The Life and Morals of Jesus of Nazareth*. New York: World Publishing, 1942.

Jennings, Sibley. "Artistry as Design: L'Enfant's Extraordinary City." *Quarterly*, 36, no. 3 (1979): 225–78.

Johansen, Bruce. *Forgotten Founders*. Boston: Harvard Common Press, 1982.

———. comp. *Native American Political Systems and the Evolution of Democracy: An Annotated Bibliography*. Westport, Conn.: Greenwood Press, 1996.

———. "Notes from the 'Culture Wars': More Annotations on the Debate Regarding the Iroquois and the Origins of Democracy." *American Indian Culture and Research Journal* 23 (1999): 165–75.

Johansen, Bruce, and Donald Grinde, Jr. "Reaching the Grassroots: The Worldwide Diffusion of Iroquois Democratic Traditions." *American Indian Culture and Research Journal* 27 no. 2 (2003): 77–91.

Joseph, Frank. *The Atlantis Encyclopedia*. Franklin Lakes, N.J.: New Page Books, 2005.

———. ed. *Discovering the Mysteries of Ancient America*. Franklin Lakes, N.J.: New Page Books, 2006.

Jung, Carl. *The Archetypes and the Collective Unconscious*. Edited by H. Read et al., translated by R.F.C. Hull. Bollingen Series 20, vol. 9 (pt. 1). Princeton, N.J.: Princeton University Press, 1975.

———. *Four Archetypes: Mother, Rebirth, Spirit, Trickster*. Translated by R.F.C. Hull Bollingen Series 20, vol. 9 (pt. 1). Princeton, N.J.: Princeton University Press, 1970.

———. *On the Nature of the Psyche*. Translated by R.F.C. Hull. Bollingen Series 20, vol. 8. Princeton, N.J.: Princeton University Press, 1973.

———. *Psyche and Symbol*. Edited by V.S. de Laszlo. New York: Doubleday, 1958.

———. *Two Essays on Analytic Psychology*. Edited by H. Read, M. Fordham, and G. Adler, translated by R.F.C. Hull. Bollingen Series 20, vol. 7. Princeton, N.J.: Princeton University Press, 1953.

"The Kabalyon Key Website." *www.kabalyonkey.com.* Accessed October 5, 2007.

Kerényi, Karl, and Carl Jung. "Prolegomena." In *Essays on a Science of Mythology*. Translated by R.F.C. Hull. Bollingen Series 22. Princeton, N.J.: Princeton University Press, 1969.

Kimball, David. *The Story of the Liberty Bell.* Philadelphia: Eastern National Park and Monument Association, 1989/1997.

Krippner, Stanley, and Alberto Villoldo. *The Realms of Healing.* Millbrae, Calif.: Celestial Arts, 1976.

Kuersteiner, Kurt. *The Unofficial Guide to the Art of Jack T. Chick: Chick Tracts, Crusader Comics, & Battle Cry Newspapers.* Atglen, Pa.: Schiffer Publishing, 2004.

Kuhn, Thomas S. *The Structure of Scientific Revolutions.* Chicago: University of Chicago Press, 1970.

Labunski, Richard. *James Madison and the Struggle for the Bill of Rights.* New York: Oxford University Press, 2006.

Lee, Antoinette, and Pamela Scott. *Buildings of the District of Columbia.* New York: Oxford University Press, 1993.

Ligou, Daniel. *Dictionnaire de la Franc-maçonnerie.* Paris: Presses Universitaires de France, 1987.

Lloyd, James. *Beyond Babylon.* Jacksonville, Oreg.: Christian Media, 1995.

MacArthur, John. "Ben Franklin on the Rattlesnake as a Symbol of America." *GreatSeal.com. www.greatseal.com/symbols/ rattlesnake.html.* Accessed August 15, 2007.

Mann, Nicholas. *The Sacred Geometry of Washington, D.C.* Somerset, England: Green Magic, 2006.

Marrs, Texe. *Dark Majesty: The Secret Brotherhood and the Magic of a Thousand Points of Light.* Austin, Tex.: Rivercrest, 2004.

———. "Magic, Alchemy, and the Illuminati Conquest of Outer Space. The Eagle Has Landed!" Power of Prophecy Website. *www.texemarrs.com/ 032003/eagle_has_landed.htm.* Accessed June 28, 2007.

Martucci, Dave, ed. "A Panoply of American Flags." *North American Vexillological Association NAVA News* 31, no. 2 (April–June 2006): 4–13.

Maslow, Abraham. *The Further Reaches of Human Nature.* New York: Penguin, 1978.

————. *Religious Values and Peak Experiences.* New York: Penguin, 1977.

Masser, Edward, ed. *Cesare Ripa Baroque and Rococo Pictorial Imagery: The 1758–60 Hertel Edition of Ripa's 'Iconologia' with 200 Engraved Illustrations.* New York: Dover, 1971.

Maxwell, Jordan. *Matrix of Power: How the World Has Been Controlled by Powerful People Without Your Knowledge.* Escondido, Calif.: Book Tree, 2000.

May, Rollo. *The Courage to Create.* New York: Bantam, 1976.

————. *The Cry for Myth.* New York: W.W. Norton & Co., 1991.

————. *Man's Search for Himself.* New York: W.W. Norton & Co., 1953.

McCullough, David. *1776.* New York: Simon & Schuster, 2006.

————. *John Adams.* New York: Simon & Schuster, 2002.

McGrath, Ken. *The Secret Geometry of the Dollar.* San Diego, Calif.: AuthorHouse, 2002.

McKeown, Trevor. "Anti-Masonry Frequently Asked Questions, Section 2, Version 2.9." Grand Lodge of British Columbia and Yukon Website. *freemasonry.bcy.ca/anti-masonry/anti-masonry02.html* Accessed June 2, 2007.

Meeks, Carol. "Pantheon Paradigm." *The Journal of the Society of Architectural Historians* 19, no. 4. (Dec. 1960): 135–44.

Merriam, Eve. *The Voice of Liberty: The Story of Emma Lazarus.* New York: Farrar, Straus & Cudahy, 1959.

Meyer, Jeffrey. *Myths in Stone: Religious Dimensions of Washington, D.C.* Berkeley, Calif.: University of California Press, 2001.

Millegan, Kris, ed. *Fleshing Out Skull & Bones: Investigations into America's Most Powerful Secret Society.* Walterville, Oreg.: TrineDay, 2003.

Moreno, Barry. *The Statue of Liberty Encyclopedia.* New York: Simon & Schuster, 2000.

Morris, S. Brent. *The Complete Idiot's Guide to Freemasonry.* New York: Penguin, 2006.

Mr. Dreyfuss Goes to Washington. Dir. Rachel Lyon. A&E Television Networks, 2001.

Musès, Charles, and Arthur Young, eds. *Consciousness and Reality*. New York: Outerbridge & Lazard, 1972.

Nakkach, Silvia. "The Secret Power of Sound: Listen and Heal." Public Programs Newsletter, May 2006.

National Treasures: Signs and Symbols of the U.S. Founding Fathers. Dir. William Henry. New Science Ideas, 2005.

Neumann, Eric. *Art and the Creative Unconscious*. Translated by R. Manheim. Bollingen Series 41. Princeton, N.J.: Princeton University Press, 1974.

———. *The Great Mother*. Translated by R. Manheim. Bollingen Series 47. Princeton, N.J.: Princeton University Press, 1970.

New York Public Library and the Comité Officiel Franco-Américain pour la Célébration du Centenaire de la Statue de la Liberté with Pierre Provoyeur and June Hargrove. *Liberty: The French-American Statue in Art and History*. Harper & Row, 1986.

Newman, Eric. *The Early Paper Money of America*. Iola, Wisc.: Krause Publications, 1990.

"Not Your Typical Ballpark." Philadelphia Phillies Website. *philadelphia .phillies.mlb.com/phi/ballpark/not_your_typical_ballpark.jsp*. Accessed October 15, 2007.

O'Connell, Brian. "An Irishman's Diary." *The Irish Times* Website. *www.ireland.com/newspaper/opinion/2006/0904/ 1156791362900.html*. Accessed October 15, 2007.

Odajnyk, Walter. *Jung and Politics*. New York: Harper & Row, 1976.

"Our Society Is Falling Apart." Pushing Hamburger. *www.pushhamburger.com/falling_apart.htm*. Accessed July 16, 2007.

Ovason, David. *The Secret Architecture of Our Nation's Capital*. New York: HarperCollins, 2000.

———. *The Secret Symbols of the Dollar Bill*. New York: HarperCollins, 2004.

———. interview by Dr. Bob Hieronimus, *21st Century Radio* radio program, February 11, 2001.

Paige, John C. *The Liberty Bell of Independence National Historical Park: A Special History Study.* Denver, Colo.: National Park Service, 1985.

Parker, Arthur. "The Constitution of the Five Nations." In *Parker on the Iroquois*, edited by W.N. Fenton. Syracuse, N.Y.: Syracuse University Press, 1968.

———. "The Double-Headed Eagle and Whence it Came." *The Builder* (April 1923).

Patterson, Richard. *The Great Seal of the United States.* Washington, D.C.: Department of State Publication 8868, 1976.

Patterson, Richard, and Richardson Dougall. *The Eagle and the Shield.* Washington, D.C.: Department of State, 1976.

"Peace Bell." Hiroshima Peace Site. *www.mickeyhart.net/Pages/ tootpd11.html.* Accessed September 1, 2007.

Pike, Albert. *Morals and Dogma of the Ancient and Accepted Scottish Rite of Freemasonry.* Charleston, S.C.: Southern Jurisdiction, F.M, 1906.

"Presidential Signing Statements." The American Presidency Project Website. *www.presidency.ucsb.edu/signingstatements* Accessed February 19, 2008.

"Presidential Signing Statements." Congresspedia Website. *www.sourcewatch .org/index.php?title=Presidential_signing_statements* Accessed February 19, 2008.

Preble, George. *History of the Flag of the United States of America.* Boston: A. Williams & Co., 1880.

"Procter & Gamble Sued Two Amway Corp. Distributors." *Wall Street Journal,* August 1, 1990.

Progoff, Ira. *Depth Psychology and Modern Man.* New York: McGraw-Hill, 1973.

Quayle, Steve. "The Fourth Reich? Nazi Symbols Creeping Up in 'Land of the (Once) Free'." Steve Quayle Website. *www.stevequayle.com/ News.alert/NOW/020405.Nazi.stamps.html.* Accessed August 20, 2007.

Ray, Paul, and Sherry Anderson. *The Cultural Creatives: How 50 Million People Are Changing the World.* New York: Harmony, 2000.

Reed, Henry. *The United States Capitol Its Architecture and Decoration.* New York: W.W. Norton & Company, 2005.

Richards, A., and F. Richards. "The Whole Person." *Journal of Humanistic Psychology* 14, no. 3 (1974): 21–27.

Riddles in Stone: The Secret Architecture of Washington D.C. Dir. Christian Pinto. Antiquities Research Films, 2007.

Robbins, Alexandra, interview by Dr. Bob Hieronimus, *21st Century Radio* radio program, February 22, 2004.

———. *Secrets of the Tomb: Skull and Bones, the Ivy League, and the Hidden Paths of Power.* New York: Little, Brown & Co., 2002.

Robison, John. *Proofs of a Conspiracy.* Boston: Western Islands, 1967.

Rogers, Carl. *Client-Centered Therapy.* New York: Houghton Mifflin, 1965.

Rubincam, M. "A Memoir of the Life of William Barton, A.M. (1754–1817)." *Pennsylvania History* 12 no. 3 (1945): 179–93.

Savage, Candace. *Eagles of North America.* New York: Greystone Books, 2000.

Schoch, Robert, and Robert McNally. *Pyramid Quest: Secrets of the Great Pyramid and the Dawn of Civilization.* New York: Jeremy Tarcher, 2005.

Scott, Pamela. *Temple of Liberty: Building the Capitol for a New Nation.* New York: Oxford University Press, 1995.

Scranton, Laird. *The Science of the Dogon: Decoding the African Mystery Tradition.* Rochester, Vt.: Inner Traditions, 2006.

Secrets of the Dollar Bill. Dir. Alex Kohler and Carol White. A&E Television Networks, 2006.

"Shwedagon Pagoda." Wikipedia Website. *www.en.wikipedia.org/wiki/Shwedagon_Pagoda.* Accessed October 4, 2007.

Silverman, Kenneth. *A Cultural History of the American Revolution.* New York: Thomas Crowell Company, 1976.

Singer, June. *Androgyny: Toward a New Theory of Sexuality.* Garden City, N.Y.: Anchor Books, 1977.

————. *Boundaries of the Soul.* Garden City, N.Y.: Anchor Books, 1973.

Sora, Steven. *Secret Societies of America's Elite.* Rochester, Vt.: Destiny Books, 2003.

Sparks, Jared. *The Writings of Washington. Vol. 11.* New York: Harper & Bros., 1848.

Spenser, Robert Keith. *The Cult of the All-Seeing Eye.* Hawthorne, Calif.: Christian Book Club of America, 1968.

Stauffer, Vernon. *The Bavarian Illuminati in America: The New England Conspiracy Scare, 1798.* Mineola, N.Y.: Dover Publications, 2006.

Stebbing, Lionel. *The Secrets of Numbers.* London: New Knowledge Books, 1969.

Stirling, William. *Canon: An Exposition of the Pagan Mystery Perpetuated in the Cabala as the Rule of All the Arts.* Whitefish, Mont.: Kessinger Publishing's Rare Reprints. Originally published 1897.

Sutton, Antony. *America's Secret Establishment: An Introduction to the Order of Skull and Bones.* Walterville, Oreg.: Trine Day, 2002.

"The Story of the Mental Health Bell." Mental Health Association in High Point Website. *www.MHAHP.org/bell.htm.* Accessed September 1, 2007.

Thomson, Doug. "Bush on the Constitution: 'It's Just a Goddamned Piece of Paper'." Capitol Hill Blue's The Rant Website. *www.capitolhillblue.com/artman/publish/article_7779.shtml.* Accessed November 1, 2007.

Thompson, Jeffrey. "Methods for Stimulation of Brainwave Function Using Sound." Encinitas, Calif.: Center for Neuroacoustic Research, 1990.

Thomson, I.L. "The Great Seal of the United States." In *Encyclopedia Americana. Vol. 13.* New York: American, 1962.

Tillich, Paul. *Dynamics of Faith.* New York: Harper & Bros., 1958.

Tompkins, Peter. *Secrets of the Great Pyramid.* New York: Harper & Row, 1971.

Totten, Charles. *The Great Seal of the United States, Its History and Heraldry. Vols. 1 and 2.* New Haven, Conn.: Our Race Publishing, 1897.

"The Unified Conspiracy Theory." Sweet Liberty. *www.sweetliberty.org/issues/hoax/unified.htm.* Accessed July 16, 2007.

The United States Capitol: A Place of Resounding Deeds. Dir. Norman Bishop. Finley-Holiday Film Corp., 2005.

The U.S. Capitol: A Vision in Stone. Executive Producers E. Samantha Cheng and Charles Crawford. Heritage Series, 2001.

Unveiling the Masonic Symbolism of Washington, DC. Dir. Majd Elias. E-Square, LLC & EMI Global, 2005.

Waite, A.E. *Devil-Worship in France with Diana Vaughan and the Question of Modern Palladism.* York Beach, Maine: Red Wheel/ Weiser, 2003.

Wallace, Paul A.W. "The Return of Hiawatha." *New York State History* 39 (1948): 385–403.

———. *The White Roots of Peace.* Saranac Lake, N.Y.: Chauncy Press, 1986.

Warner, Christian. *Global Unity Now.* Baltimore, Md.: End Time Messages, n.d.

"Washington, D.C. Planned by Masonic Founding Fathers as the Most Powerful Occult Capitol in World History! Part 2." The Cutting Edge Website. *www.cuttingedge.org/News/n1493.cfm* Accessed October 16, 2007.

Watts, Alan. *The Book.* New York: Collier Books, 1967.

Webb, Thomas. *The Freemasons Monitor or Illustrations of Masonry.* Salem, Mass.: Cushing and Appleton, 1821.

Webster, Nesta. *Secret Societies and Subversive Movements. 9th edition.* Originally published in 1924. N.p.: Christian Book Club of America, n.d.

Weisberger, Bernard. *The Statue of Liberty: First Hundred Years.* New York: American Heritage Publishing, 1985.

Weiss, Philip. "Masters of the Universe Go to Camp: Inside the Bohemian Grove." Sociology Department, UC Santa Cruz Website. *sociology.ucsc.edu/whorulesamerica/power/ bohemian_grove_spy.html* Accessed September 15, 2007.

Westcott, W. *Numbers: Their Occult and Mystic Virtues.* New York: Allied Publications, n.d.

Westcott, Wendell. *Bells and Their Music.* New York: G.P. Putnam's Sons, 1988.

Westbrook, Jr., Charles. *The Talisman of the United States: America's Oldest Secret, The Mysterious Street Lines of Washington D.C., Signature of the Invisible Brotherhood.* Ayden, N.C.: Westcom Press, 1990.

————. *The Talisman Newsletter* 1, no.1&2, October 31, 1990.

Wilhelm, Richard. *The I Ching or Book of Changes*. Bollingen Foundation. Princeton, N.J.: Princeton University Press, 1967.

Wilson, Robert Anton, and Robert Shea. *Illuminatus: Part 1, the Eye in the Pyramid*. New York: Dell, 1975.

Wolf, Fred Alan. *The Dreaming Universe*. New York: Touchstone, 1994.

"The World Peace Bell." The Verdin Company Website. *www.verdin.com/ info/world-peacebell.asp*. Accessed October 4, 2007.

Yates, Frances. *The Rosicrucian Enlightenment*. London: Routledge & Kegan Paul, 1972.

Zieber, J.J. "Charles Thomson, the Sam Adams of Philadelphia." *Mississippi Valley Historical Review* 45 no 3. (1968): 464–80.

The Zohar. Translated by Harry Sperling and Maurice Simon, vol. 2. London: Socino Press, 1978.

INDEX

ABOUT THE AUTHOR

obert R. Hieronimus received his PhD for the doctoral thesis, *An Historic Analysis of the Reverse of the American Great Seal and Its Relationship to the Ideology of Humanistic Psychology,* from Saybrook Institute in 1981 under Dr. Stanley Krippner. Dr. Hieronimus's research on the Great Seal has been used in the speeches, literature, and libraries of the White House, the State Department, and the Department of Interior. In June 1976, President Gerald Ford used Hieronimus's research in his speech at the opening of the centennial safe during the American bicentennial. In 1976 and again in 1981 Hieronimus was invited to the White House to discuss the history and meaning of the two Great Seals of America. His Independence Hall speech on the bicentennial of the Great Seal was published in the Congressional Record, and his research was shared in a personal meeting with former Egyptian president Anwar El-Sadat. He and his wife, Zohara, lobbied the House and Senate on the Great Seal Act after decades of speaking about the symbolism of the reverse of the Seal in hundreds of interviews for print media, radio, and TV (including *Voice of America*), and on the lecture circuit to colleges and universities, and conferences around the country.

Dr. Hieronimus is also an artist and has included American symbols in dozens of murals including the 2,700-square-foot *Apocalypse* at Johns Hopkins University and the 800-square-foot *E Pluribus Unum* at Lexington Market in Baltimore. (*E Pluribus Unum* also contains portraits of all the Founding Fathers who have eaten at the Lexington Market, including George Washington, Ben

Franklin, and Thomas Jefferson.) During the summer of 1968 he shared his research with Elektra recording artists including Jimi Hendrix and Timothy Buckley. His Artcar VW bus "Light" (better known as "the Woodstock bus") was photographed by the Associated Press and *Rolling Stone* at the original 1969 Woodstock, and is still seen today regularly reprinted in media all over the world. A diecast model of Hieronimus's painted Woodstock bus will be produced by Sunstar Diecast in 2008 in recognition of the 40th anniversary of Woodstock.

Since 1988 Hieronimus has hosted the radio talk show, *21st Century Radio,* which explores the unknown with the world's leading-edge thinkers, researchers, and practitioners in such fields as parapsychology, holistic health, UFOs, and the environment. In the early 1990s, Hieronimus & Co. produced *21st Century News* for the local FOX-TV channel and cable TV, promoting environmental solutions, scientific advances in alternative fields, and cultural heroes such as the Negro Leagues baseball players, the legendary Babe Ruth, and the works of J.R.R. Tolkien. More about Hieronimus & Co. can be learned at *21stCenturyRadio.com.*

In 2002 he published *Inside The Yellow Submarine: The Making of the Beatles Animated Classic* (Krause) after decades of research. *Animation World Magazine* called it "an indispensable companion to the movie." In 2006 *Founding Fathers, Secret Societies* was released by Destiny Books, an updated and expanded version of Hieronimus's 1989 book, *America's Secret Destiny.* Hieronimus has appeared in documentaries airing repeatedly on the National Geographic and History channels and worldwide. In 2006 he painted his Mercedes 300SD to become an Artcar called "The Founding Fathers." It runs on biodiesel, a non-polluting fuel that can be grown from renewable non-food crops supplied by American farms.

More information about *The United Symbolism of America,* including supplementary photos and additional text, can be found at *UnitedSymbolismofAmerica.com.*